Gregory the Great

Gregory
the Great

ASCETIC, PASTOR, AND FIRST MAN OF ROME

George E. Demacopoulos

University of Notre Dame Press

Notre Dame, Indiana

Manufactured in the United States of America

Library of Congress Cataloging-in-Publication Data

Demacopoulos, George E.
    Gregory the Great : ascetic, pastor, and first man of Rome /
George E. Demacopoulos.
        pages   cm
    Includes bibliographical references and index.
    ISBN 978-0-268-02621-9 (pbk. : alk. paper) —
    ISBN 0-268-02621-1 (pbk. : alk. paper)
    1. Gregory I, Pope, approximately 540–604.   I. Title.
    BX1076.D46   2015
    270.2092— dc23
    [B]
                                                    2015023757

CONTENTS

ACKNOWLEDGMENTS

In some respects, I have been working on this book for more than fifteen years. I wrote my doctoral dissertation at the University of North Carolina at Chapel Hill on Gregory's distinctive approach to spiritual direction. That project expanded to include additional authors in my first monograph, *Five Models of Spiritual Direction in the Early Church* (University of Notre Dame Press, 2007), which concluded with a chapter on Gregory. A second monograph, *The Invention of Peter* (University of Pennsylvania Press, 2013), on Petrine discourse in the early Church similarly concluded with a chapter that investigated Gregory's contribution. While those projects were intellectually satisfying in their own ways, it was not until I began working on the present study that I was able to articulate with some semblance of clarity how it was that Gregory's ascetic and pastoral commitments fit alongside his pragmatic administration of the Roman Church.

This project began in earnest during the fall of 2011 with the combined support of the Carpenter Foundation and a Fordham Faculty Fellowship. It was late in the year, however, before I began—the sabbatical had been devoted primarily to *The Invention of Peter*—and I was only able to dedicate a few months to rereading Gregory's large corpus and to developing what I hope is an original approach to the material. Thus, I have written the majority of this book in short bursts of a few days at a time over the course of the past few years.

Along the way, I benefitted a great deal from the generosity of friends in the academy who were willing to share their time and insight.

Kristina Sessa has proven to be an invaluable conversation partner for all matters regarding the Roman Church in late antiquity. Her insight and patience are beyond compare. Carole Straw read an early draft of the manuscript, providing pertinent critiques and identifying many lacunae. Joseph Lienhard, S. J., a longtime friend at Fordham, also read the manuscript and offered many helpful suggestions for revision. Although they did not contribute directly to this project, I would be remiss if I failed to acknowledge Aristotle Papanikolaou and Ben Dunning, who continuously provide intellectual stimulation, models of scholarly excellence, and friendship.

Finally, this book is dedicated to Peter Iver Kaufman. It was Peter who first pushed me to think more carefully and more comprehensively about the multiple strands within Gregory's thought and action. As both friend and mentor, Peter has provided me more than I can ever hope to repay.

Introduction

Pope Gregory I, known among Western Christians as St. Gregory the Great and by Eastern Christians as St. Gregory the Dialogist, was born around the year 540 to an aristocratic family well connected to the Roman Church. Gregory's great-great-grandfather was likely Pope Felix III (bishop of Rome from 483–492), and Pope Agapetus (bishop of Rome from 533–536) was presumably a distant uncle.[1] Three of Gregory's aunts (on his father's side) are known to have been estate-dwelling ascetics.[2] Gregory's father, Gordianus, held the administrative rank of *defensor* in the Church of Rome, which would typically mean that he served as a property and legal manager for a portion of the Church's extensive landholdings.[3] Gregory's family was wealthy, and he possessed all of the advantages of an aristocratic youth, including a palatial estate on the Caelian Hill and the best education available at that time.[4] Unfortunately, Gregory tells us little about his youth or the specifics of his studies.[5]

At the time of his birth, Italy and the city of Rome were shadows of their former selves. For most of his childhood, the "Roman" armies of the East waged a destructive war against the Ostrogoths for supremacy of the Italian peninsula. Between 546 and 547 alone, control of the city of Rome switched three times between imperial and Gothic hands.[6] We know nothing about how Gregory's family responded to the calamity of the initial siege of the capital in 546, when famine is said to have ensnared even the wealthiest of the city's districts. One of Gregory's early-twentieth-century biographers, F. Homes Dudden, speculated that the family may have retreated to the relative safety of its Sicilian estates to escape the devastation of the siege, but no evidence survives to support that idea.[7] However Gregory's family weathered the crisis, the Gothic wars dramatically hastened an already steep decline for the once mighty capital of the Roman Empire.[8] By the time that Gregory reached adolescence, a great percentage of the city of Rome, including many of its greatest monuments, was abandoned.[9] Indeed, it is not too hard to imagine why Gregory's writings are, at times, so apocalyptic in character—he was living in a nearly deserted city.[10]

Although Justinian's armies finally routed the Goths and established a permanent stronghold of Eastern Roman influence at Ravenna in the 550s, by 568 another Germanic tribe, the Lombards, crossed the Alps into Italy. That migration, and the wars that resulted from it, only furthered the desperation of the local populations and increased the political complexities for Rome's civil and religious leaders.[11] It was onto this shifting stage that Gregory stepped when he entered public life so auspiciously in 573 as the *praefectus urbi* (prefect of the city). In former times, the urban prefect would have been the head of the Senate, with both legal and civil jurisdiction over the city and everything within one hundred miles of it.[12] By Gregory's tenure, the authority of the prefecture's office was likely diminished, but there is little denying that Gregory would have been seen as one of the leading men in the city, responsible for public works, finance, supply lines, and military defenses.

It is often noted that Gregory held this post for only a single year before abandoning public service to pursue the contemplative life of monasticism. It is not often described, however, just how traumatic that year would have been. First, it was during this year that Lombards threatened the city for the first time, temporarily suspending all communication with Ravenna and Constantinople.[13] Second, Pope John III (bishop of Rome from 561–574) died, leaving an uncommonly long vacancy until the election of Benedict the following year.[14] And, third, the famous Byzantine general Narses, who was responsible for protecting the city, also died. However unpopular the tax-happy Narses might have been among the aristocrats of Rome, his death left Gregory alone to address the multifaceted needs of the city's inhabitants.[15] We know nothing of how Gregory actually dealt with the problems he faced; we have only a brief comment, made years later, in which Gregory emphasized the spiritual burden that this period placed upon his soul.[16] But as we will see, Gregory's experience of civic leadership, however brief, helps to explain both the competence for public administration and the commitment to service that would become hallmarks of his tenure as Roman bishop.

Despite the immense pressure that public service would have placed upon the young Gregory, there is little reason to believe that he chose monasticism as a means to escape responsibility. Indeed, Gregory's commitment to the ascetic life seems to have been absolute. He donated his family's patrimony, endowed six monasteries in Sicily, and transformed his Roman estate into a seventh, St. Andrew's, which he entered as a novice under the instruction of Valentius, the abbot.[17] According to his medieval biographers, the future bishop subjected himself to an unusually rigorous asceticism, likely causing the frequent ill health he suffered later in life.[18] As chapter 1 will demonstrate, Gregory's entire outlook was formed by a particular vision of the ascetic life that he no doubt began to develop during this period.

In 579, at the start of his pontificate, Pope Pelagius II (bishop of Rome from 579–590) recalled Gregory from his monastic retreat, ordained him to the diaconate, and appointed him *apocrisiarius* (i.e., papal representative to the emperor in Constantinople).[19] Given the intricate and overlapping concerns of the See of Rome with the city of Rome, Gregory's responsibilities in the Eastern capital included religious, political, military, and economic interests. Gregory spent nearly seven years in Constantinople in this capacity, but the emperor's preoccupations with Eastern affairs left Gregory free to devote a good deal of his time to study and the supervision of a small community of Latin ascetics from St. Andrew's who had accompanied him to Constantinople.[20] It was in this environment that Gregory began what would become his voluminous *Moralia in Iob*, which runs a dizzying eighteen hundred pages in the modern critical edition. The experience also provided Gregory with important contacts and a behind-the-scenes look at the imperial court and the Church of Constantinople, both of which would prove valuable in Gregory's future negotiations with the civil and ecclesiastical leaders of the East.[21]

In 585 Gregory returned to Rome and St. Andrews, where he may have assumed the role of abbot. In 590 he was selected to be Pelagius's successor as bishop of Rome. Unlike so many episcopal elections in Rome and elsewhere, Gregory's rise to the throne of Peter seems to have been uncontested. Indeed, as Peter Kaufman wryly noted, the only person who seems to have been upset about the appointment was Gregory himself.[22] The lone contemporary account is that of Gregory of Tours, who devotes a few lines to the election, emphasizing (in hagiographic fashion) Gregory's many attempts to avoid the papal office.[23] Gregory the Great served as bishop of Rome from September of 590 until his death in March of 604. In some respects, he may have been the most accomplished pontiff of the entire late-ancient period. Some of his achievements include the daily feeding of Rome's indigent, the refurbishing of the city's defenses, the introduction of monastics to the papal administration (he was himself the first monk-pope), and the reintroduction of Roman Christianity to England.[24] Added to these pragmatic endeavors are the pontiff's important theological, exegetical, and hagiographic works, which likely did more to shape the theological landscape of the Latin West in the Middle Ages than those of any other author, save Augustine. To be sure, Gregory's accomplishments required a determination and assertiveness that belie the irenic presentation of Gregory's medieval biographers, who characterized him as a gentle-minded contemplative.

Perhaps what is so fascinating about Gregory's thought and activity is that his achievements in many ways came despite a deep theological and ideological pull toward the seclusion of ascetic detachment. Indeed, if there is any single axiom that explains Gregory as both theologian and papal actor, it is that he felt ever conflicted between his inclination for ascetic ideals (namely humility and retreat) and a Ciceronian-like compulsion to public service.

Interpreting the Life and Thought of Gregory the Great

Modern assessments of Gregory's life and thought are, of course, confined by the availability of the historical sources. In many ways, we are fortunate to have access to so many of Gregory's writings—biblical commentaries, sermons, hagiographic works, a treatise on pastoral care, and more than eight hundred letters survive. With the availability of so much material, it is easy for interpreters to make the mistake of thinking that we have access to everything and that we can know a great deal more about his career than we actually can. At least one estimate suggests that there may have been as many as twenty thousand papyrus letters in the corpus before it was transposed to vellum by Carolingian editors at the end of the eighth century.[25] It is impossible to know what may have been contained in the missing letters. It is equally difficult to ascertain the reasons why certain letters were preserved and others jettisoned. But we should be ever aware that editorial erasure could be a powerful tool in the shaping of ecclesiastical memory. In short, we must be cognizant of the fact that what remains of Gregory's corpus is very much a construction of Gregory's Carolingian editors.[26]

It is also important to recall that the production of the earliest biographies of Gregory, such as they exist, might also have been born from an attempt to create and control a particular papal narrative. It is remarkable, in fact, that no Roman biography of Gregory, apart from a brief and apathetic entry in the *Liber Pontificalis*, survives from before the latter part of the eighth century.[27] And while it is likely that Gregory's medieval biographers, Paul the Deacon (d. ca. 799) and John the Deacon (d. prior to 882), may have had access to sources that no longer survive, it is equally true that they were motivated to present Gregory and his papacy in a way that accommodated the partisan concerns of their respective eras, particularly as they related to the spread of papal authority.

Among modern studies, Erich Caspar's monumental *Geschichte des Papsttums* (Berlin, 1930−1933) remains a pivotal moment in papal historiography because it offers a means for studying the papacy and individual pontiffs that was self-consciously divorced from the apologetic studies of the papacy that had preceded it. Caspar traces the development of the papal ideal and its corresponding ideology in the early Church. Significantly, he shows only marginal interest in Gregory because he interprets him as having done little to advance either the papacy or its ideology. But Caspar's focus on the development of the papal institution has since blossomed into a cottage industry among medieval historians, some of whom read Gregory as having been instrumental in the development of an independent and powerful institution. Of these, Walter Ullmann stands out for arguing, among other things, that Gregory's famous mission to Kent was precipitated by a desire to free the papacy and the Western Church from the shackles of Byzantium and its Caesaro-papist emperors. Although that thesis has been definitively refuted by Robert Markus and others, when we compare it to Caspar's interpretation we are presented with a startling range of possible interpretations of where Gregory fits in the narrative of the papal history.

Gregory's modern biographers have offered similarly divergent accounts, albeit through different means. The discrepancy of these studies is in large part dictated by whether or not one privileges his exegetical and hagiographic works or his voluminous and pragmatic correspondence. Among those studies that emphasize the exegetical works, Carole Straw's *Gregory the Great: Perfection in Imperfection* (Berkeley, 1988) provides an important constructive analysis of Gregory's thought at the close of the twentieth century. Straw explains the apparent inconsistencies in Gregory's thinking as a deliberate mental comprehension of dialectical opposites being complementary forces on a single continuum.[28] She aptly points to several readily apparent binaries in Gregory's corpus, including his spirituality versus his pragmatism, his intellectual exegesis versus his promotion of populist saint-cult, his desire for retirement versus his commitment to service, and especially his ability to find perfection in an imperfect and fallen world. But it is the spiritual versus carnal binary that most illumines Gregory's integration and serves as the primary axiom for her investigation. For Straw, the only way to make sense of these binaries is to comprehend the "mental processes and the various configurations of ideas that structure his thought," but to do so one must combine the "skills of a literary critic, anthropologist, and historian."[29] It is, perhaps, telling that she does not include "theologian" in the list of academic skills, despite her occasional foray into what would otherwise be considered Gregory's theological outlook.[30]

Claude Dagens's 1977 biography was one of the first modern attempts to detail Gregory's theology, although it is a very different sort of analysis than typical studies of early Christian theologians.[31] Indeed, Dagens offers an uncommon degree of direct citation of Gregory's works, which he intends to transform into an appreciation for the experience of the Christian life rather than an assessment of Gregory's ideas per se. In part, this might derive from Dagens's presumption that Gregory's dogmatic theology was largely derivative of Augustine.[32] Dagens emphasizes, instead, a different kind of theology—one that seeks to understand the values and pastoral possibilities that Christianity offers to its practitioners. Despite its length, Dagens's study offers a relatively limited assessment of the range of Gregory's interests, and even those aspects of his thought that are emphasized (such as his moral and pastoral concerns) are not especially differentiated from those of other ascetically inclined bishops of the period.

The beginning of the twenty-first century has seen a marked increase in the number of theological assessments of Gregory's work among European scholars. Of these, Katharina Greschat's study of Gregory's *Moralia* stands out as a fine example of a newfound appreciation for Gregory's exegetical sophistication.[33] On Greschat's reading, the life of Job is interpreted by Gregory as a kind of allegorical bridge between his Christological commitments and his pastoral concerns—thus, Gregory's preachers, like Christ himself, must inspire their followers to commit themselves fully to God but must simultaneously assist those around them. Like many scholars before her, Greschat's interpretation of Gregory's theological vision is largely confined by an Augustinian spectrum, but she nevertheless provides detailed assessments of the *Moralia* and rightly appreciates its author's emphasis on spiritual leadership.

Rade Kisić has more recently offered an account of Gregory's eschatology, linking it both to the pontiff's ascetic inclinations and to his ultimate pastoral concerns.[34] For Kisić, Gregory's eschatological vision is ultimately positive because of the eschatological hope made possible by the resurrection of Christ. In part, this optimistic reading of Gregory's theology fuels an interpretation of Gregory as a bridge between East and West. While that position is not original in itself, the emphasis on eschatology allows Kisić to argue his thesis in a fresh way.

The common revisionist theme in Greschat, Kisić, and other recent studies of Gregory's theology is that the pontiff was a more creative and sophisticated thinker than most twentieth-century scholarly assessments had acknowledged.[35] Gregory was creative, Greshat or Straw would argue, even when he remained within an Augustinian framework. But what binds all of these assessments of Gregory's theology is a clear favoritism for Gregory's exegetical and hagiographic works. We learn very little about

Gregory's activity as bishop, public administrator, or diplomat, or how that activity may have been motivated by his theological commitments. Thus, the present study is differentiated from these previous assessments of Gregory's thought in two principal ways. First, it situates Gregory's ascetic commitments and the uniqueness of his ascetic theology as the baseline for his other theological investments. Second, it seeks to build upon the analysis of Gregory's thought by seeking ways to understand how his theological commitments are revealed in his pastoral, administrative, and diplomatic activities.

JEFFREY RICHARDS'S BIOGRAPHY, *Consul of God: The Life and Times of Gregory the Great* (Routlege, 1980) offers something of a polar extreme to these theological assessments in the sense that it pursues a political and administrative account of Gregory's career, drawing primarily on the bishop's extensive correspondence and largely ignoring his exegetical and hagiographic works. To be sure, Richards's account is a thorough appraisal of the geopolitical forces at work in Gregory's world and nicely addresses the significance of Gregory's interaction with the Lombards and Merovingians. Throughout, Richards shows a particular interest in Gregory's contribution to the development of the papacy as a political and economic institution that would continue to develop in the Middle Ages, but does so without much of the anachronism that characterizes Ullmann's assessment.

Perhaps the first serious attempt to offer a comprehensive study of Gregory's life and thought since Dudden was that of Robert Markus, whose 1997 biography reflects a lifetime's study of Gregory.[36] Although most at home in his examination of the pontiff's correspondence and the political and administrative aspects of his career, Markus does acknowledge Gregory's commitments to ascetic idealism and rightly understands the pastoral motivations that governed much of Gregory's decision-making process. Indeed, for Markus, Gregory is nothing if not a pragmatic and efficient administrator of the Roman See whose dedication to his cause prompted his expansion of Rome's influence into Gaul, Kent, and elsewhere. It is one of the great achievements of Markus's biography that he views Gregory as a loyal son of the empire, even if that empire was now centered in Constantinople, and Gregory did not always see eye to eye with the emperor.

If one were to critique Markus's account, one might find the most fault with his assessment that Gregory was a derivative thinker, someone who drew his ideas from Augustine and John Cassian and, apart from attempting a synthesis of the two, showed few signs of theological creativity or innovation. Indeed, it will be one of the central efforts of this volume to demonstrate that Gregory was, in fact, a unique and nuanced theologian, whose subtlety is often missed by scholars who wrongly assume that theological originality must be of a dogmatic nature or who fail to see the ways in which his particular theological commitments to asceticism and pastoral ministry informed his approach to administrative and diplomatic tasks.

More recently, Barbara Müller's 2009 biography, *Führung im Denken und Handeln Gregors des Grossen*, provides a thorough account of Gregory's view of "leadership" (*Führung*) based upon an analysis of his career and writing. Her study progresses according to a diachronic narrative of Gregory's life but does so in such a way as to reflect in detail upon several of his texts. Müller is determined to show that context always framed Gregory's actions and his state of mind as he wrote and preached. Although most of Gregory's major works (as well as the *Libellus responsionum*[37]) receive a dedicated chapter, Müller largely ignores his famous *Moralia in Iob*,[38] which Gregory had initially delivered as a series of homilies during his stay in Constantinople. It is perhaps surprising that she chose to exclude the *Moralia*, both because it is widely regarded as his most sophisticated theological work and because Gregory has so much to say about leadership within the text.[39] Indeed, one could argue that a great portion of the treatise is an extended digression about the way in which spiritual directors are to provide effective leadership to those in their care.[40]

There are a number of common pursuits between Müller's analysis of Gregory's concept of leadership and certain components of the present study. The reader will notice rather quickly, however, that there also exist significant differences in both method and interpretation. Whereas Müller follows a strict chronological narrative that examines only the ideas of individual treatises as they fit into the sequence of Gregory's biography, I start with an assessment of his theological and pastoral ideals before beginning to interpret his actions in light of those commitments. This simple difference of approach leads to some surprising differences in conclusion, particularly as they relate to the uniqueness of Gregory's ascetic theology and the extent to which it informed his approach to certain pastoral and diplomatic decisions.

Indeed, I will argue that an adequate understanding of Gregory's activity in Rome and his diplomacy abroad requires a thorough understanding of his theological commitments and that those commitments are best understood within an ascetic and pastoral framework. Through a careful reading of the *Moralia* and other theological texts, I argue that Gregory's ascetic theology predisposed him to approach leadership in general and spiritual direction more specifically from a particular (and largely unique) vantage point. I then interpret his theory of pastoral theology as well as his specific responses to the crises of his day from that assessment of his ascetic commitments. For example, whereas Müller's discussion of the *Book of Pastoral Rule* is situated at a precise moment in Gregory's biography and seeks a plausible interpretation of key words that he employs, my investigation of the *Pastoral Rule* is routinely supplemented with direct comparisons to the ascetic and pastoral commitments that Gregory first articulated in his musings on leadership in the *Moralia*. By interpreting the *Pastoral Rule* in light of the *Moralia* (and other treatises from his early tenure as bishop), I hope to offer a more holistic view of the connection between Gregory's ascetic theology and his strategies for spiritual leadership. What is more, whereas Müller's study never strays far from a traditional narrative history, the present investigation routinely incorporates discourse and other forms of literary analysis to demonstrate the sophistication of Gregory's thought and the subtle ways in which he was able to pursue multiple ends through various endeavors.[41]

Gregory was a man compelled by conflicting impulses. On the one hand, he believed that the Christian confession of faith demanded humility—not merely a rhetoric of humility or a nod to a passé protestation against self-interest, but an authentic, convicting, and lifelong commitment that could only be sustained through ascetic detachment. On the other hand, Gregory simultaneously felt a deep draw to the service of others. Capable men, in Gregory's eyes, do not forsake civic responsibility to wall themselves off in a monastery; no, the faithful must hear the call to serve. Whereas the sources for Gregory's impulse for Christian humility are rather easy to surmise—it came largely from his ascetic reading—the impulse to public service cannot be as easily iso-lated. As we will see, threads of theological and classical sources, as well as a variety of experiences, were woven into the tapestry of Gregory's thinking in the years prior to his election as Roman bishop.

It is the thesis of this book that Gregory's ascetic and pastoral the-ology both informed and structured his administration of the Roman Church. To that end, I have divided the present volume into three parts so as to provide a more integrated assessment of Gregory's thought and life than currently exists. Part 1 examines the particular characteristics of his ascetic theology and then traces some of the consequences of his ascetic commitments to other aspects of his thought. It is remarkable, given the depth of Gregory's ascetic reflection and the degree to which it was unique among his contemporaries, that no extensive study of Greg-ory's ascetic theology exists. Part 2 explores the various dimensions of his pastoral theology, showing the extent to which it can be understood as the culmination of his ascetic vision and his sense of responsibility as a public servant. Part 3 then traces some of the most important diplomatic crises and administrative initiatives of his tenure as Roman bishop, in-cluding the expansion of Roman influence throughout Italy and Gaul and his various efforts to improve the quality of Christian life among the Germanic tribes. Throughout, I will resist the temptation to divide Greg-ory's world or his response to it between the customary binaries of East and West, Greek and Latin, or imperial and Germanic. In doing so I follow the lead of the recent collection of essays for Brill's *A Companion to Gregory the Great*, edited by Bronwen Neil and Matthew Dal Santo.[42] As we will see, Gregory's administration of the Roman Church, his diplomatic efforts among the northern tribes, and his negotiations with Eastern rulers were often directly integrated and always tangentially con-nected. It is hoped that the extensive foregrounding of the pontiff's theo-logical commitments will illuminate in new ways the means by which he responded to the world of his day.

Part One

Gregory as Ascetic Theologian

While the first part of this study will not be able to offer an exhaustive examination of all of Gregory's theological commitments, it will assess those features that most informed his policies and show the extent to which he was a creative, if subtle, theologian in his own right. The idea that Gregory was a creative theologian has not always been the dominant view. For his harshest critics, Gregory's intellectual crime was that he had inherited a rich and sophisticated religious outlook from Augustine, Jerome, and Ambrose, only to exchange it for a superstitious world full of mythical tales of saints, relics, and demons.[1]

Even those scholars who are more sympathetic to Gregory often view him as a derivative thinker. The majority of twentieth-century commentators, in fact, see Gregory as little more than a monastic sieve between Augustine and the Middle Ages. Robert Markus well characterized that interpretation when he noted that, despite the fact that Gregory read widely in the Latin fathers who preceded him, "in all essentials it was Augustine's conceptual structures that shaped the world of his imagination."[2]

Since the turn of the twenty-first century, however, a number of French, German, and Italian monographs have sought to show that Gregory was in fact a sophisticated thinker — even if he remained steadfastly within Augustine's theological shadow. As noted in the introduction, these scholars have emphasized different aspects of Gregory's theology—ranging from his eschatology to his exegetic style—to correct the Gibbonesque narrative that Gregory represents the intellectual decline into the Middle Ages. Even Gregory's *Dialogues*, which had been the source of so many hostile interpretations,[3] now routinely receive positive assessments.[4]

While Gregory's appropriation of the hagiographical topoi that fill his corpus, especially his *Dialogues*, may not have been typical of the Latin theologians of the late fourth century, there is little reason to conclude that his literary decisions or fascination with the mystical realm demonstrate any intellectual or theological deficiency.[5] On the contrary, part 1 will show that the use of these ascetic topoi well illustrate the extent to which Gregory was able to synthesize a variety of ideas to produce his own creative adaptation of literary and theological traditions in response to the various needs of those with whom he interacted.

THE ARGUMENT OF part 1 is that Gregory's theological outlook was primarily shaped by his commitments to a specific form of ascetic practice that emphasized service to others.[6] To claim that Gregory's theological outlook is an ascetic one is not groundbreaking: Gregory's personal monastic piety and his popularization of the legendary acts of Italian ascetics are well known. Thus, the purpose of this section is not so much to demonstrate that Gregory's theological vision was ascetic in general terms as it is to show the important implications that individual subthemes within his particular vision of ascetic behavior have for other aspects of this theological thought and instruction.

To that end, this examination begins with a careful analysis of the specific dimensions of Gregory's ascetic theology before moving on to consider more broadly some of the consequences of that outlook. In the later chapters of part 1 we will learn, for example, that Gregory's ascetic commitments contributed greatly to what I have previously termed his "participationist" soteriology, a perspective that led him to advocate simultaneously for the necessity of grace and human initiative.[7] We will also see the extent to which Gregory's dedication to the ascetic topos of humility was incongruent with many of the claims of papal privilege that steadily increased during the fifth and sixth centuries. Gregory was not oblivious to or unconcerned with securing Roman ecclesiastical authority, but his rhetorical promotion of Roman claims was always in tension with an equally powerful discourse of ascetic humility. The resulting ecclesiological vision greatly differentiated Gregory from other bishops of Rome in the late-ancient period. Part 1 concludes with an analysis of some of the mystical characteristics of Gregory's theology[8]—including his understanding of the function of miracles and his promotion of the cult of the saints—characteristics that further demonstrate his unique appropriation of and contributions to the ascetic and literary traditions of the late-ancient period.

CHAPTER ONE

A Theology of Asceticism

On November 30th of 591 or 592, Gregory delivered a brief homily to those who had assembled for the Feast of St. Andrew the Apostle. The Lectionary reading for the feast, appropriately enough, was Matthew 4:18–22 (Christ's call for the four fishermen, Andrew, Peter, James, and John, to follow him). For Gregory, the meaning of the passage was clear: the saints, when called, abandon their desires in order to follow Christ. Using charity as a measuring stick for conviction, Gregory was distressed that people in his own time appeared to lack apostolic zeal, which left them unable to follow Christ truly. Anticipating those who might claim that they have no possessions to abandon, Gregory instructs his listeners that they need to sacrifice desire itself.[1] How does one know if he has abandoned the desires of the world? Gregory asks rhetorically. We know it, he says, if we fear not for ourselves but for our neighbor; if we seek not our own gain, but the prosperity of those around us; if we desire the sufferings of our enemies to become our own; and if we offer our own souls as a sacrifice to God.[2] Gregory concludes the homily with a turn, again, to the virtue of St. Andrew and enjoins his audience to begin the process of withdrawal from the world. Through ascetic discipline, he promises, they will advance "step by step," as they progress from the abandonment of desire for another's goods (i.e., greed) to the abandonment of desire for one's own goods (i.e., charity), which ultimately leads to a willingness to suffer for others.[3]

While Gregory describes a linear progression from the abandonment of desire to the willingness to suffer for others, it is characteristic of his homilies that he would present action, motivation, and the grace that fuels them both as a mysteriously integrated and mutually implicated collection of forces. While Gregory could not control the mystical flow of divine grace, he could hope to inspire his audience to see that willfully serving others was the best way to answer the call of Christ.

On another occasion early in his pontificate, Gregory found himself preaching a similar message at the shrine of an unnamed martyr.[4] The Lectionary passage for that day was John 15:12–16, a pericope of some Trinitarian significance but one from which Gregory chose to emphasize the relationship between the denial of self and the love of neighbor.[5] The "ancient enemy," Gregory warns, uses our envy and greed to drive a wedge between us and our neighbor. Whereas Christians should sacrifice all that they have, even for their enemies, most Christians resist their enemies because they fear the loss of possessions through enemies.[6] To overcome this, Gregory reasons, Christians must learn to abandon their selfishness: only then will the desire for earthly things be transformed into a burning desire for the things of the Lord; only then will Christians be able to imitate the saints.[7] Gregory concludes the homily by noting that although it is unlikely that his listeners will have the opportunity to suffer martyrdom like the saint for whom they have assembled, they should nonetheless conquer their souls, because such a sacrifice is pleasing to God. For Gregory, this sacrifice is a struggle or contest (*certamen*) of the heart.[8] This is a "spiritual" contest, one that is won by forgiving enemies and those who have wronged us, but that also requires an indifference to material possession in the sense that only those who are indifferent to material loss can gladly forgive those who have taken from them.

I have chosen to begin my analysis of Gregory's theology of asceticism with a snapshot of these two public homilies because they evince well the core presumptions underlying his commitment to the ascetic life. For Gregory, cultivation of ascetic practices was one of the most basic consequences—moral applications, if you will—of a Christian's faith in Christ. While these particular examples emphasize the rejection of material possessions, Gregory's ascetic register incorporated all of the typical forms of early Christian renunciation (including the regulation of food, the divestiture of money and family, and the rejection of sexual desire). Thus, Gregory reasoned, a moral or ascetic commitment was expected of everyone who believed that Christ was God.

To be clear, the term *asceticism* is largely a modern scholarly tag for a set of personal commitments that were often linked to specific physical and spiritual regimens. When I speak of Gregory's "asceticism," his "ascetic register," or his "ascetic idiom," I hope to convey the particular aspects of Gregory's ascetic thinking. In general terms, many early Christians believed that their faith in God required them to limit those pursuits that led to temporal ends or fleeting pleasure (e.g., the acquisition of money, luxurious food, comfort, or fame). These adherents sought to rechannel their energies toward endeavors that they hoped would bring spiritual growth (e.g., fasting, charity, sexual renunciation, and humility). And, to be sure, both the renunciatory and aspirational dimensions of ascetic discipline could be physical or contemplative, and often they were some combination of the two. By the time of Gregory's writing, ascetic writers had developed a sophisticated intellectual, hermeneutical, and physical apparatus for connecting what we might loosely call an "ascetic commitment" to their practice of Christianity. In the pages that follow, I will demonstrate the ways in which Gregory's ascetic theology drew from these general tendencies but was also unique in key respects.

Indeed, the two homilies just reviewed do more than illuminate Gregory's asceticizing hermeneutic (a characteristic that was typical of many exegetes of the period); they also demonstrate what was distinctive about Gregory's theology of asceticism: its social dimension. Gregory, perhaps more than any other Latin author of the Patristic Era, consistently argued that the true ascetic was the one who cared so little about himself that he would willingly suspend his own enjoyment of the contemplative life to be of service to others. Indeed, within Gregory's enormous corpus we find an embroidery of many ascetic threads, all of which advocate an asceticism for others.

Scripture, Knowledge of God, and an Asceticizing Hermeneutic

As we delve deeper in the "logic" of asceticism in Gregory's thought, it is important to analyze the extent to which Gregory's understanding of the ability of a Christian to have knowledge of God and to comprehend the revelation of God through the Scriptures was intrinsically linked to the pontiff's own "asceticized" reading of the Scriptures.[9] In her masterful *Reading Renunciation: Asceticism and Scripture in Early Christianity*, Elizabeth Clark elucidates the many ways in which late-ancient authors successfully "recontextualized" the words and verses of the Bible to endorse an ascetic reading of Scripture that was in line with and reinforced their own predispositions for the life of renunciation.[10] "Professing to remain faithful to the biblical passages at hand, ascetically inclined church fathers nonetheless produced new meaning that made the entire Bible speak to the practical as well as theological concerns of Christian renunciants."[11] Though Pope Gregory lay beyond the chronological scope of Clark's study, the pontiff's inclination to interpret Scripture, history, and theology through the medium of his own ascetic commitments is readily discernable.[12] And it is through this medium that his epistemological and hermeneutical perspectives converge.

Indeed, Gregory argues that the knowledge of God derives, primarily, from a study of the Scriptures. The Scriptures contain "divine speech"[13] and provide "food and drink" for the soul.[14] Not only are they the foundation of Christian beliefs, they also serve as the inspiration for a life in Christ.[15] Although some of the truths contained in the Scriptures are beyond human comprehension,[16] all Christians who strive for knowledge of God are able to gain something from the Bible. But Gregory's theological topography (like that of other Christian intellectuals of the period) is hierarchical and axiological—meaning that some Christians are able to understand the Scriptures better than others. According to Gregory, those Christians who couple an exceptional degree of ascetic progress with authentic humility are more equipped than others to discern the mysteries of the sacred texts and their source (i.e., God). Establishing these points in his commentary on the prophet Ezekiel, he notes, "Many things were written simplistically so that the youthful might be nourished, whereas other things surely were concealed in obscure notions (*obscurioribus sen-*

tentiis) that occupy [the minds of] the strong because things that are comprehended after great effort are the more gratifying."[17]

For Gregory, it is through discernment (*discretio*) that one obtains the mystical insight to interpret Scripture properly.[18] The connection between *discretio* and knowledge of God lies in the belief that this "spiritual" insight is a basic requirement for the accurate interpretation of Scripture, which is, in turn, the primary conduit for true knowledge.[19] Making this precise point in his homilies on Ezekiel, he argues that *discretio* is vital to acquiring knowledge from Scripture because it guarantees a proper interpretation; if left to our own interpretive abilities, we will believe that we are reading Scripture spiritually when, in fact, we are being deceived by our carnal impulses, which lead to a false reading.[20] Elsewhere, Gregory warns that a carnal life prevents the reader of Scripture from accessing its divine truths.[21] Conversely, we may infer that it is through ascetic accomplishment that one is most able to acquire the gift of discernment.[22]

Although Gregory does offer several positive statements about the ability—even the necessity—of the mind's activity in the acquisition of knowledge,[23] those statements are rarely isolated in Gregory's corpus from a discussion of the knowledge that is mediated through Scripture. Moreover, by describing cognition as something contingent upon both humility and grace, Gregory's characterization of the mind's acquisition of knowledge simply mirrors his treatment of discernment, which is, in itself, a kind of discussion about mental activity.[24] Underpinning these epistemological statements is Gregory's conviction that the acquisition of knowledge, whatever the source, is preconditioned by a life that is both renunciatory (i.e., engaged in physical ascetic acts) and contemplative.[25] But once knowledge is obtained, another form of balance—the balance between the active life and the contemplative—conditions the retention and dissemination of knowledge.[26] In other words, what is attained through contemplation or through a study of the Scriptures is not pursued for its own sake, nor is it to be kept to oneself. Rather, Gregory believes that the spiritually advanced receive knowledge of God for the benefit of others and themselves. As we will see, properly balancing the two (i.e., self and neighbor), allows the spiritual director to fulfill the commandment to love both God (contemplative) and neighbor (active).[27]

In the twentieth century, scholars were keen to differentiate Gregory's biblical commentaries from the *Dialogues* because of their supposed difference in genre, content, and sophistication. And while it is true that these texts emphasize different literary styles, the discrepancies between them may be overblown.[28] Note, for example, that Gregory's famous dictum (from the *Moralia*) that there are three distinct modes for the interpretation of Scripture (i.e., the historical, the allegorical, and the moral) never seems to have compromised his inclination to employ all three methods to derive ascetic inspiration—inspiration that was ultimately in line with the moral prescriptions of the *Dialogues*.[29] Indeed, the pontiff's asceticizing hermeneutic seems to enable the primary goal of his didactic practice, which is to lead his audience to a moral and practical application of the biblical text—an application that is almost always expressed through an ascetic register.

Even a cursory reading of Gregory's biblical commentaries will yield a dizzying number of examples that evince the ascetic character of his interpretive strategies. His repeated discussions of Adam's Fall, for example, almost always occur within an ascetic idiom. Whether he describes the Fall as act of "gluttony" or an act of "pride," or whether he interprets the prelapsarian state as one of "perfect contemplation" that ultimately gave way to a postlapsarian imprisonment of "external concerns," there is no denying that Gregory's interpretive imagination exists within the ascetic's horizon, the ascetic discourse.[30] Other examples, of course, abound.[31] In his *Commentary on Ezekiel*, the warm and cold winds are interpreted to represent virtue and vice;[32] so too do the steps of the gate (see Ezek. 40:6).[33] He interprets Ezekiel 1:23 ("every one with two wings covered his body") as a call to an ascetic discipline of the body and Ezekiel 4:2 ("build a siege wall against it") as representing the spiritual director who instructs his disciples to guard against vice.[34] In the *Moralia*, Job's sons are routinely castigated for their gluttonous behavior,[35] his wife is accused of seeing the world through carnal rather than spiritual eyes,[36] and the animal sacrifice of the Jewish priesthood is allegorized to represent various acts of ascetic repentance.[37] One of Gregory's best-known interpretative maneuvers, of course, is to interpret the animals of Scripture in allegorical and/or morally instructive ways, including (rather famously) the rhinoceros, whose horn is the quintessential symbol of pride.[38]

For Gregory, the intersection of ascetic practice and scriptural medita-tion occurs in multiple and overlapping ways. His personal ascetic train-ing and his supervision of ascetic communities (both before and after his election as bishop of Rome) predispose him to seek and find ascetic mes-sages within the biblical text. Those "mystical messages," in turn, fuel his belief in the necessity of ascetic commitment, and they provide the basis upon which he structures his pastoral teaching. Even passages that appear to have little obvious ascetic content are spun, in Gregory's hands, into an appeal for renunciatory practice, and they are communicated in an ascetic idiom.[39]

Dividing the World into Virtues and Vices

Perhaps one of the most discernable ways in which we can docu-ment the growing influence of ascetic communities on the broader Church in the late-ancient period is through traceable shifts in linguistic patterns and theological categories. Within the ascetic communities of late antiquity (particularly those of the Egyptian desert), there was a par-ticular emphasis on the internalization of the spiritual battle. The legisla-tive enjoinders found in Scripture (e.g., do not kill, do not steal, do not commit adultery) presented a moral imperative, but through the process of intensive self-reflection, ascetic activists began to identify sin where it had gone unnoticed before. For example, they scrutinized the vices (i.e., inner depravations that led to spiritual or physical sin) and developed cata-logs of spiritual antidotes (i.e., the virtues) for their control and eventual eradication.[40] In this discourse of virtue and vice, fasting prevented glut-tony, charity corrected greed, and humility guarded against pride.[41]

Whereas Ambrose and Augustine had typically employed the four cardinal virtues according to the classical Greco-Roman models (i.e., pru-dence, temperance, fortitude, and justice), Gregory's corpus reveals a near universal appropriation of the ascetic idiom for describing virtue and vice.[42] In fact, Gregory is probably the Latin theologian most responsible for mediating the concept of the seven vices (later known as the seven deadly sins) to the Middle Ages.[43] The asceticizing discussion of virtue and vice permeates every genre of Gregory's writing. In the *Dialogues*, for example, the miracles of saints are said to spring from preexistent virtue. Similarly, the didactic value in describing these miracles along with other acts of the Italian saints serves as an active promotion of ascetic virtues (especially fasting, almsgiving, chastity, and humility). In the *Pastoral Rule*, the ascetic register for virtue and vice becomes a primary filter by which a candidate for the priesthood is described as being either qualified or unqualified for office.[44] And the promotion of virtue and the correction of vice dominates book 3 of the same treatise, which is intended to serve as the foundation for the spiritual leadership offered by Gregory's priestly readers.

It is in the biblical commentaries, however, that we find the most exhaustive discussions of the asceticized categories of virtue and vice. The most explicit listing of the seven vices, all of which spring from their "mother" (i.e., pride), is in book 31 of the *Moralia*.[45] This particular discussion develops as an extended metaphor on war and battle and is drawn from Job 39:25. Other occasions offer extended analyses of one or more particular vices and the need for their eradication.[46] Gregory is especially concerned that his readers understand the extent to which the vices are interconnected—a vice that is left untreated will almost certainly be the source of others.[47] Although he is far less interested than Evagrius had been to show that the devil or his demons are the tempting force behind the vices, the idea is certainly not alien to his thinking.[48] Here Gregory follows Cassian in understanding the demons as more of an external than an internal threat.[49]

Gregory's emphasis on the virtues and vices no doubt derives from the fact that they offered an effective means of bridging the gap between the spiritual and physical worlds and of communicating the necessity of constant introspection in a ready-made taxonomy of good and bad behavior. As we will explore in chapter 7, Gregory believed that every Christian was spiritually unique—everyone had distinct spiritual talents and challenges.[50] The spiritual director was charged with discerning these idiosyncrasies in his disciples and setting them upon a proper path to spiritual correction through the encouragement of ascetic discipline. Thus, the language of virtue and vice made simple both the diagnosis of sin and the prescription for reform.

Among the things to which Gregory was keen to alert potential directors was the fact that vices could very often masquerade as virtue[51] and that virtue unaccompanied by humility is no virtue at all.[52] Of course, there was more to the appropriation of ascetic language than simple fearmongering—Gregory repeatedly held up the saints as examples of virtuous living and encouraged his audiences to imitate their modes of renunciation.[53] Indeed, the meditation on the lives of the saints (the biblical heroes, the martyrs, and the ascetics of the *Dialogues*) offers an important vehicle for Christians to cultivate virtue.[54] Although no saint is in possession of every virtue, every saint is in possession of the most important virtue—humility.

Humility and Asceticism

Among the many things that one learns from reading Gregory's exhaustive correspondence is that he was deeply suspicious of those in power, whether civil or ecclesiastical. More often than not, the pontiff's expressed concern related to what he perceived to be an inherent link between the exercise of authority and the acquisition of pride.[55] It is noteworthy, in fact, that the occasions on which Gregory was most willing to confront the Roman emperor Maurice were precisely those occasions on which he believed that Maurice had enabled others (especially clerics) to act with pride.[56] So, too, the pontiff's strongest words against the Merovingian rulers related to his critique of simony in their realms, which in Gregory's theological reckoning was an unlawful disruption of the rightful structure of the Church and always born of pride.[57]

Gregory's concern with pride and his promotion of humility, however, ran much deeper than a simple platform for critiquing his ecclesiastical and secular rivals. Indeed, the pontiff understood the entire cycle of humanity's fall and redemption to be located within the pride/humility paradigm. Gregory begins book 31 of the *Moralia* with a summary of this view, identifying Satan's temptation of Adam in the Garden of Eden as the manifestation of pride and Christ's birth, death, and resurrection as the ultimate personification of humility.[58] It is through pride, Gregory reasons, that we distance ourselves from God, and it is through humility that we escape sin. One might say that the balanced antitheses of pride and humility, and good and evil, are at the heart of Gregory's theological outlook.[59]

Gregory's ideas about pride and humility, of course, have long been noticed by scholars.[60] Claude Dagens stressed the place of humility in Gregory's understanding of the virtues.[61] Conrad Leyser has more recently made a great deal of what he calls Gregory's "rhetoric of vulnerability."[62] While Leyser is certainly right to note the shifting parameters of late-ancient discourse (which between the periods of Augustine and Gregory came to emphasize the Christian virtue of humility and the extent to which a "rhetoric of humility" could serve to activate or retain authority), there is good reason to believe that Gregory's theological outlook was in large part shaped by an ascetic framework that understood humility to be the quintessential Christian virtue. In other words, just as it would be foolhardy to believe that Gregory had nothing to gain from his frequent protestations of weakness and vulnerability (one of Leyser's primary points), so too would it be wrong to presume that such protestations were made without some theological commitment (Leyser's analysis does not engage humility as a theological conviction). But to evaluate this clearly one needs to see the balance between Gregory's ascetic theology and his theology of humility, particularly as the two converged to produce an ascetic vision that emphasized service to others as the climax of the spiritual and ascetic life.

To be sure, Gregory was not the first ascetic theologian to esteem humility. Evagrius of Pontus and John Cassian offer the two most obvious antecedents, both of whom either directly or indirectly helped to shape Gregory's outlook.[63] And there are countless examples in Gregory's corpus of his endorsement of humility and warning against pride,[64] which, in his theological understanding, is the most powerful obstacle to holiness and the acquisition of divine knowledge.[65] But two things distinguish Gregory's treatment of humility from that of most other theologians of the late-ancient period: his eagerness to mine the "weaknesses" of the saints to draw out their ultimate goodness, and the way in which Gregory reconfigures the link between asceticism and humility so that the most successful ascetics are the ones who care so little for themselves that they suspend their own contemplation for the sake of others.

In the opening pages of book 2 of the *Moralia*, Gregory offers a theoretical explanation for why the Scriptures reveal the weaknesses of the saints. This is true, Gregory reasons, not only so that we may "learn what we ought to fear" (i.e., anything that is a hardship for the saints will certainly be a hardship for us) but also so that we may learn of the great power of humility through the examples of the saints.[66] Indeed, it is one of the defining characteristics of Gregory's exegetical interests to mine the failures, sins, and shortcomings of the saints. The most obvious examples, of course, are King David, St. Peter, and St. Mary Magdalene (whom Gregory famously conflates with the unnamed woman caught in adultery [Jn. 8:1–11]).[67] Gregory was unique among the late-ancient bishops of Rome in his willingness the hold up the errors, sins, and shortcomings of St. Peter.[68] But Gregory was also willing to mine the errors of other, less obviously flawed saints (including Paul, Benedict, and even Job) so as to provide a saintly exemplar for the power of humility.[69] And it was more than the saintly exemplars whom God allowed to fall into sin; Gregory believed that all of the "elect" fall into certain sins so that they can personally learn humility and so that others can be inspired by the power of their repentance through humility.[70]

Whereas the most influential ascetic writers of the late-ancient period had not been involved with the selection and supervision of a large network of clerics, Gregory's unique contributions to the development of ascetic theology were likely shaped by that responsibility. It is thus important to understand the extent to which his discussions of humility fit within a complex matrix of ascetic and administrative concerns. Indeed, Gregory in many ways refocused the theology of humility by emphasizing its social possibilities. Whereas Evagrius, Cassian, and others stressed humility as an exercise in self-abasement through the recognition of personal sin and fault, Gregory encouraged his readers to learn that humility could be cultivated through denying oneself spiritual joys, particularly the joys of contemplation and retreat.[71] Indeed, unlike ascetic collections such as the *Apophthegmata Patrum*, which were filled with ideological quips about humility as an antidote to pride, Gregory looked beyond such sentiments in his search for a balance between authentic humility and effective leadership.

For example, in the ninth homily of his *Commentary on Ezekiel*, Gregory explores the complex relationship between authority, pride, retreat, and humility. He cautions that just as it is likely that the one in authority will be susceptible to pride, so too will the one who resists a position of leadership fail to obtain humility because he has acted out of fear of responsibility rather than true humility in refusing to serve others.

"Therefore, freedom and pride, humility and fear must always be differentiated so that fear does not mask itself as humility nor pride pretend to be freedom."[72] For Gregory, the more one comes to know God, the less one thinks of himself, and, as a consequence, the more capable one is to offer effective leadership to others.[73]

An Asceticism for Others

The notion that ascetics should put themselves in the service of others was not a Gregorian invention—Basil of Caesarea famously encouraged his monks into active social ministry.[74] Even Cassian, who is sometimes understood to have promoted a sectarian view of the monastic life that had little interest in the outside world, can be interpreted as having endorsed a tentative outreach in the last installment of his *Conferences.*[75] But in Gregory's hands the very summit of ascetic perfection is redefined. Whereas both Basil and Cassian understood the goal of the ascetic life to be a mystical union with God that was ultimately achieved through a state of contemplative *apatheia*, Gregory argued that the apex of the spiritual life was to be found in the sacrifice that corresponded to service for others.

Gregory's emphasis on a balance between contemplation and active ministry has, of course, been noted by several scholars.[76] Perhaps the most sophisticated analysis of this aspect of Gregory's thought belongs to Carole Straw, who understood the pontiff's repeated encouragement of "active contemplation" as a kind of third way, a "mixed life" reciprocally balanced between the lives of contemplation and action.[77] This concept is central to Straw's thesis that Gregory found perfection in the balancing of binary ideals. While her analysis of symmetry in Gregory's thinking is quite helpful, I propose a slightly different means of interpretation. Namely, I would like to suggest that if we reflect upon Gregory's active contemplative life within the context of late-ancient ascetic theology more broadly, we find that the pontiff is advocating for a nuanced vision of ascetic perfection. And, as part 3 of this volume will demonstrate, it was precisely that nuanced vision that informed and structured Gregory's administration of the Roman See.[78]

The contemplative life was important—even fundamentally necessary—in Gregory's eyes. But Gregory distinguished himself from other late-ancient ascetics, even those committed to the service to others, with the idea that no one could achieve perfection in the stillness of contemplation alone. One had to be willing to suspend those spiritual joys for the sake of others, even if doing so meant losing some measure of contemplative progress.[79] In his fifth homily in the *Commentary on Ezekiel*, Gregory chastises those ascetics who are so selfish in their contemplative efforts that they refuse to be a light to others. "The man who leads a good life in secret but is of little assistance for the advancement of others is like a coal" (i.e., a source of energy that remains cold).[80] In the seventh homily in the same collection, he notes that the "perfect" are those who not only weep for their own sins but also stretch out the wings of their virtues for others.[81] In book 6 of the *Moralia* he goes so far as to argue that there is no advantage to ascetic discipline if the practitioner is unwilling to have compassion for his neighbors.[82] And then, in book 7, he maintains that the love of God that is isolated from love of neighbor is an impoverishment of the spiritual life.[83] These are but a few examples that exist in Gregory's lengthy biblical commentaries.

It is in *Dialogues*, however, that we find the most comprehensive and orchestrated presentation of Gregory's argument for the importance of service to others. For example, in book 3 of that text we find a story of two brothers who enter monastic life together. One of the brothers becomes the abbot of the community; the other pursues a more eremitic form of asceticism. The abbot is said to lack the spiritual capacity to perform miracles, whereas the recluse is graced with the ability to perform them regularly. But, in the end, it is not the one who performed miracles in isolation but the one who served others who is shown to be the monk of consistent virtue. And the way in which this manifests itself in the story is that the recluse is unable to properly deal with the sins of others, which leads him to fall victim to pride and anger. His brother, by contrast, proves to be a model of patience, humility, and sanctity.[84]

It is the account of St. Benedict in the *Dialogues*, of course, that most effectively communicates Gregory's vision of an asceticism for others. Indeed, when we compare Gregory's *Life of Benedict* to the literary accounts of other famous late-ancient ascetics (e.g., Athanasius's account of Anthony, Theodoric's account of Symeon the Stylite, or Sulpicius Severus's account of Martin of Tours), we find that the story of Benedict is unique in its emphases. Whereas the other accounts place the narrative arc on the acquisition of ascetic skill and the contest against demonic forces that stand in its way, Gregory's *Life of Benedict* begins with its hero acquiring ascetic virtue without need of a mentor.[85] Thus, the narrative development does not lie in Benedict's asceticism; rather, it lies in his challenge to offer effective spiritual direction to others. Indeed, the vast majority of Benedict's miracles are not ascetic feats or personal conflicts against demonic forces but events in the supervision of unruly monks who continuously challenge his authority. Through discernment and pastoral condescension, Benedict leads his disciples in the face of insubordination, attempted assassinations, and demonic attack. Like the heroes of other late-ancient Christian biographies, Benedict encounters the devil and his demons repeatedly. But unlike the dark forces that challenge St. Anthony or St. Martin, Benedict's spiritual foes typically pose a pastoral rather than an ascetic challenge. Indeed, when compared to those early hagiographies, Gregory's *Life of Benedict* redefines both the purpose of ascetic purgation and the summit of monastic perfection in terms of spiritual supervision.[86]

In part 2 we will explore the dynamics of Gregory's understanding of spiritual direction in greater detail. In the present context, what is most important is the extent to which he understood service to others as an important component of his ascetic theology. Like many of the great ascetic writers of the late-ancient world, Gregory viewed all of theology through the prism of his own ascetic experience. His ascetic convictions predisposed him to understand the relationship between God and humanity in a particular way (both what could be known of God and what kind of behavior was expected of humans). Those same convictions also predisposed him to read Scripture in a certain fashion and to have that reading reinforce his advocacy of specific ascetic behaviors. As we will see in the chapters that follow, Gregory's ascetic vision, even in its particularities, was so sweeping that it provided the foundation for nearly all of his other theological commitments. This was perhaps nowhere more obvious than in his interpretation of the Fall of Adam and Redemption through Christ.

CHAPTER TWO

Fall, Redemption, and the Ascetic's Filter

In her *Gregory the Great: Perfection in Imperfection*, Carole Straw dedicates a chapter to the "logic of asceticism" in Gregory's thought.[1] I call attention to Straw's discussion of asceticism now, in the context of the Fall and Redemption (rather than in the preceding chapter), because I believe that her interpretation reflects a predetermined Augustinian framework for considering Gregory's theological anthropology, his view of original sin, and the extent to which his ascetic outlook was a consequence of those theological commitments (rather than the reverse).[2] Straw, of course, is not the only modern interpreter to view Gregory's soteriology and theological anthropology through an Augustinian prism; Katharina Greschat offers a more recent rendition of that position.[3] And however much it may be the case that Augustine's anthropological pessimism overlaps with what we might describe as a general ascetic vision of human weakness,[4] there were more theological options for understanding the Fall and Redemption available to Gregory than the Augustinian one.[5] Particularly relevant is the extent to which Gregory's understandings of the body and the potential of humans to contribute to their salvation distinguish his position from Augustine's.[6] While a few scholars have noticed that Gregory's soteriology, and especially his understanding of grace, diverge from Augustine's (many of these scholars criticize Gregory for it!), this chapter aims to show how Gregory's particular ascetic commitments both enable and explain his understanding of the Fall and the possibility of human redemption.[7]

Original Sin and the Fall of Adam

Whereas Augustine's later views of the Fall and original sin were in large part forged by theological conflict (especially related to the protracted debates with Pelagius and Julian of Eclanum), Gregory's reflections were steeped in a brew of personal meditation and were always expressed within a pastoral context.[8] Like Augustine, the pontiff believed that humanity inherited Adam's punishment (i.e., death and corruptibility),[9] but unlike Augustine, Gregory did not argue that Adam's sin corrupted the human condition to the point that it prevented Christians from the possibility of contributing freely to their salvation. The Fall gave rise to a series of human limitations such as hunger, exhaustion, and menstruation, but Gregory did not understand those frailties to be sinful in themselves.[10] It was true, of course, that these physical limitations could become a source for temptation—the need for food could lead to gluttony, the need for sleep could lead to laziness, and the need to procreate would, almost certainly, lead to lust.[11] Capitulation to those temptations could lead to sinful habits that were nearly impossible to overcome.[12] In fact, Gregory often linked sin (whether Adam's or everyone's) to the willful pursuit of desire.[13] We might characterize Gregory's view as one that understands pleasure to be the danger and asceticism to be the cure.[14] And, in framing the spiritual battle in such a way, Gregory's position does resonate with certain Augustinian elements.[15]

By describing sin as the consequence of desire, and doing so within the context of pastoral instruction, however, Gregory was able to present a remedy for sin through the renunciation of desire (i.e., asceticism). And it is in this respect, especially, that we see the ways in which Gregory's ascetic theology most tangibly offers alternatives to the Augustinian framing of a postlapsarian anthropological pessimism. Indeed, for

Gregory, the ascetic life offers an escape from the endless cycle of sin and death. If Christians submit themselves to ascetic discipline and the supervision of a spiritual advisor, Gregory reasons, the appetite for pleasure can be rechanneled into love for God.[16]

As noted in the previous chapter, Gregory repeatedly argues that humanity is susceptible to vice, but he also counsels that individual vices can be overcome through penance and the cultivation of virtue. For example, Adam's fall is sometimes described within the asceticizing idiom of gluttony, vanity, and avarice.[17] But abstinence deliberately pursued, Gregory argues, wards off the sin of gluttony, humility prevents pride, and prayer averts worldly concern.[18] As such, Gregory admonishes everyone (monastic and married alike) to the degree of ascetic discipline befitting their position in life: "I want to advise you to abandon everything, but I do not venture to do so. If you cannot abandon all worldly things, then hold on to the things of this world in such a way that you are not held in the world by them; so that you possess earthly things and they do not possess you."[19] In short, ascetic renunciation neutralizes, at least in part, the limitations of the Fall. It can even reverse the Fall through merit that thereby leads the Christian to God.

To comprehend the extent to which Gregory subtly positions his ideas as distinct from Augustine's, it is helpful to recall that the pontiff typically resisted Augustinian language for "original sin." Note, for example, that whereas Augustine employed the phrase *peccatum originale* (a phrase that he coined) more than five hundred times, Gregory used it on only five occasions.[20] Even more significant is the fact that Gregory softened the theological consequences of the Augustinian doctrine by differentiating the actual sins of Adam from the culpability of his descendants for that sin.[21] And, although he concurred with Augustine that children who died before their baptism would be consigned to Hell, Gregory's explanation for this was a de facto rejection of Augustine's emphasis on grace, predicated on the salvific value of good works.[22]

Perhaps the bishop of Rome's most deliberate break from Augustine concerned the latter's teaching that original sin passed from parent to offspring through the physical act of sex.[23] On at least three occasions, Gregory contested that view. In *The Book of Pastoral Rule*, the *Moralia*, and his *Libellus responsionum* (equally designated in scholarship as the *Responsa* or the *Libellus*), the pontiff argued that sex could be free of lust.[24] Even marital sex that lacked procreative intent, though not recommended, is pardoned according to Gregory.[25] Thus, humanity shares Adam's mortality through nature, not the procreative process.[26]

Free Will, Grace, and Human Initiative

Without revisiting the countless scholarly appraisals of the fifth-century soteriological debate between the Augustinians and the so-called semi-Pelagians (who are generally thought to have derived much of their inspiration from John Cassian),[27] I propose simply to outline Gregory's own view of the relationship between grace and free will as he presents it in his biblical commentaries and public sermons. As I have argued previously, Gregory's view is distinctively "participationist," by which I mean that he believes that salvation is made possible by a mystical (i.e., unknowable in its details) fusion of God's grace and freely chosen human initiative.[28] For the most part, the pope advocates for this position in two ways: he defends the idea of the freedom of human action, and he subtly implies that there is an eternal reward for the performance of good works, especially works of ascetic renunciation.

For example, in the third of his *Homilies on the Gospels*, Gregory notes that "St. Peter could not have suffered for Christ, had he been unwilling" (*nollet*).[29] This echoes a passage from the *Moralia* in which our author suggests that Paul's effectiveness among the Gentiles stemmed from a combination of the saint's efforts and divine grace.[30] Similar assertions exist throughout the corpus.[31] The impetus of each is encapsulated in the following salient example. Commenting on Job 4:16 in the context of a broader discussion about the importance of contemplation, Gregory turns to Moses's reception of the Law as a quintessential meeting between God and humanity. Moses, Gregory notes, did not receive the covenant on level ground—he ascended Mt. Sinai. By extension, the Lord presents himself only to those who "advance much" (*multum proficientibus*).[32] Just as Moses climbed the mountain to meet God, so, too, must humans climb (via contemplation) to accept God's grace. Although no human can fully comprehend God in his substance, it is possible to speak of the "participation" of God's faithful servants in the sense that our pursuit of God is a combination of our climb and his descent.[33]

Gregory's frequent use of the asceticized language of virtue and vice, of course, provides a convenient mechanism for him to proffer that Christians are capable of choosing to do well. This is because the virtue/vice idiom allows him to link virtue to physical and spiritual achievement; it also enables him to propose that vice stems from a capitulation to desire and a lack of spiritual vigilance. In other words, the virtues are a measuring stick of ascetic progress; the presence of vice indicates a failure in the spiritual contest. So, too, hagiography provides yet another ascetic medium for conveying his participationist views by highlighting the stunning achievements of past and present ascetic saints.[34]

Because so many of Gregory's statements on this subject derive from pastoral occasions (his biblical commentaries, sermons on the Gospel, and *Dialogues* all had pastoral motivations), the pontiff often exaggerates the benefit of pious acts (at times ignoring altogether the role of grace) in order to communicate the importance of a particular virtue. For example, in many homilies and particularly in the *Moralia*, Gregory identifies obedience as the ultimate expression of free will successfully applied.[35] He maintains that it was disobedience that expelled Adam from his lofty perch and that it is obedience "of our own will" that will restore humanity to unity with God.[36]

Gregory's voluminous correspondence further testifies to the ways in which his personalized instructions for moral reform encouraged ascetic behavior by holding out the promise of an eternal reward.[37] So, too, the pontiff's famous *Pastoral Rule* contains a series of pastoral prescriptions based on a varied set of spiritual and physical conditions.[38] Like his hagiographic anecdotes, these enjoinders assume the salvific potential of human effort.

In short, there is a mutually reinforcing link between Gregory's ascetic commitment and his theological interpretation of the Fall and Redemption. Not only does Gregory read the Fall through an ascetic filter that predisposes him to view Adam's errors within a register of ascetic anxieties, but he also develops a sophisticated participationist soteriology that places an important theological value on ascetic behavior.[39]

CHAPTER THREE

Ecclesiology and the Rhetoric of Episcopal Equality

Shifting now from Gregory's understanding of the Fall and Redemption to his ecclesiology—particularly with respect to the organization of the Christian world into discrete episcopal jurisdictions and the authority that the bishops of those jurisdictions were believed to possess—we see further the extent to which he was predisposed to express his theological ideas within an ascetic discourse. Indeed, an appraisal of Gregory's ecclesiological statements reveals how significantly his theological commitment to humility (admittedly interconnected with his rhetorical strategies) bound the discursive presentation of his ideas. It is important to note from the outset, in fact, that the great majority of Gregory's ecclesiological statements arose in the midst of specific diplomatic controversies—his more reflective works offer only a few snippets of an ideological commitment on these matters.[1] In order to gain the most comprehensive view possible of Gregory's thinking on the matter, this chapter begins with those surviving ecclesiological statements that are less obviously connected to specific diplomatic concerns before mov-

ing on to consider more fully the circumstances and rhetorical perform-
ances that constitute his ecclesiological diplomacy.

Like nearly all bishops of his era, Gregory presumed that the episcopal office was descended from the apostles and that, as a consequence,
each bishop possessed both the spiritual authority to "bind and loose"
the sins of his congregation and the administrative authority to run his
diocese as he saw fit (so long as he did not lapse into heresy or unfairly
prosecute members of his clergy).[2] Whereas many bishops of Rome from
the fourth century onward developed a series of rhetorical and theological arguments to justify expansion of the Roman See's jurisdictional
authority over other dioceses (both in Italy and abroad), Gregory's understanding of the Roman bishop's role in the broader Church and the
rhetorical choices he pursued to express his views indicate both nuance
and ambivalence. Indeed, when compared to other dominant papal personalities in the late-ancient period (e.g., Leo I or Gelasius I), Gregory's
promotion of Roman authority, particularly as it derived from an associ-
ation with the apostle Peter, was anomalous.[3]

In the twenty-sixth of his *Homilies on the Gospels* (a sermon devoted to
John 20:19–29), Gregory offers a brief statement regarding his belief
that the bishops of his day are the spiritual heirs of the apostles: "Their
place in the Church is now held by the bishops."[4] The point of the
sermon, which was likely intended for Gregory's ascetic community in
Rome (and possibly the clergy of Rome more generally), is that all
spiritual directors (both bishops and other clerics) need to be ever aware
of the danger that pride presents to anyone in a position of leadership.
The apostles, Gregory reasons, were uncommonly humble, and it should
be the primary goal of all spiritual directors, but especially bishops, to
imitate that humility because the authority to bind and loose sin—
even the obedience that one receives by virtue of being in a position of
leadership—often leads to pride. Beyond the obvious comparison between the apostles and bishops, however, the sermon and its biblical ref-
erent are of ecclesiological significance because there is no discussion in
either Gregory's sermon or the Johannine passage of a specifically Petrine prerogative. Whereas the Gospel of Matthew narrates Christ giving the ability to bind and loose sin directly to Peter, the Gospel of John
presents this gift as having been delivered to all of the apostles equally

through the vehicle of the Holy Spirit.[5] While Gregory mentions the Matthew passage in multiple settings within his corpus, it is unfortunate that his surviving Gospel homilies do not include a detailed examination of Matthew 16, which might have afforded an interesting comparison to the Johannine passage and thereby clarified Gregory's understanding of how the two biblical authorizations of apostolic privilege relate to one another.

Contained within Gregory's *Dialogues* we find a few stories that offer some further confirmation that the promotion of Roman ecclesiastical authority was not the most important concern driving some of the bishop's ecclesiological statements.[6] In book 1 of the *Dialogues*, Gregory tells the story of a pious but rustic abbot, Equitius, who comes under the censure of the Roman clergy and an (unnamed) pope for public preaching (Equitius was not a cleric, and the passage presupposes that preaching was reserved for the clergy).[7] The point of the story is to emphasize Equitius's piety and humility, which Gregory contrasts against the flattery and pride of the Roman clergy. Near the conclusion of the account, Gregory's interlocutor asks with some amazement how the pope could have been so wrong about "this man of God." Gregory responds by reminding him that no bishop of Rome is a prophet, and yet, even the prophet David himself made great mistakes.[8] Clearly, in this setting, Gregory was comfortable showing that the bishops of Rome could be wrong and that their piety could pale in comparison to that of a simple monk.[9]

Book 4 of the *Dialogues* contains a more ecclesiologically complicated account of Roman episcopal dignity. In recounting the story of a Roman deacon by the name of Paschasius, Gregory navigates a careful line between the spiritual benefits of personal piety and the consequences of failing to recognize papal authority.[10] Paschasius, according to Gregory, had been a deacon at the time of the schism of Symmachus and Laurentius (ca. 498–507)—a brutal contest that submerged the Roman Church in a period of violence and vitriol.[11] Gregory notes that Paschasius was "highly orthodox," the author of "brilliant books on the Holy Spirit," a man of "outstanding sanctity," and "zealous in his almsgiving."[12] Unfortunately, Paschasius also supported the wrong candidate during the disputed election, and even after the consolation council(s) that confirmed the election of Symmachus, Paschasius refused to recognize his authority. Gregory's treatment of Paschasius is remarkable for its unevenness. He criticizes Paschasius for having failed to recognize Symmachus "when he [i.e., Symmachus] had been accepted unanimously by both parties."[13] But Gregory also attributes the healing of a demoniac to Paschasius's tomb.[14]

Gregory's final anecdote about the saint only further complicates our picture of him. According to Gregory, years after Paschasius's death (and presumably after his tomb had already performed its miracle), another holy man (Germanus, the bishop of Capua) had a vision in which he saw Paschasius serving as the attendant at a Roman bath. Scandalized, Germanus asks Paschasius how could have sunk to such a role. Paschasius responds, "The reason that I am serving here, is that I supported the party of Laurentius against Symmachus. So I beg you to pray for me."[15] The bishop prays for Paschasius's soul, and we are left to believe that the prayers of the bishop have freed the late deacon from any further turmoil.

The theological point of this sequence of stories lies in the power of prayer and the potency of the miraculous. But what does the account say about Gregory's presentation of the sovereignty of the Roman bishop? On the one hand, it suggests that holiness and miracles are not confined to the Roman Church or its administrative institutions. On the other hand, it also seems to suggest that the extent of one's holiness can be compromised by failing to recognize episcopal (perhaps papal) authority.[16]

Contained within Gregory's correspondence we find many more detailed statements about ecclesiological matters, particularly as they relate to the pontiff's attempts to curb what he perceived to be unwarranted efforts by others to seize authority. In nearly every case, Gregory's intervention betrays his ascetic predispositions, in terms of both his willingness to support monastic communities against episcopal encroachments and the way that he forcefully employs the rhetoric of a pride/humility paradigm to squash episcopal self-aggrandizement.[17] For our present purposes, the latter example is the most relevant—the ways in which Gregory chose to censure those bishops whom he believed to be usurping authority unjustifiably.

The case of Maximus of Salona offers an important insight into Gregory's understanding of the traditional reach of Roman jurisdiction. The Archdiocese of Salona, which lay on the western coast of modern-day Croatia, had long been subordinate to the See of Rome. As the *Codex Thessalonicensis* demonstrates, the See of Rome had asserted itself in the region since the late fourth century.[18] The area was more recently the home to a small patrimony of farms that helped to sustain the Roman Church.[19] When its bishop died in 593, the candidate preferred by the Constantinopolitan court, Maximus, was elected over the candidate preferred by Rome.[20] For years, Gregory refused to recognize Maximus's election and forbade his agents in the Balkans to concelebrate Mass with him. Gregory's blunt directives that Maximus not celebrate Mass without papal permission and that he come to Rome to stand trial for his usurpation of the see fell on deaf ears. The pontiff's correspondence from this period suggests that he viewed Maximus, the Eastern emperor, and the patriarch of Constantinople all to have been culpable in usurping Roman episcopal authority.[21]

Gregory's rhetorical strategies during the controversy reveal the connection between the pontiff's ecclesiological statements and the purchase that the ascetic idiom afforded him. He accused Maximus of having fallen victim to the "heresy" of simony by resorting to bribes to pursue his prideful lust for authority.[22] Gregory presented Maximus's unwillingness to submit his election to Roman review as indicating a "lack of humility" and a lack of "obedience" to the canonical traditions of the Church.[23] Similarly, when he wrote an open letter to the clergy of Salona, Gregory claimed that whether the charge of simony was accurate or not, Maximus was revealing the extent of his "pride" by failing to submit himself to an investigation.[24]

Speaking directly to the question of Roman authority in Salona, Gregory insisted that the adjudication of the matter must occur in Rome (rather than Salona, as both Maximus and the emperor preferred), owing to the long tradition of Roman jurisdiction in the region.[25] But perhaps the most intriguing of the diplomatic choices that Gregory pursues in the controversy is his decision to play the Petrine trump card. Gregory repeatedly refers to his see as "Peter's see" and presents Maximus's prideful behavior as an "affront to St. Peter." He even promises Maximus that if he will submit himself to a trial in Rome he can be assured that "justice" will prevail through the "intervention of St. Peter."[26] While these statements do not directly address the framework within which Gregory understood the See of Rome to serve as the de facto locus for ecclesiastical adjudication—nor do they speak in any way to his understanding of the role of the See of Rome with respect to sees beyond Rome's traditional superjurisdiction—these statements do, nevertheless, implicitly seek to assert Roman privilege through its most effective symbol of primacy (i.e., St. Peter).[27]

Of course, the diplomatic crisis that prompted the most extensive and rhetorically rich of Gregory's ecclesiological statements was the controversy over John of Constantinople's use of the title "Ecumenical Patriarch"—a title that Gregory took to be an unprecedented assertion of pride and that, according to Gregory, upended the entire episcopate. Having explored this controversy at some length in previous publications, I will confine my analysis of the controversy to Gregory's ecclesiological statements and the extent to which (if at all) we can presume that those statements might reflect a theological vision more permanent than the occasional and contested context in which the statements arose.[28]

It is generally well known that the Greek title *oikoumenikos* (ecumenical) was translated into Latin as *universalis* (universal) by Gregory and his scribes.[29] In the initial rounds of the controversy, it was precisely this "universal" character of the title that Gregory attacked the most vehemently. From his perspective, the use of the title implied that John was claiming to be, in effect, the "only bishop," with the result that all other bishops received their authority through him.[30] Writing directly to John, Gregory argues that the bishops of the Church are like the stars of the sky, but John's arrogant title suggests that he alone will ascend to heaven and that he will trample upon all other bishops in the process.[31] He notes, "Certainly Peter, the prince of the apostles, himself was but a member of the holy and universal (*universalis*) Church; Paul, Andrew, John—what were they but the heads (*capita*) of individual communities? Were not all the [apostles] members under one head [i.e., Christ]?"[32] The notion that John's self-promotion was an attack on the dignity of all bishops, not just the See of Rome, was Gregory's key rhetorical strategy in his letters to the patriarchs of Antioch and Alexandria.[33]

Gregory's use of the ascetic idiom in his censure of John is all the more interesting because John was, himself, a renowned ascetic—his epithet, in fact, is "the Faster." As noted in previous chapters, however, Gregory consistently argued that ascetic discipline divorced from humility was ultimately fruitless. And Gregory said as much, repeatedly, in his letters to John and others.[34] According to Gregory, it is inconceivable that John could simultaneously insist upon such a presumptuous title and offer effective pastoral supervision, a spiritual activity that requires humility and the assistance of grace.

Not surprisingly, Gregory also played the Petrine card throughout the controversy over the ecumenical title. Writing to the emperor in 595, Gregory notes, "Behold, Peter received the keys of the kingdom of heaven, he was granted the power to bind and loose sin, and the care and authority of the entire Church was committed to him, and yet even he is not called the universal apostle."[35] In other words, if the title was too grand for St. Peter, it was surely too grand for the current patriarch of Constantinople. As in the controversy in Salona, Gregory could use the link between Peter and the See of Rome to exert rhetorical pressure to achieve a specific diplomatic goal. That he did so primarily in correspondence likely says more about Gregory's creativity as a diplomatic strategist than it actually reveals a consistent ecclesiological vision.

That supposition is evinced, at least in part, by the way that Gregory altered the rhetorical application of Peter's authority as the controversy wore on. After years of making very little progress on the matter, even among other bishops, Gregory altered his approach by sharing his Petrine capital with the patriarchs of Antioch and Alexandria. The ecumenical title, Gregory reasoned, was a usurpation of Petrine authority, an authority that belonged exclusively to the three ancient sees that had a link to his legacy: "Therefore, while there are many apostles with respect to preeminence, the see of the prince of the apostles has become more valid in authority, which in three is unified as one. For [Peter] exalted the see in which he deigned to rest and complete the present life [i.e., Rome]; he adorned the see to which he sent his disciple the Evangelist [i.e., Alexandria]; and he established the see in which he sat for seven years, even though he would eventually leave it [i.e., Antioch]."[36] To Gregory's great disappointment, he never did convince the patriarch of Antioch or the Roman emperor to support his cause, nor did he ever succeed in persuading John of Constantinople (or his successor) that he should drop the title *Ecumenical.*[37]

How, then, are we to incorporate the statements born of Gregory's diplomatic efforts (whether against John of Constantinople or Maximus of Salona), with all of their rhetorical finesse, into our appraisal of Gregory's ecclesiological vision? To be sure, there are some elements that appear without contravention in Gregory's corpus. First among them is the idea that all (orthodox) bishops are the spiritual successors of the apostles and, as such, possess the authority to bind and loose sin for the individual members of their flock. So, too, does Gregory believe in the sacramental authority of the bishops to preside over the celebration of the Mass and to administer baptisms.

Where it gets a little more complicated, however, is within the realm of inter-episcopal hierarchies, particularly as they relate to the adjudication of miscreant clergy and the resolution of contested episcopal elections. Indeed, the spark that lit the ecumenical title fire was a tit-for-tat squabble between Constantinople and Rome over whether or not an Eastern cleric could appeal his Constantinopolitan condemnation to the Roman bishop.[38] While it is certainly true that Gregory was willing to employ forceful rhetorical arguments for the defense of Roman claims, it is equally true that there is little evidence in Gregory's corpus that he ever did this to expand Roman claims. In other words, in both the cases rehearsed above, Gregory seems to have understood himself to be defending ancient Roman privileges (whether it was its superjurisdictional authority in Salona or the right to adjudicate any clerical judgment in Rome); he was not seeking to extend Roman authority in new ways.[39] But the one element that is perhaps the most consistent of all of his ecclesiological statements (whether drawn from his treatises or his diplomatic initiatives) is that he always communicated his positions in an ascetic idiom that proscribed any effort that could be construed as prideful.

CHAPTER FOUR

Some Mystical Attributes of Gregory's Ascetic Theology

Eschewing the more complex scholarly definitions of mystical theology that are often reflective of a later period, I would like to use the language of "mystical" and "mysticism" to capture, simply, Gregory's understanding of the "hiddenness" of certain elements of the divine–human relationship. By "hiddenness" I mean that Gregory believed that God's interaction in the world (particularly the mysterious ways in which grace interacted with and spurred the will) were, ultimately, incomprehensible to the postlapsarian mind.[1] But, in spite of our limited ability to comprehend the dynamics of God's activity, Gregory proffered that there are several reasons that Christians should have confidence in the truth of God and his activity. Indeed, Gregory repeatedly describes the miracles and relics of the saints as physical symbols for the invisible operations of God. Similarly, he instructs his readers that ritualized behavior (particularly the sacramental rituals) elicits divine favor or serves a purgative penitential function. As in the preceding chapters, we will here engage these mystical aspects of Gregory's theology from the perspective that they flow from his own ascetic practice and were understood and articulated within an ever-ascendant ascetic discourse that had fully integrated what scholars might divide into the "intellectual" and "popular" forms of Christian thought and practice at the close of Christian antiquity.

To be sure, both Gregory's understanding of the mystical qualities of the spiritual life and his idiom for expressing them are reminiscent of several other writers and collections (Eastern and Western) of the period (e.g., *Apophthegmata Patrum*, the "Sayings" of the Desert Fathers, and John Cassian). And while scholars have long since identified the theological richness of those other texts and traditions, most twentieth-century interpreters of Gregory view his discussion of miracles and relics (particularly in the *Dialogues*) as a source of embarrassment or, at the very least, bewilderment.[2] Even though the overall appraisal of Gregory's theological sophistication is beginning to improve among European scholars—most noticeably in the monographs by Greschat, Müller, and Kisić—such appraisals are less frequently drawn from an examination of the *Dialogues*.[3]

While the *Dialogues* may not reveal theological sophistication in the traditional sense, they certainly indicate the kinds of behavior and an approach to life that Gregory wishes to impart upon those with whom he interacts. Consequently, they provide an important witness to the richness and comprehensiveness of Gregory's theological outlook.[4] In the same way that a figure such as Athanasius was able to convey some of his most important theological, ecclesiological, and pastoral convictions through the hagiographic idiom, so too was Gregory able to employ hagiography as a literary device for the dissemination of his ascetic and pastoral convictions.[5]

Miracles

The most complete study of the function of miracles in Gregory's thought belongs to William McReady, who sought to defend not only the theological significance of the *Dialogues* but also Gregory's fundamental belief in the miracles that they relate.[6] The question of Gregory's belief in the veracity of these miracles, however, may not be the most important, nor does an answer to that question (assuming one is possible) necessarily preclude us from investigating the more comprehensive rhetorical, literary, and theological functions of the miraculous in the *Dialogues* or other Gregorian texts.[7]

Indeed, Gregory employs the miraculous in the *Dialogues* to multiple ends, not the least of which is the promotion of ascetic behavior.[8] For example, the consequence of the first miracle narrated in the *Dialogues* was that it enabled a young man to cultivate a form of abstemiousness that would have been otherwise impossible.[9] Not only does this story promote the importance of fasting (and, by extension, the value of ascetic discipline more broadly), it also repudiates all who dismiss that importance.[10] Further episodes in the *Dialogues* detail the other ways in which specific miracles enable additional feats of fasting and chastity.[11] And, as we have already discussed, many of Benedict's miracles (as narrated in book 2 of the *Dialogues*) were for the purpose of achieving specific pastoral objectives.

Thus, one of the primary literary functions of the miraculous in Gregory's writing (whether in the *Dialogues* or elsewhere) relates to the process of conversion and spiritual growth more broadly.[12] Throughout the *Dialogues*, Gregory refers to the power of the Italian saints to bring those around them to Christianity or, at the very least, to soften the barbarity of some Lombards (and also, but less frequently, the Goths).[13] He also uses the hagiographic topos of miraculous visions to suggest that one can overcome the limitations of the Fall.[14] Even in his own day, Gregory understood there to be a direct connection between a missionary's ability to preach the gospel and his power to perform miracles. Indeed, the pontiff boasted to the patriarch of Alexandria that Augustine of Canterbury's numerous miracles led directly to the conversion of eight thousand Angli on Christmas Day in the year 597.[15]

It is especially noteworthy that whenever Gregory explains the "function" of miracles in the context of the apostolic era, his discussion is linked to the swift spread of the faith through miracles. Apostolic miracles, he contends, hastened the spread of Christianity because they provided a physical confirmation of the invisible faith that the apostles preached.[16] The frequent narration of apostolic miracles, of course, led some in Gregory's time to ask why their own age did not experience the miraculous.[17] Gregory's typical response to this line of questioning is multidimensional. On the one hand, he argues that there was a greater need for miracles in antiquity when the faith was in its infancy and the message of Christ was less well known.[18] On the other hand, Gregory often insists that miracles continuously occur in his own day but do so in less visible ways (such as when a priest invisibly exorcises demons in the context of a baptism).[19] In fact, he argues that when "holy preachers" are able to perform miracles, they often do so for the purpose of bringing others (presumably Christians) closer to God.[20]

A discussion of whether or not Gregory understands the sanctity of the holy man to be the source of his miraculous power or the reverse (i.e., that the performance of miracles marks a man as holy) emerges throughout the course of the *Dialogues*, in the dialectic between Gregory and his interlocutor, Peter. Indeed, Peter repeatedly offers his view that the ability to perform miracles is the reason that someone ought to be considered a saint. Gregory repeatedly censures this perspective, arguing rather that the ability to perform miracles is an outward manifestation of an interior presence of sanctity that preexists miraculous signs.[21] To focus on the external show rather than their interior source, Gregory reasons, is to misunderstand both the source of sanctity and the lesson of the saints.[22] And there is little denying the extent to which Gregory believed the lesson of the saints, and especially their relics, to be of great spiritual value.

The Saints and Their Relics

One of the hallmarks of ascetic writing in the fifth century was the way by which the lives and sayings of the saints could be used to promote a specific form of ascetic theology or behavior. John Cassian, for example, used his *Institutes* and *Conferences* to communicate moral and ascetic lessons through the words and actions of legendary figures. The strategic purpose of that approach lies in the connection between the recognized authority (i.e., the ascetic hero) and the behavior or idea that the author hopes to inspire. By taking the persona of a reporter, Cassian was able to transmit his own ideas as the undisputed tradition of past ascetic saints.[23] Gregory was able to do the same thing, whether through the explicit telling of saints' lives via the *Dialogues*, the anecdotes about various holy men and women that appear in his *Homilies on the Gospels* and *Epistles*, or the presentation of biblical heroes in the *Pastoral Rule*, *Moralia*, and *Homilies on Ezekiel*.

In the opening pages of the *Dialogues*, Peter beseeches Gregory to instruct him with regard to the miraculous activities of Italian saints by differentiating the benefit that comes from a meditation on Scripture from the benefit derived from knowing about the saints. Peter notes, "An explanation of holy Scripture instructs us concerning the acquisition and preservation of virtue, but a description of the miracles [of the saints] shows us how virtue reveals itself in those who possess it."[24] What is more, Peter reasons, the meditation on the saints inspires humility because we see our own shortfalls through the examination of holiness in others.[25]

Like Cassian, Sulpicius Severus, and the ascetic writers of the East, Gregory encourages his audiences to reflect upon the lives of the saints precisely because they provide examples for virtuous living.[26] In the *Commentary on Ezekiel*, Gregory notes that it is through the saints that we come to learn of all the virtues—no single saint possesses every virtue, but through a study of different kinds of saints we find multiple examples of holiness.[27] Just as the saints imitate Christ, so too should Christians imitate the saints.[28]

Not surprisingly, Gregory turns to Peter and Paul more than other saints to promote specific theological, pastoral, and moral interests. Indeed, anecdotal recourse to their lives (whether scriptural or legendary) fills Gregory's biblical commentaries. But even the *Dialogues*, which are ostensibly about sixth-century Italian saints, make repeated reference to Peter and Paul,[29] although the same texts say relatively little about the sixth-century popes, Peter's supposed successors.[30] As we will explore in greater detail in the final chapter, Gregory's interest in St. Peter (and the relationship between Peter and Gregory's own authority) was multifaceted but unique among the late-ancient bishops of Rome.

For our present purposes, let us recall that Gregory frequently pointed his audiences to Peter's weakness as the means by which the pontiff hoped to convey a pastoral or ascetic message.[31] It is, in fact, a peculiar characteristic of Gregory's hagiographic style to maximize the weakness of the saints (whether Peter's, David's, or Mary Magdalene's) to show their ultimate virtue. Indeed, for Gregory, sanctity could be born of weakness. In fact, Gregory was likely one of the first theologians to emphasize progress through weakness and suffering as a distinctively saintly topos.[32] In many cases he uses the weakness of the saints to convey the spiritual potential of ritualized repentance.[33] In his twenty-sixth homily on the Gospels, he even suggests that Thomas's lack of faith is more instructive for our spiritual reformation than the otherwise pious examples of other saints.[34]

Of course, the other obvious connection between Gregory's interest in St. Peter and our understanding of the pontiff's mystical theology relates to the fact that Gregory attributed "countless" and "daily" miracles to Peter's tomb and relics.[35] The utilization of these material objects was likely Gregory's greatest contribution to the expansion the Petrine legacy.[36] Not only did the pontiff employ Peter's tomb as the locus for the swearing of oaths (both papal agents and recalcitrant clerics were ordered to swear an oath at Peter's tomb), he also disseminated Petrine relics to nearly a dozen patrons and clients around the Mediterranean and among the Merovingians.[37]

Indeed, it is a characteristic of Gregory's mystical theology that he views the relics of the saints as more than the mere remains of a sanctified body—relics are, in Gregory's estimation, proof of the afterlife, of heaven, and of the truth of Christianity. They are the embodiment of an eschatological promise in the resurrection of the body and soul.[38] According to Gregory, Christians have empirical evidence of the resurrection through the miraculous activity of relics, which can both heal and terrify. The *Dialogues*, not surprisingly, contain several stories in which the relics of the saints serve as the conduits for miraculous healing. Thus, the text attests to the need for Christians to respect the shrines of the saints and refrain from tampering with them in any way that diminishes their dignity.[39] Gregory confirms this point on multiple occasions in his correspondence, both when he agrees to distribute Petrine "relics" and when he refuses to release the actual bones of the saints that rest in Roman churches.[40]

Placing Gregory's discussion of postmortem saintly miracles into a precise historical context, Matthew Dal Santo has convincingly shown that the *Dialogues* further functioned as an apology for the burgeoning cult of the saints at a time when churchmen in Rome and Constantinople were beginning to question both the orthodoxy of the saintly cult and the expediency of prayers for the dead.[41] Among other things, Dal Santo demonstrates that Gregory's views were significantly different from Augustine's and largely in line with key contemporary theologians in the East.[42] Not only were miracles performed by the saints at their shrines clear evidence, to Gregory, that the saints were active after their deaths, but the saints also take on a "sacramental" quality in the sense that they "constantly displayed in their bodies and miracles the changed order of creation after the incarnation."[43]

Ritualizing the Mystical

One final aspect of Gregory's mystical theology for our examination is the relationship between Christian ritual—particularly sacramental ritual—and the miraculous. Several of the miracles Gregory chronicles in the *Dialogues* are set within the context of liturgy—whether it is the Eucharistic Mass, the service of Vespers, or the veneration of relics within a liturgical setting more broadly. For example, in book 3 of the *Dialogues*, Gregory offers an account of a miracle performed by Pope Agapetus during his celebration of the Mass.[44] The same book reports that a man was brought back to life through the intervention of a holy man's liturgical prayer.[45] In this latter example, the holy man took dust from the altar table at the conclusion of the service and placed it upon the dead man's face—ritualized acts that ultimately brought the man back to life.

The mysterious connection between liturgical prayer, physical objects, and the miraculous is confirmed elsewhere in the *Dialogues*. In a rare autobiographical account, Gregory reports that he personally witnessed a miracle in which the ritualized procession of relics into a former Arian church forced a demon out of the sanctuary.[46] Elsewhere in the text he narrates a rather disturbing story of a woman who fell victim to a demon because she dared to be present at a liturgical procession of relics the morning after she had coupled with her husband.[47] Through these very different stories, Gregory seeks to impart to his readers the remarkable power of relics, particularly relics in liturgical procession, to disrupt or otherwise harass demonic forces that remain active in the world.

Similar statements reflecting the link between ritual and the miraculous occur throughout his corpus. For example, Gregory notes that the prayers for the dead offered during the Mass can have a salvific effect.[48] Similarly, the ritual of the altar can provide the spiritual force that assists heretics in returning to the true faith. Gregory combines this assertion with the declaration that the ritualized acts of heretics are of no value whatsoever.[49] In fact, the links between ritual, divine grace, and the miraculous offer an important nexus for both the championing of orthodox worship and the censure of errant rituals (whether pagan, heretical, or Jewish). Note, for example, Gregory's accusation that God took away the "sacraments" from the Jewish priesthood.[50]

In Gregory's theological view of the world, God remains active with his creation through visible and invisible ways. The miracles of the saints and their relics, like the miracles enabled through ritualized prayer, procession, and penance, attest to God's mercy. They simultaneously inspire and terrify. For the holy man, the ascetic, and all those who have committed themselves to a life of spiritual growth, the mysteries of God's intervention in the world are a source of comfort and hope. For those who have not sufficiently embraced the ascetic and moral requirements of the Christian life, or for those who have done so without the requisite humility, the mysteries of God are a source of fear and confusion.

Gregory, Theology, and the Ascetic Idiom

In part 1 I have argued that Gregory's theological vision was in large part shaped by his ascetic experience and his commitment to the life of renunciation. Gregory's articulation of his theological commitments, in fact, was almost always communicated through an ascetic idiom that both presupposed and promoted ascetic concerns. As we have seen, that idiom included the frequent use of the virtues and vices (especially the pride/humility paradigm), the hagiographic genre, and the active promotion of the cult of the saints. But, even more importantly, it is the content of Gregory's message that is so closely associated with the ascetic communities of his day. Regardless of audience or genre, Gregory encourages his readers and listeners to submit themselves more fully to renunciatory behavior because, he reasons, it is the moral requirement of faith in Christ.

The reach of Gregory's ascetic commitments and inclinations is particularly revealing when we look at specific facets of his theology, such as his soteriology and his ecclesiology. As we have seen, Gregory's understanding of the Fall and his expressed confidence in the ability of the Christian to participate in his or her own salvation clearly reveal his predispositions to "read renunciation" into humanity's history and ultimate salvation. So, too, in our investigation of Gregory's ecclesiology, we found the striking degree to which his articulation of his positions (whether in defense of Roman prestige or in the critique of another's self-aggrandizement) is always framed by an ascetic discourse that never strays far from the pride/humility paradigm.

Finally, it is worth noting the extent to which Gregory's ascetic theology was distinctive from other voices in the late-ancient/early medieval period. Specifically, Gregory's ascetic vision was a social one. But more than simply encouraging communal monasticism or the need for monks to take on social ministry, Gregory actually recast the summit of ascetic perfection as a willful suspension of divine contemplation for the love of neighbor. Whereas Cassian, Gregory Nazianzen, Basil, and others had all recognized the importance of pastoral leaders' suspension of their contemplative efforts for the sake of others, Pope Gregory was the first to actually identify pastoral service combined with contemplation (rather than contemplation alone) as the summit of the spiritual life. As we will see in part 2, Gregory believed that every Christian's path to God was distinct, and as a consequence, the degree and form of renunciation expected and pursued was to be varied. But it took the keen spiritual eye of an experienced director to discern that path.

Part Two

Gregory as Pastoral Theologian

Within a few months of ascending the papal throne, Gregory sent the first copy of his *Liber Regulae Pastoralis* (*Book of Pastoral Rule*) to Archbishop John of Ravenna.[1] A few years later, he sent a copy to an old friend he had known in Constantinople, Leander, who had since become the bishop of Seville.[2] With time, Gregory's *Pastoral Rule* would become the most widely circulating and influential treatise on spiritual direction in Christian history.[3] The initial spread of the text can be attributed in part to the fact that Gregory was so well connected: through his relationships at the imperial court, the *Pastoral Rule* was translated into Greek, making him perhaps the only late-ancient Latin author whose works circulated in Greek during his lifetime.[4] But the text is also the most comprehensive pastoral treatise from the Patristic Era, touching upon a wide array of elements related to spiritual leadership, including both "pastoral care" and "spiritual direction," which are often differentiated by modern practitioners.[5] Gregory's most sophisticated ideas and the majority of the text in the *Pastoral Rule* are concerned with spiritual direction, but it is worth noting that the current distinction between the pastoral care and spiritual direction would probably have made little sense to him: he understood the spiritual director to be the person most prepared to offer pastoral care to those in need, and he understood that task to exist within the framework of spiritual direction.[6]

Like Gregory Nazianzen, John Chrysostom, Ambrose, and Augustine before him, Pope Gregory distinguishes between those who should and those who should not assume spiritual responsibility. Also like previous authors, he identifies many of the leader's responsibilities and impending challenges.[7] But unlike his predecessors, Gregory includes a lengthy section in his treatise in which he offers a prototype for spiritual counseling based upon a dizzying array of personality profiles set in opposition to one another. For example, he differentiates between men and women, rich and poor, and old and young and then identifies the specific pastoral considerations that a spiritual director should take into account when he engages with or preaches to these individuals.[8]

Anyone familiar with Gregory's corpus knows well that his interests in spiritual leadership are not confined to the *Pastoral Rule*.[9] His commentaries on the books of the Hebrew Bible, which were initially delivered to the members of his ascetic communities in Rome and Constantinople, are prime examples of the pontiff's preoccupation with spiritual direction. These texts not only scrutinize the qualifications for leadership (many in the audience, in fact, went on to serve as priests and bishops in Gregory's administration), but also repeatedly digress into discussions of spiritual supervision, which we might assume reflects a concern for spiritual direction both within the ascetic community and in the broader Christian environment. For example, as the *Moralia* progresses it focuses all the more directly on roles, conditions, challenges, and strategies for effective spiritual direction.[10] Several of its later portions jettison the narrative of Job entirely and simply view various passages of biblical text through the prism of ministry.[11] So, too, the digressions in the *Commentary on Ezekiel* frequently relate to the considerations of spiritual direction.[12] Gregory's forty homilies on the Gospels offer fewer direct statements about the qualifications for leadership than the *Moralia* or *Commentary on Ezekiel*— the audience for most of the public sermons collected as *Homilies on the Gospels* typically included laypersons—but the concern for the tactics of spiritual supervision dominates their structure and argument. What is more, the pontiff's correspondence is filled with both gentle and not-so-gentle admonitions to non-Roman clerics about their responsibility to provide quality spiritual leadership. Even the *Dialogues*, which ostensibly have little to do with clerical supervision, can be viewed as both a tool for recruiting ascetics into the clergy and a series of holy examples of pastoral ministry successfully conducted.

The fact that Gregory reflected upon the "art" of spiritual direction for diverse audiences and in a variety of genres requires us to consider the broad range of figures who might be entrusted with its authority. Indeed, although he first distributed his *Pastoral Rule* to a fellow bishop, there is little reason to hold, as scholars once did, that Gregory's ideas about spiritual authority were restricted to the office of the episcopate.

On this count, Gregory's terminology for the spiritual director in the *Pastoral Rule* is particularly relevant. The most common term is *rector*, which he employs more than forty times. But he also uses a variety of other terms to refer to the practitioner of spiritual leadership, including *sacerdos*, *praedicator*, and *pastor*.[13] Intriguingly, *episcopus* is not one of them. Nevertheless, several twentieth-century commentators presumed that Gregory was writing solely about the episcopate.[14] Such a position not only fails to account for the pontiff's terminology, but also underappreciates the extent to which Gregory advanced very similar ideas about spiritual leadership, particularly the need for ascetics to undertake the role of "preacher" (*praedicator*) and "pastor" (*pastor*) in other treatises and letters that were composed for ascetic audiences.[15] This is particularly true of the *Moralia*, which was first delivered to Gregory's monastic community in Constantinople and is in many ways an extended excursus on the qualities and techniques of spiritual leadership.[16]

While it is certainly true that Gregory's idealized *rector*, *praedicator*, or *pastor* would likely be a cleric—a *sacerdos*—his language was inconsistent enough and his conception of spiritual direction fluid enough that we should resist the temptation to assume that Gregory was always speaking about or to priests and bishops. As his correspondence demonstrates, the pontiff frequently wrote to leaders of monastic communities, providing specific suggestions or even rebukes concerning their pastoral efforts.[17]

With all of this in mind, part 2 explores the theoretical and practical considerations of Gregory's pastoral theology. The central argument is that Gregory's approach to spiritual direction is consonant with and mutually reinforced by the particular emphases of his ascetic theology. For example, Gregory's contention that the summit of ascetic perfection is to be found in sacrifice for others can be seen as bearing directly upon his insistence that renunciants embrace positions of spiritual leadership. The same presuppositions no doubt lie behind Gregory's belief that the spiritual director was the most exalted in his taxonomy of faithful Christians (i.e., directors, ascetics, laypersons). The pontiff's commitment to the ascetic life also helps to explain the standards by which he evaluated potential candidates for the priesthood, as well as the strategies for supervision that he encouraged all spiritual authorities to pursue. But before delving deeply into these specific issues, we will begin with a survey of Gregory's understanding of the purpose and significance of the "art" of spiritual direction.[18]

CHAPTER FIVE

The Importance of Spiritual Leadership

Following in a pedagogical tradition with both Greco-Roman and Christian antecedents, Gregory was deeply committed to the idea that individuals benefit from the insights and advice of their spiritual leaders. The philosophical schools of the classical world, for example, had a long-standing tradition of thinking that an experienced elder or teacher could help a disciple's spiritual and philosophical growth.[1] That master–disciple dynamic provided an obvious model for spiritual direction undertaken by Christians in the ascetic communities of late antiquity.[2] The Christian Scriptures provided another important antecedent for the master–disciple model: early Christian interpreters of the New Testament presupposed that the apostles and their successors were graced by the Holy Spirit to instruct their communities according to the precepts and moral implications of the faith.[3]

However important the classical and scriptural traditions may have been, however, it was probably Gregory's own experience of the monastic life that most directly shaped his ideas concerning the "art" of spiritual direction and the role of the director in the practice of that art.[4] Indeed, within most ascetic and monastic communities of the late-ancient period, the master–disciple relationship was the most significant mechanism for theological and moral instruction.[5] What is so significant about Gregory's contributions to the practice of spiritual direction is that he, more than anyone else in Christian antiquity, brought the practices and theory of spiritual direction from the ascetic and monastic world into the broader Christian community. He did this in part by placing experienced ascetics in prominent clerical positions in the Western Church and in part by advocating a specific model of spiritual renewal that was, in effect, a laicizing of monastic strategies for spiritual advancement.[6] In a sense, what we find in Gregory's vision of spiritual leadership is an ascetic-branded Christian refashioning of Cicero's public servant, who commits himself not to the service of Rome per se, but to the service of the Roman Church.[7]

To understand Gregory's deep investment in the master–disciple relationship, it is important to recognize the extent to which the pontiff understood the Christian's ascent to God to be a long and gradual process.[8] In book 22 of the *Moralia* he compares the spiritual development of a Christian to the growth of a tree, from seed to sapling to full maturity.[9] In his *Commentary on Ezekiel* he holds that even those disciples who progress well will inevitably regress (due to either temptation or pride) and that it is the duty of the spiritual mentor to identify and remedy the situation through rebuke or encouragement.[10] Indeed, it is precisely because Christians sin, and because they are typically incapable of even knowing that they have done so, that they need the discerning eye of a spiritual mentor. For these reasons, Gregory's *Pastoral Rule* frequently stresses the need for spiritual directors to take a long-term approach when issuing spiritual advice — not only should they not rush disciples into ascetic exercises for which they are not ready, they must equally understand that the suppression of one vice might lead to the progression of another.[11] Within this framework, Gregory came to see the director's responsibility for his disciples as fundamentally linked to his own potential for salvation.[12]

And it was precisely because Gregory understood that the spiritual director's task is so important (and so difficult) that he came to view the Christian community according to a three-tiered taxonomy of believers — spiritual directors, ascetics, and married laypersons (*praedicatores/rectores, continentes, boni coniugati*) — that emphasizes the superiority of the spiritual director.[13] In this conceptualization, the spiritual director (most often identified in the *Moralia* as *pastor* or *praedicator* and in the *Pastoral Rule* as *rector*) is a hybrid, deliberately situated between the activity of the world and the life of retreat. We gain a sense for the progress of Gregory's thinking on the matter in the prefatory letter for the *Moralia*, which he sent to Leander of Seville. Here Gregory recalls that when he was a younger man, he became aware of the divide between the active and contemplative lives, and his struggle was in abandoning the one for the other. Only in hindsight, after he had progressed from ascetic to priest (which he frames as his commitment to "serve the altar"[14]), did he come to understand that either a life in the world (as a layperson) or a life in a monastery (as an ascetic) would have been easier than the task and responsibility that he faces as a spiritual leader, burdened by the weight of pastoral care (pondus est curae pastoralis iniunctum).[15] It is only now, years after becoming a bishop, that he realizes the significance of the effort to pursue a life of active service without sacrificing the inner vision that derives from the contemplative life.[16]

In fact, going back to the original creation of the *Moralia*, we might speculate that Gregory pursued the lengthy examination of Job when he did (during his time in Constantinople) because the project offered an intellectual and spiritual escape from the interstitial trap of being *apocrisiarius* in the Eastern capital.[17] In other words, as both committed monk and ambassador to the imperial court, Gregory would have been pulled between the ideal of peaceful contemplation and a degree of secular involvement that few other clerics could have experienced. We might say that the protracted examination of Job (of all biblical figures!) provided a vehicle for study and reflection that could make sense of Gregory's otherwise unsustainable existence.[18]

But from this reflection on the ancient *vir sanctus*, and the examination of other heroes of the Hebrew Bible that would follow, Gregory became increasingly willing to see the world through a three-tier division that prioritized both the challenge and the superiority of the life of pastoral leadership, which was restricted to those ascetics who embraced others—in other words the active contemplative life.[19] Indeed, Gregory's spiritualizing analysis of Job's activity routinely turns to an encomium for the superiority of the "mixed" life, which combines the spiritual insights gained through contemplation and the service for others that could only be pursued through active engagement. It is particularly significant that even though Job was not a priest, Gregory is able to emphasize Job's role as "preacher" and "holy man" precisely because he struck the proper balance of action and contemplation. Through Job's example, Gregory repeatedly encourages his readers to aspire to the life of spiritual leadership—a life that is most evident through preaching. For example, in book 6 of the *Moralia* Gregory emphasizes the inadequacies of both active and contemplative life. Effective spiritual leadership—and, in particular, successful preaching—requires the insights of contemplation and the good works of active engagement.[20]

One of the most explicit engagements of the three-tiered taxonomy derives from his exegesis of Ezekiel 14:14 and his multiple (if indirect) references to that passage elsewhere in his biblical commentaries.[21] According to the scriptural text, the prophet suggests that despite the impending destruction of Israel, God will preserve Noah, Daniel, and Job, even if he does not preserve any of their children. For Gregory, their "survival" provides the basis for the taxonomy (*ordines*) of the faithful, which he believes comes into effect at the time of the apostles.[22] In other words, Noah represents the spiritual leaders (designated alternatively as *pastor* and *praedicator*[23]), Daniel the ascetics, and Job the married. Among the many interesting elements of the typology is that the biblical figures do not easily fit Gregory's categories. For example, Noah, who is supposed to represent spiritual leaders, is married—Gregory routinely proscribed married clergy.[24] And although Job, too, was married, Gregory routinely employs Job as a model for preachers. It is thus rather perplexing that Noah serves as the model for spiritual leaders rather than Job. In the *Commentary on Ezekiel*, Gregory acknowledges the flaws in his typology but continues to use it.[25]

For our purposes, what is most significant about Gregory's three-tiered division of the faithful is not the peculiar reference to Ezekiel 14:14, but rather what this division says about his understanding of the importance of spiritual direction. Clearly, Gregory was dissatisfied with the standard ascetic/married binary that circulated widely in Christian discourse in the period. By privileging those in public roles over those who remained focused on the contemplative life, Gregory was further elaborating on his belief that the summit of ascetic perfection was to be found in the service of others. And while it is noteworthy that the three-tiered paradigm never appears explicitly in the *Pastoral Rule*, we might take its prominence in the biblical commentaries to be a marker of Gregory's own hermeneutical dispositions.[26] Indeed, the three-tiered paradigm is an important consideration as we approach Gregory's commentaries because it helps to explain why the majority of his interpretive digressions are focused on various aspects of the art of spiritual direction and emphasize the necessity of service for others.

CHAPTER SIX

The Recruitment of Leaders

Gregory believed strongly that the ascent to God was facilitated by the careful supervision of an experienced director. It therefore stood to reason that those directors would themselves need to have been instructed by someone else. There were, however, some notable exceptions to this pattern. John the Baptist and Moses offered obvious biblical alternatives. In Gregory's day, too, there were a few ascetics who were so graced by God that they did not need the instruction of others before being able to offer inspired advice. In the *Dialogues*, Gregory submits that neither St. Benedict nor St. Honoratus was in need of personal instruction because they were so filled with the grace of the Holy Spirit.[1] While Gregory is keen to praise these particular saints, he is also careful to note that their stories are exceptional. Anyone, the pontiff reasons, who presumes to lead others without having first submitted himself to the instruction of others must be tested. And to guard against those who falsely proclaim to possess the Holy Spirit, he argues that true sanctity will be revealed by two signs: miraculous powers and humility.[2] When we move beyond the *Dialogues*, we see that it is humility, far more than the ability to perform miracles, that marks the potential for spiritual leadership.

Gregory's selection and recruitment of spiritual directors, in fact, is in certain respects reminiscent of Plato's "philosopher king." Whereas Plato holds that the only one worthy to be king is the philosopher, Gregory similarly insists that the only one who is qualified to govern the souls of others is the one who is too humble to desire this authority.[3] While there is ultimately more to Gregory's criteria for spiritual authority than humility, that asset holds a certain primacy within Gregory's pantheon of virtues, not only because of its intrinsic value, but also because the person who has obtained it is also likely to possess many of the other ascetic qualifications that the pontiff values in spiritual leadership.

Credentials (Ascetic and Otherwise)

In book 1 of the *Pastoral Rule*, Gregory identifies the qualities that exemplify spiritual leadership.[4] He notes that the ideal *rector*

> must be devoted entirely to the example of good living. He must be dead to the passions of the flesh and live a spiritual life. He must have no regard for worldly prosperity and never cower in the face of adversity. He must desire the internal life only. His intentions should not be thwarted by the frailty of the body, nor repelled by the abuse of the spirit. He should not lust for the possessions of others but give freely of his own. He should be quick to forgive through compassion, but never be so far removed from righteousness as to forgive indiscriminately.[5]

Several of these attributes, of course, reflect Gregory's ascetic concerns. Note, for example, the rhetorical contrasts in his framing of "passion" versus "spiritual living" or "body" versus "spirit."

The ascetic idiom is perhaps even more evident in those passages where Gregory marks the vices that disqualify a potential candidate from consideration. He mentions pride, of course, but also vainglory, greed, lust, and desire for prestige as the most obvious problems. Particularly revealing is Gregory's allegory of Leviticus 21:17–18 (a list of physical disfigurements that preclude someone from the Jewish priesthood). He compares a blind man to "one who is ignorant of the light of heavenly contemplation" because he is "oppressed by the darkness of the present life."[6] He similarly suggests that one with a "small nose" lacks spiritual discernment (*discretio*)—"just as the nose discerns the difference between a sweet smell and a stench, [a successful pastor] applies discernment to distinguish between sin and virtue."[7]

Gregory's allegory of the Leviticus passage may emphasize his point by negation (i.e., it emphasizes what is missing, not what is good), but it is clear from this excerpt that he considers *contemplatio* and *discretio* to be two of the most important attributes of successful spiritual direction. By the sixth century, *contemplatio* had long been synonymous with the ascetic retreat—a life of prayerful meditation.[8] *Discretio*, similarly, had long been used within ascetic literature to describe the key supernatural gift bestowed by God upon a worthy spiritual advisor. The Egyptian abbot Ammonas marks discernment as the most important spiritual gift; John Cassian dedicates an entire conference to the subject; and Benedict of Nursia identifies *discretio* as the most crucial quality of a potential abbot.[9] It is one of Gregory's most enduring legacies that his model of spiritual direction brought these aspects of ascetic practice to the broader Christian community.

Not surprisingly, Gregory's biblical commentaries and *Dialogues* repeatedly confirm his view of the standards for spiritual leadership. In the *Dialogues*, for example, St. Benedict and St. Equitius are described as having taken on disciples only after they had conquered the temptation of lust.[10] Another holy man, St. Libertinus, refuses to perform a miracle (even though he has the grace to do so) because he is so concerned about maintaining his humility.[11] Viewed from the perspective of Gregory's precise pastoral considerations, the *Dialogues* prove to be a far more sophisticated presentation of Gregory's theological and pastoral interests than most acknowledge them to be.

It is the *Moralia*, however, that offers the most persistent presentation of the ascetic credentials that are needed for a successful pastoral ministry.[12] In a passage that could have come from the Egyptian desert in the late fourth century, Gregory argues that only those who are experienced in renunciation and contemplation know how to pray for the gift of discernment.[13] Similarly, he notes that only those who wish to be "dead to the world" will be called to a position of leadership by the Lord.[14] As elsewhere, he differentiates between good leaders and bad leaders, with the primary distinction between them being the commitment to asceticism—not only the commitment to personal renunciation, but also the ability and willingness to instruct others in the life of renunciation.[15] What is more, the distinction between good and bad directors is often presented within the pride/humility paradigm.[16] Here, too, Gregory notes the link between the absence of virtue and the inability to acquire the discernment necessary for successful leadership.[17] And, with Job as the ultimate example, our author also stresses the willingness of holy men to suffer injustice, particularly for the sake of instructing others.[18]

As we already saw in Gregory's censure of Maximus of Salona and John of Constantinople, the pontiff's criticism of insubordinate or rival clerics often reflected—at least rhetorically—his notion that successful ministry required ascetic detachment that was manifest in both a reputation for renunciation and a public display of humility. In the case of Gregory's interaction with John, because the pride/humility paradigm had become so integrated into Gregory's notion of renunciation, the pontiff was able to claim that his rival in Constantinople lacked the credentials for effective ministry when, in fact, he was renowned for his renunciation. As we will see in chapters 11 and 12, Gregory routinely presented his censure of incompetent priests and bishops as a failure to adhere to the pontiff's exacting moral and ascetic standards.

Strategies for Recruiting Reluctant Candidates

One of the responsibilities that Gregory faced as bishop of Rome was filling clerical vacancies with suitable candidates. Not only did he find that there were too many unqualified pretenders putting themselves forward, but those he deemed to be the most qualified (i.e., experienced ascetics) were all too often unwilling to abandon the monastic life for the toil of priestly service. Ironically, it was this unwillingness that made them so desirable, because it could evince, to Gregory's reasoning, their possession of humility.

In book 1 of the *Pastoral Rule*, Gregory confronts directly the reluctance of ascetics to assume positions of pastoral leadership. Acknowledging their renunciatory and spiritual credentials, he begins, "For there are several who possess incredible virtues and who are exalted by great talents for training others; men who are spotless in the pursuit of chastity, stout in the vigor of fasting, satiated in the feasts of doctrine, humble in the long-suffering of patience, erect in the fortitude of authority, tender in the grace of kindness, and strict in the severity of judgment."[19] In other words, these men possess everything Gregory values in a spiritual leader. But a few lines later he warns, "If they refuse to accept a position of spiritual leadership (*culmen regiminum*) when they are called, they forfeit the majority of their gifts—gifts that they received not for themselves only but for others as well. When these men contemplate their own spiritual advantages and do not consider anyone else, they lose these goods because they desire to keep them for themselves."[20] As he continues, he characterizes them as "preferring the mystery of stillness" and of taking "refuge in the solitude of spiritual investigations."[21]

There is little doubt that Gregory refers here to professed ascetics.[22] But rather than further commend their renunciation or praise their humility, Gregory warns instead that they have, through the guise of false humility, acted with self-interest and failed to answer the call to service. Indeed, he argues that "no one is truly humble if he understands by the judgments of the Supreme Will that he ought to govern but then refuses to do so."[23]

Following the same concerns through Gregory's other works, we find that the pontiff employed a series of strategies in his attempt to recruit qualified but reluctant individuals. As we saw in the example from book 1 of the *Pastoral Rule*, one of Gregory's most striking arguments was that if worthy candidates refuse to assume a position of leadership out of selfishness, then God will forsake those ascetics and the virtues that would have otherwise made them compelling candidates. In the *Moralia* he similarly maintains that ascetic achievements will be of no salvific value for those who have failed to acknowledge the needs of their neighbors: "For what advantage is it to restrain the flesh in chastity if the soul is not broadened in the love of neighbor through compassion? For the chastity of the flesh is nothing if it is not recommended by the sweetness of the mind."[24] Pursuing the same theme later in the text, he decries those who lack the humility to suspend the spiritual joys of inward contemplation for the sake of their neighbors.[25]

The Mary/Martha paradigm offered Gregory a frequent source of reflection about the active/contemplative binary. Whereas most ascetic authors of Christian antiquity praised Mary and chastised Martha, Gregory's analysis was not nearly so straightforward. To be sure, reflection on this passage did occasion Gregory's promotion of the monastic and contemplative life,[26] but it also provided an opportunity for the pontiff to reiterate the importance of service. Twice in his *Commentary on Ezekiel* Gregory takes up the Mary/Martha paradigm. In the third homily of book 1 he begins with the stock position that the contemplative life is superior to the active life, but he soon transitions into a more daring proclamation that no one can obtain salvation who is confined entirely to one mode of life (i.e., either the active or the contemplative).[27] Of course, anyone familiar with the Gospel passage will realize that Gregory's position is not easily enabled by the text itself, and as a consequence our author's argument lacks cohesion. Perhaps even more surprising, however, is the second treatment of the passage in the second homily of book 2, wherein Gregory goes to great lengths to rehabilitate Martha's service.[28] Drawing on the story of Leah and Rachael (Jacob's wives) for confirmation, Gregory here offers the startling suggestion that a life of contemplation that lacks service is barren (like Rachael) and will be rejected by God: "For Rachael is beautiful but barren, because the contemplative life is splendid in the spirit but does not bear sons through preaching since it would rather seek the rest of silence."[29]

A related strategy that Gregory employed to recruit men to positions of leadership was appealing to their sense of responsibility without simultaneously threatening them with divine retribution. This milder approach appears repeatedly in the *Moralia*, with the basic theme that all Christians are expected to employ the talents with which God has graced them.[30] Similar passages can be found in the *Commentary on Ezekiel* and even the *Homilies on the Gospels*.[31] In fact, in both the first and seventh homilies of book 2 of the *Commentary on Ezekiel*, Gregory insists that leaders must willingly sacrifice their own spiritual joys for the sake of others.[32]

Of course, Gregory used other tactics as well, including a series of rhetorical presentations that cast the priesthood as something to which all successful ascetics should aspire. As noted, he repeatedly implies that the office of preachers is the highest and most significant order within the Christian community—a claim that was at least partially intended to make the role of the spiritual director more appealing to potentially reluctant ascetics because, he argues, advancement in the spiritual life requires that they take on this role.

In the *Commentary on Ezekiel*—which is from a later period than the *Pastoral Rule*, *Moralia*, or the *Homilies on the Gospels*—Gregory introduces a new element to his long-standing effort to recruit ascetics.[33] In three of these homilies, Gregory maintains that the practice of spiritual direction can actually be beneficial to the cultivation of one's own spiritual life. Whereas Gregory had encouraged ascetics to embrace spiritual leadership in previous treatises, sermons, and letters, he simultaneously acknowledged that the assumption of spiritual responsibility could detract directors from their own fulfillment—a regression that was necessary to adhere to the commandment to love one's neighbor. But in the *Commentary on Ezekiel*, Gregory states more confidently that the assumption of spiritual leadership would be spiritually beneficial.

For example, in the tenth homily of book 1, Gregory submits that the ascetic who possesses the virtue of chastity can make further progress in that virtue by encouraging others to pursue it as well. "If the mind [of the leader] is ever tempted by the impurity of lust, it can amend itself with the very zeal with which it corrected others."[34] In a later homily he reminds his readers that if they remain alone in their ascetic pursuits, they will develop pride. But if they willingly submit themselves in humility to the spiritual trauma of serving others, they will have the opportunity to grow from their own weakness.[35] And then, in a passage that would appear to be a complete contradiction of certain warnings he offers in the *Pastoral Rule*, Gregory suggests that it is possible for a preacher to learn about particular virtues by preaching about them, even if the one speaking does not presently possess those virtues he discusses in public.[36] The contradiction is unexplained, and we are left to assume that Gregory chose an alternate rhetorical objective for his homily on Ezekiel.

One additional strategy that Gregory employed to convince otherwise reluctant ascetics to accept the responsibility of spiritual direction is the appeal to a saintly exemplar. The creation and circulation of hagiographic texts served multiple purposes, of course, but the most important was that it allowed an author to advance a specific interpretation of the significance of the saint's life.[37] We have already rehearsed some of the ways in which Gregory's *Dialogues* subtly reflects his interests. At this juncture, however, it is important for us to recall the extent to which his presentation of many of the Italian saints, especially St. Benedict, reflects a specific concern for the recruitment of experienced ascetics to active ministry. A careful reading of the life suggests, in fact, that Benedict is praised, first and foremost, for his willingness to suspend his own spiritual joys for the sake of others.[38] In other words, Gregory presents Benedict's holiness in the context of his spiritual supervision. The same is true for other heroes in the *Dialogues*.[39] And we can see that Gregory pursued a similar tack in the *Moralia*, where he repeatedly defines holiness as the willingness to serve others.[40]

CHAPTER SEVEN

The Tasks of the Spiritual Leader

In book 2 of the *Pastoral Rule*, Gregory identifies the many tasks and challenges that confront the spiritual director. Some of the specific responsibilities he lists include the need for the spiritual director to be willing to serve others, discerning in speech, compassionate to all who seek his counsel, and confident in the reproach of those who need it. All the while, the director must learn to balance the ministry of service with the continued (if modified) pursuit of heavenly contemplation. As with the other aspects of his pastoral theology, Gregory's discussion of the tasks before the spiritual director is not confined to his treatment in the *Pastoral Rule*, and it is through a consideration of the full corpus that we gain the most complete picture of his thinking.

Preaching and Interpreting the Gospel

Like Gregory Nazianzen and Augustine before him, Gregory believed that the most fundamental responsibility of the clergy was to preach the good news of Christ.[1] Of course, what the pontiff means by this is not simply the repetition of Matthew, Mark, Luke, and John, but rather a thoughtful interpretation of the whole of Scripture, including the Hebrew Bible, that would inspire the spiritual and moral reform of the audience. One way to gauge Gregory's interest in preaching is by a simple analysis of the words that he employs to name the spiritual director. Indeed, in both the *Pastoral Rule* and the *Moralia* one of the terms he uses most frequently to describe the spiritual leader is *praedicator*, or "preacher."[2] What is more, he frequently interchanges *rector* ("leader" or "ruler") with *praedicator*. As noted, some modern interpreters have argued that the pontiff understood the art of spiritual direction (and especially the audience of the *Pastoral Rule*) to be reserved for the episcopacy.[3] Such a view, however, fails to take into account the extent to which Gregory repeatedly encouraged monastic audiences to reflect upon similar matters and to concern themselves with the "art" of spiritual direction made manifest through preaching. For example, a careful analysis of the typological digressions contained within the *Moralia* reveals that there is a steady progression from a specific description of Job's activity—"the holy man did"—to a more generic "we see that holy men do." By the later portions of the work, the progression continues from "holy men" to "holy preachers."[4] In this way, Gregory subtly suggests that all who wish to be holy like Job must master the art of preaching.

Naturally, we find more specific discussions of the content and scope of the preaching of morality in Gregory's works. In the *Dialogues*, for example, the pontiff offers the rather significant argument that the invisible conversion of a sinner to repentance through a director's preaching is more powerful than the miracle of bringing the dead back to life.[5] The *Moralia* repeatedly speaks to the importance of preaching, whether it is the examples of Job, Paul, and others or the function of preaching in the repentance and ultimate salvation of sinners.[6] Indeed, the first half of book 18 is an extended excursus on the importance of preaching, which is enabled through Gregory's interpretation that Job's activities should be understood as a metaphor for excellent preaching. In the prefatory letter for the text, Gregory seems to take the significance of public preaching for granted when he emphasizes for Leander's benefit the three-part interpretative method that the preacher should employ in his public exegesis.[7] The *Commentary on Ezekiel* similarly directs spiritual directors to understand their responsibility to preach well, to preach the truth, and to pay attention to the details of grammar and diction so that their message might not be undercut by inadequate preparation.[8]

Discernment

Of all of the aspects of spiritual direction Gregory investigates for the benefit of other leaders, the element that he engages most often is the need for discernment, *discretio*.[9] Following the lead of John Cassian, Gregory understood discernment to be more than merely a gift of self-knowledge (as many early Christian and Greco-Roman writers had understood it).[10] Through discernment, a spiritual director could perceive the unique spiritual strengths and flaws in his disciples and then deliver an inspired message. In book 30 of the *Moralia*, Gregory summarizes a lengthy discussion of the art of spiritual direction by showing the mutual dependence of renunciation, preaching, grace and discernment. In this setting, he suggests that discernment is the trigger for the other elements. The "preacher" who carefully preserves discernment in his instruction of disciples will be strengthened by grace, "for when the discernment in teaching is carefully preserved by the preacher, a greater fullness of [the grace] of preaching is given by the divine."[11] This supernatural assistance enables the director to love and sympathize with his disciples. It helps him to understand that there is a proper "season" for preaching renunciation and another season for the promise of mercy.[12] Gregory is thus arguing that the gift of discernment facilitates individualized care that is simultaneously just, reasonable, and merciful. In short, discernment is both the spiritual mechanism by which the master understands the needs of his disciples and the map onto which he charts the course for spiritual progress. The latter aspect, of course, shows Gregory's understanding of discernment to have moved further than previous Christian conceptions of discernment as a "discernment of spirits."[13]

In contrast to the earlier ascetic writers, who typically defined discernment as a mystical gift of grace bestowed upon experienced and humble renunciants, Gregory's discussions of the source of discernment are less consistent.[14] To be sure, he frequently described it as a gift from God that enabled directors to parse virtues and vices in their disciples or to enable the correct interpretation of the Scriptures.[15] But, as just noted, Gregory was also willing to suggest that a fruitful use of discernment could be the trigger for grace that ultimately enabled better preaching. Of course, discernment was also a spiritual tool that could be lost if a director failed to maintain humility during his interactions with disciples.[16]

The majority of Gregory's observations about discernment concerned either the way it aided in the diagnosis of spiritual ills or its role in the prescription for spiritual healing. Concerning the former, he repeatedly argues that it is impossible to identify the proper spiritual regimen if the director is unable to understand his disciple's unique condition.[17] The director must especially be on the watch for vices that masquerade as virtues.[18] So too must he discern if a disciple's acts of renunciation are genuine or for show.[19]

In Gregory's view (which was derivative of both contemporary medicine[20] and Christian doctrine), everyone was susceptible to different vices and to different degrees of those vices. As a consequence, it was the responsibility of the director to know the strengths and weaknesses of everyone with whom he interacted and then establish an individualized path for spiritual advancement.[21] This also entailed knowing how sternly a disciple could be reprimanded, based on his or her experience with the life of penitence.[22] Indeed, the whole of book 3 of the *Pastoral Rule* was an extended excursus on the diagnosis and treatment of spiritual faults.[23]

Gregory's comments concerning the role of discernment in a mentor's spiritual advice are more about the need for common sense than they are an elaboration on the theme of discernment as a mystical quality. Although *discretio* is sharpened by contemplation, Gregory understands it to be sublimely rational—the keenest and most incisive rationality and perception.[24] It is not just the ability to "see" something; it is the ability to weigh and consider its importance. It is the ability to appreciate how distant something is from the target of perfect action. It is precisely because Gregory desires that spiritual advice and pastoral reprimands be applied appropriately that he understands discernment to be such a critical attribute for effective ministry.[25] Being too harsh or too lenient is a failure of discernment.[26] More often than not, the mentor needs to chart a course for gradual correction that leads the penitent step-by-step to spiritual health.[27] The advisor will continue to monitor his disciple's progress and adjust the spiritual medicine as needed.[28]

At times, Gregory reasons, a pastor's instruction will require a bending of canonical rules. It may even necessitate that the advisor allow one vice to grow temporarily so that the destruction of a more immediately threatening behavior may occur.[29] Here, too, Gregory follows Cassian in the application of the pastoral concept of *condescensio* (*oikonomia* in

Greek ascetic literature), a temporary suspension of a prescribed repri-
mand for a greater pastoral good.[30] More than simply adapting the rules
for a pastoral benefit, the concept of *condescensio* could also be applied by
a spiritual director to exaggerate the danger of a particular vice so as to
shake the disciple into action.[31] On these points, as in other cases, Gregory's letters offer confirmation of his application of *condescensio* according to his own discernment of the pastoral context.[32]

The idea that spiritual counseling should be tailored to the individual
needs of the disciple was, of course, not a Gregorian invention — as noted,
it had both Greco-Roman and Christian antecedents. But Gregory's discussion of particularities of this concept was not only much more comprehensive than that of any other Patristic author, it was also the register
by which he evaluated and encouraged reform. This demonstrates a level
of ascetic commitment that is stronger than all other episcopal discussions of spiritual formation from the era.

Encouragement of Asceticism and Moral Reform

To the extent that the purpose of spiritual direction was to assist
Christians in their ascent to God, we might say that Gregory understood
the outcome of a successful ministry to be reflected in the ascetic and
moral reform of the spiritual director's community. We have already investigated Gregory's ascetic theology in detail, and we have also evaluated the extent to which he understood the prerequisites for spiritual authority to entail, more than anything else, ascetic credentials. What we
have not yet had occasion to explore is the extent to which Gregory encouraged specific spiritual regimens in order to cultivate ascetic and moral
discipline.

Like other late-ancient ascetic authors, Gregory frequently encourages
his readers (and, in a sense, the disciples of his readers) to all of the customary acts of Christian renunciation, including fasting, charity, chastity,
and vigil. He does this explicitly through admonition in his correspondence,[33] but he also does it implicitly by highlighting the ascetic feats of
the biblical heroes and ascetic saints. As important as those specific external acts of renunciation are, Gregory is also keen to promote a form of in-

ternal introspection and renunciation that is less obvious and less corporeal, but even more essential to the development of humility.

The cultivation of humility was one of the ways that a Christian could pursue the internal dimensions of the spiritual life. It is therefore noteworthy that Gregory rarely provides specific advice for how one is to obtain it—he typically just states that it is necessary. But the one "practice" that Gregory does identify as leading to humility is penance (*paenitentia*), and he encouraged it in every genre of his writing.

On nearly a dozen occasions in his biblical commentaries, Gregory speaks of the relationship between penance and humility.[34] He is particularly interested in the tears of repentance, which he takes to be a physical marker of authentic regret and a sign of yearning for reform: "For truly, when sin (*culpa*) is washed by the tears of repentance (*paenitentiae lamentis*) and the crimes that were perpetrated are so bewailed (*plaguntur*), a great confidence arises in the mind so as to ponder the joy from above, as the face of our hearts is lifted up."[35] True reform, in fact, is differentiated from temporary guilt by the presence of the tears of penitence.[36] In book 9 of the *Moralia* Gregory offers an extended discussion of the difference between authentic and inauthentic tears. Authentic tears of humility, he notes, are born from a desire for the heavenly kingdom and a recognition of impurity; they are not born simply from the absence of what we desire.[37] In book 11 he differentiates between sins of act and sins of thought, noting that recognition of sins of thought requires vigorous self-inspection, and they can be purged only by weeping and self-chastisement.[38] Gregory reminds his readers that the saints provide a model for this kind of continuous internal introspection, and their penitence flows unprompted through an authentic yearning for God.[39] But it is the responsibility of the spiritual director to teach his disciples of the need for penance. This can be done in a number of ways, including the assigning of penance, the promise of its reward, and the example of the saints.[40]

Not surprisingly, Gregory's correspondence contains dozens of discussions of penitence in a variety of settings. One of the more arresting examples that has drawn the attention of scholars is Gregory's practice of sending both malcontent clergy and laypersons to monasteries as veritable prisoners, where they were expected to perform penitence under the supervision of the abbot or the local bishop.[41] Although Gregory understands the monastery to be a place of spiritual healing, these letters demonstrate that he was willing to force a penitential routine upon the most stubborn offenders of his code of discipline.

Not all of Gregory's statements about penitence and moral reform in his correspondence were so draconian; the majority, in fact, offer direct instruction and reproach. Writing to Boniface, the bishop of Reggio in Campania, Gregory attempted to thread the needle between praising the man's charitable action and criticizing his penchant for boasting of his own good works.[42] Writing to the congregation of Rimini, Gregory declares that the entire community is in need of penance, owing to the fact that they have behaved so badly with respect to their bishop that he has become incapacitated and is unlikely to be able to return to his position.[43]

The surviving evidence concerning Gregory's spiritual and moral admonitions to his correspondence stems largely from letters to aristocratic men and women far removed from the city of Rome. In such a role, Gregory corrects errant belief, reproves the ways that the wealthy treat their slaves, and repeatedly encourages his correspondents to the spiritual rewards made available through charity.[44] Our knowledge of these relationships is, in most cases, confined to one or two letters, but some of these correspondences are considerably longer. Venantius of Syracuse provides one of the most revealing examples of a long-running spiritual relationship between the pontiff and an aristocratic "disciple." Indeed, Gregory uses these letters to repeatedly encourage a level of ascetic discipline suitable to married life.[45] Venantius of Syracuse was an ex-monk who had left the ascetic world in order to marry a well-placed lady, Italica. In the first letter of the surviving correspondence, Gregory laments that Venantius has abandoned his commitment to God (i.e., his monastic profession) and has chosen, instead, the way of the world.[46] Although Gregory encourages Venantius to change his course, he promises not to abandon him, and indeed, the correspondence runs for more than a decade and eventually expands to include Venantius's wife and daughters.[47]

Additional Responsibilities

The spiritual director must consider many other aspects of leadership in his supervision of his disciples, including the need to set a proper example, the necessity of administering the sacraments, and the where-withal to not lose sight of his own spiritual well-being. Gregory has plenty to say about the need for the director to set a good example. Indeed, we might view a large portion of book 2 of the *Pastoral Rule* as an extended discussion of the extent to which the *rector*'s behavior will be scrutinized and imitated by those under his direction.[48] Here, the thrust of Gregory's argument is that everything of value that the *rector* might offer through preaching will be undermined if his behavior shows him to be a hypocrite or simply sets him up for public scrutiny. But the pontiff also engages the link between action and imitation in positive ways as well. One might say that the very purpose of the *Dialogues* was to show that the life of virtue leads to the imitation of virtue. In fact, several of the stories of the *Dialogues* suggest that the presence of sanctity can soften the heart of even the fiercest barbarians, precisely because God "inhabits" the holy man and reveals his power through him.[49]

While there is little doubt that Gregory believed in the potency of the sacraments and the need for the clergy to take their sacramental responsibilities seriously, by comparison he rarely speaks to the sacramental responsibilities of the clergy in the context of his other lengthy discussions about spiritual direction.[50] The *Pastoral Rule*, for example, does not offer any extensive analysis of the sacramental obligations of the clergy or their soteriological importance in the way that Chrysostom's *On the Priesthood* describes the significance of the baptismal and Eucharistic roles of the priest.[51] This is not to say that Gregory ever explicitly denies the importance of the sacraments—in fact, he offers multiple testimonies to the occurrence of miracles in a sacramental setting and repeatedly claims that there is no salvation without baptism. But it is noteworthy that his more prolonged treatments of the tasks of the spiritual director provide only minimal discussion of the priest's liturgical roles.[52]

The one remaining issue to which Gregory directs a great deal of his attention is the need for the spiritual director to maintain the life of contemplation within, and despite, his engagement with active ministry.[53] We know from the pontiff's correspondence the degree to which his own episcopal career was consumed with secular responsibilities that were far beyond the traditional rhythms of the "activity" of spiritual ministry.[54] On many occasions he laments the extent to which he is consumed by the affairs of the world when he would prefer to return to the solace of the monastic life.[55] And yet he reminds himself and his readers that there is a great benefit to be found in the nexus of active contemplation.

Indeed, Gregory's praise for the "active contemplative" exists in every genre of his surviving corpus. As we have already seen, he denies the traditional claim of ascetic writers that the summit of the Christian life is to be found in contemplation alone: perfection resides in those who are able to contemplate the divine mystery but who willingly suspend (not cease) that contemplation for service to others.[56] In the *Moralia*, Gregory repeatedly showcases Job's ability to balance the active and the contemplative life.[57] In book 18 he runs through a series of Old Testament saints (especially Joseph and Daniel) to emphasize how the saints can take responsibility for others without losing the interior life.[58] A little later he suggests that the preacher who strives for both will be more effective in his ministry and obtain greater mystical insights by maintaining a strong balance between the two, precisely because the two reinforce one another.[59] In short, even though the preacher will, no doubt, be saddled with worldly responsibility and distracted by that responsibility, he cannot allow those challenges to prevent him from attending to his own spiritual needs if he hopes to offer effective spiritual advice and be a model for imitation.[60]

CHAPTER EIGHT

The Impediments
to Effective Leadership

Having already discussed the need to retain a healthy spiritual life in the context of active ministry as a "task" of spiritual direction, we will conclude part 2 by assessing those additional elements that Gregory believed to pose the greatest impediments to quality leadership. We have repeatedly addressed the extent to which he understood the sin of pride to be the most dangerous of the vices, a view that he shared with other early Christian ascetics. In the context of spiritual direction, however, pride was especially threatening because the very exercise of authority could become an uncontrolled source of prideful temptation.[1] In book 1 of the *Pastoral Rule* he cautions, "For no one is able to acquire humility in a position of authority if he did not refrain from pride when in a position of subjection. He does not know to flee from praise when it abounds if he yearned for it when it was absent."[2] A little later he adds, "For it is very often the case that the discipline of good works, which was maintained in a time of tranquility, is ruined in the assumption of authority. For an inexperienced sailor can steer a ship in calm waters but even an experienced seaman is disordered by a storm."[3] According to Gregory, the best way for a spiritual director to compensate for the temptation of pride that accompanies authority is to dwell on the fact that he has lost the leisure of contemplation and will therefore have to be all the more alert to his own weakness and vigilant against his sins. Vigilance, of course, requires the strengthening of self-discipline, achieved through ascetic detachment—and so the cycle continues.

Another possible threat to a successful ministry that derives from the actual exercise of leadership relates to the desire to be liked.[4] For early ascetic writers such as Evagrius and Cassian, "vainglory" was the name attributed to the sinful desire to be well esteemed by others. More than the modern fixation on vanity—a desire to be perceived as physically attractive—vainglory was understood in the late-ancient ascetic register to be the desire to be held in good opinion. Thus, vainglory poses the spiritual threat preventing someone from doing what is right for fear of how they will be perceived.

Although Gregory's language is not as precise as Evagrius's or Cassian's, his concern for vainglory is readily apparent in book 2 of the *Pastoral Rule*, where he dwells in detail on the need for the spiritual leader to censure his disciples (especially those in positions of civil authority) without any fear of recrimination. The *rector* who fails to instruct his disciples out of fear of being disliked or of loss of personal comfort is the *rector* who has forsaken his spiritual responsibility.[5]

Beyond the specific concerns for pride and vainglory, however, the majority of Gregory's statements about the impediments to effective ministry typically relate to the sheer toll that an active ministry would take on the spiritual health of the *rector* and the subsequent effect on his ministry. As far as Gregory was concerned, no leader was free of this danger: not himself, not former popes, not even King David or the other saints.[6] We find Gregory's concern for the danger of spiritual direction manifest in several ways. In book 1 of the *Moralia*, for example, he includes an analysis of John 13 (in one of many digressions about the text of Job) to emphasize the point that Christ had washed the feet of his disciples because they had sullied themselves in the act of service.[7] Even though spiritual direction was clearly important to Gregory, he did not want his readers to believe that it could be assumed easily or without consequence.

Later, in book 19, he offers a similar analogy, only this time the washing is not of the disciples' feet but rather the "washing in butter" that is described in Job 29:6. According to Gregory, the passage is a warning that it is impossible to assume the office of preaching without some transgression.[8] The minister will either get unjustly irritated when a disciple disapproves of what his advisor says or, if everything spoken is accepted, swell with pride. Either way, preachers need continuous cleansing.[9] Without self-examination, penance, and the pursuit of contemplation, even the most effective ministers will have the "gift of preaching" taken away from them.[10]

THE CENTRAL ARGUMENT of part 2 has been that Gregory's pastoral theology was inextricably linked to an ascetic outlook that both measured the worthiness of a potential candidate for spiritual leadership in terms of his ascetic credentials and encouraged a type of spiritual instruction that emphasized moral reform through ascetic means. These concerns are well articulated in Gregory's famous *Pastoral Rule*, which he published at the beginning of his pontificate, but they are also well represented in his biblical commentaries, the *Dialogues*, and his correspondence. The frequency with which Gregory pursues his interests in spiritual direction in texts that might otherwise not be considered pastoral in scope, in fact, demonstrates the extent to which the challenge of providing effective ministry continued to dominate his mind. As we turn now from the theoretical and theological to the practical and diplomatic aspects of Gregory's activity, we will see that even in the most desperate and defensive of political moments, the echoes of Gregory's ascetic and pastoral concerns ring loudly.

Part Three

Gregory as "First Man" of Rome

In the thousand years between the founding of the Roman Republic and birth of Gregory the Great, the office of urban prefect, *praefectus urbi*, had granted its holder a variety of rights and responsibilities. At the onset of the imperial period, Augustus reinvigorated the role of the urban prefect, making him a quasi-mayor and granting him authority over all of the guilds and colleges, which placed several municipal duties, including supervision of grain shipments and dredging of the Tiber, under its holder's supervision. In conjunction with these significant responsibilities, the urban prefect controlled the urban police and acted as legal authority over all criminal matters. It was one of the most prestigious positions in the empire, well befitting the literal meaning of the title: "first man of the city." During the late-ancient period, as the imperial court increasingly resided outside of Rome (in either Milan or Constantinople), the prefect became the de facto leader of the city and its suburbs.

As detailed in the introduction, Gregory served as urban prefect before becoming a monk. Gregory's family had long been involved in both civil and ecclesiastical administration, and however much he may have bemoaned his secular responsibilities, Gregory was a skilled administrator of the Roman Church's property and its interests. It is the thesis of part 3 that Gregory governed the See of Rome like a seasoned and exacting executive, but he did so in a way that drew from deep theoretical convictions born of his unique views of asceticism and spiritual direction. By viewing Gregory's administrative and diplomatic decisions through the prism of these theological commitments, we learn more fully the extent to which Gregory undertook a transformation of the papal institution, and in doing so we gain a better sense of his achievements, failures, and uniqueness.

CHAPTER NINE

The Rome of Gregory's Imagination

We begin this final section, dedicated to Gregory's dual role as the leader of the Roman See and a leader of the city of Rome, by seeking a better understanding of what being a "Roman" might have meant for Gregory. Gaining a better appreciation for both the tangible and imagined elements of the epistemic horizon we will designate as *Romanitas* helps us to understand the extent to which "Roman-ness" may have played a role in Gregory's decisions as a Roman leader and in the literary and rhetorical choices he made when presenting his ideas.[1] As noted, when Gregory became bishop, the city of Rome was a shadow of its former self and the Italian peninsula had spent the better part of the past century mired in a series of destructive wars. While the empire's better days may have been in its past, the Roman people were now ostensibly Christian and, as such, had the promise of an eternal kingdom that would replace the faltering earthly one. This chapter will attempt to parse Gregory's writings for a sense of how these divergent trends may have impacted his conceptual understanding of what it was to be a

Roman Christian. Along the way, we will try to get a sense for how Gregory understood the relationship between the city of Rome and the Empire of Rome, which was now centered in Constantinople. We will further explore the meaning of *Romanitas* in Gregory's imagination by scrutinizing what he said about barbarians—the most obvious non-Romans with whom he interacted. As we will see, there may well have been larger theological purposes behind some of Gregory's most vehement critiques of barbarian otherness.

Because the Rome of Gregory's imagination was very much a Christian Rome, my investigation in this chapter follows Jeffrey Richards's contention that the intersection of *Christianitas* and *Romanitas* offers the primary lens for understanding Gregory's thought and career.[2] In some ways, Richards's position is simply the extension of a historiographic trajectory that seeks to describe the rise of the papal institution (and its corresponding ideology) as the natural replacement for the Western empire.[3] In my reevaluation of the relationship between *Christianitas* and *Romanitas* in Gregory's imagination, however, I will seek to nuance Richards's assessment by including additional interpretive strategies for comprehending Gregory's views about the state of Christian Rome, his fidelity to the empire, and the distinction between Romans and barbarians. By investigating the literary function of certain passages and by considering the possibility that his statements can also be viewed as acts of rhetorical performance, I hope to offer a greater appreciation for the theological subtlety and pastoral concerns that may have motivated Gregory's presentation of *Romanitas*. As we will see, this is true for Gregory's notion of Rome both as a place and as an idea.

The Legacy of Ancient Rome

Among the many ways that the legacy of ancient Rome may have enabled Gregory's concept of *Romanitas*, perhaps the two most obvious relate to the Latin cultural inheritance that he would have received through schooling and a shared imperial vision of the world that placed Rome at its center. Concerning the first, and like so many other aspects of his life prior to his pontificate, Gregory tells us very little about his education or intellectual pursuits. Several scholars have offered overlapping assessments of what his education likely entailed, often drawing on more explicit evidence from figures such as Cassiodorus or Augustine.[4] Historians generally assume that Gregory had some training in the *quadrivium* (geometry, mathematics, astronomy, and music) but that the core of his education would have been on the *trivium* (grammar, rhetoric, and dialectic), with its emphasis on language and the art of persuasion.[5] For his part, Gregory of Tours famously suggested that Pope Gregory was second to none in the city of Rome with respect to learning—a passage that was adopted by the pontiff's ninth-century biographers as well.[6] Gregory of Tours's statement, of course, is little more than a trope employed to affirm Pope Gregory's qualifications for leadership. The fact of the matter is that any assessment of Gregory's education or literary interests is, at some level, a matter of conjecture.

Equally frustrating for our attempts to assess the influence of Rome's literary or intellectual heritage on Gregory's sense of *Romanitas* is the fact that the pontiff offers few citations of the classical sources that he would have known. Pierre Riché concludes that Gregory's career marks a tipping point between the classical and the medieval world precisely because the pontiff was the first major Latin author to cite Scripture and the church fathers rather than the Latin ancients as proof-texts in his writing.[7] This is not to say that Gregory never drew upon pre-Christian authors—there are references, both direct and indirect. But compared to someone such as Augustine, Gregory's use of classical sources is notably rare.[8] What is more, even though Gregory does seem to have had an appreciation for the famous Latin writers and moralists (especially Cicero and Seneca), he did not attempt to replicate the style of their prose-rhythm in the way that other late-ancient Christian authors, such as Ennodius and Cassiodorus, did.[9]

We are on firmer ground trying to get a sense for the legacy of ancient Rome in Gregory's imagination by pursuing its political, especially its imperial, dimensions. Indeed, given the extent to which Gregory is sometimes characterized as antagonistic to the Eastern court, it is remarkable how much the pontiff's expressions of self-identity reflect a shared late-ancient discourse of patriotism, imperial loyalty, and Roman statesmanship.[10]

For his part, Robert Markus has demonstrated that the Roman Church in the late sixth century was an imperial church with ideological borders and possibilities that had been very much shaped by Justinian's legisla-tion.[11] Through his *Novellae*, or "New Laws,"[12] Justinian had made the Christian institution one of the most important in the empire, effec-tively equating imperial law with canon law—a transition that ulti-mately blurred the distinction between the sacred authority of the bishop and the imperial authority of secular rulers.[13] Gregory never really ques-tioned this reality or its novelty. As Markus notes, Gregory's "language reveals the hold on his mind of the established clichés of Roman impe-rial ideology. The empire or the state are, quite simply, 'the Christian empire,' . . . or 'the holy commonwealth.'"[14] Secular and ecclesiastical leaders had distinct spheres of responsibility and concern, but the two were to work together (so much as was possible in a fallen world) for the common good.[15] This is true not only in his correspondence with impe-rial figures in the East[16] but also in his letters to Saxon rulers, for whom Gregory extolled the virtues of Constantine and Helen as models for secular leadership.[17]

Gregory's acceptance of the imperial structures of his age (both the centering of the empire in Constantinople and the functional relationship between ecclesial and imperial authority) is further confirmed by com-parison to his papal predecessors.[18] For example, whereas Gelasius had an acrimonious relationship with the Eastern ruler,[19] Gregory never ques-tioned the imperial authority of the rulers of his day, nor did he deny that they had a role in promoting orthodoxy—if anything, he wanted them to be more consistent and more thorough in their concern for the admin-istration of the Church.[20] This is not to say that Gregory enforced impe-rial policies uncritically—as we will see, he resisted the emperor and his agents on multiple occasions. But when he did resist the imperial govern-ment, his actions and rhetorical tone did not appear to reflect the depth of political anxiety of those fifth- and early-sixth-century Roman bishops who saw the rise of Constantinople and the decline of the city of Rome as a loss of traditional privilege or custom.

Identifying Gregory as a loyal son of the empire has not always been the path of his biographers. Walter Ullmann argued, somewhat notori-ously, that Gregory's famous Christian mission to Kent (discussed in chapter 13) was designed as a means to spread papal influence through-out the West and to separate himself and his church from the Byzantine court.[21] Markus, among others, sufficiently demonstrated that the mission was motivated by nothing of the sort,[22] and other scholars have increasingly shown the extent to which it is an anachronism to divide Gregory's world so rigidly between the Byzantine East and the Latin West.[23] And while there is no reason to deny that Gregory fundamentally understood himself to be a citizen of the empire and a servant of the emperor (however disappointed he might become with individual emperors), there are, nonetheless, occasional rhetorical jabs at imperial authority throughout his correspondence.

A careful analysis of the rhetorical structures of Gregory's imperial correspondence demonstrates that the pontiff would often subvert certain features of imperial discourse for the purpose of promoting specific theological, pastoral, and political goals. Indeed, Gregory's letters to Maurice (Roman emperor from 582–602) often employed a series of sophisticated rhetorical features intended to steer imperial policy in a direction that conformed to Gregory's ascetic inclinations. For example, the pontiff took particular offense at an imperial law that prohibited soldiers from becoming monks.[24] In his attempt to alter that policy, Gregory developed a series of subtle arguments to elide (perhaps even subvert) the imperial kingdom to the heavenly kingdom. By linking one to the other, he gestures toward Maurice's authority but simultaneously, and not so subtly, asserts that there is both a more exalted kingdom and a more exalted ruler (i.e., God).[25] What is more, Gregory presents himself as the one who properly understands the difference between the two and can thus direct Maurice toward the appropriate policy, which in this case would allow soldiers who have been properly screened to embark upon the monastic life.

We might also consider the ways in which Gregory's imperial correspondence reformulates imperial obligation in such a way as to reorient imperial authority. To be sure, the Greco-Roman world had a series of sophisticated and ancient traditions linking responsibility to leadership — these traditions were literary (e.g., Homer), philosophical (e.g., Aristotle), political (e.g., Augustus's *Res Gestae*), and legal (e.g., *pater familias*). But Gregory shrewdly supplements (again, one might even say subverts) the traditional concepts of imperial obligation by inserting himself into the decoding of where and how that obligation should be employed. A careful analysis of Gregory's letters to Maurice during the crisis over the ecumenical title shows that the pontiff is implying that the emperor cannot be left to interpret the obligations and responsibilities of imperial leadership on his own, nor should he be instructed by tradition or Roman law alone.[26] Rather, Gregory implies that, as an ambassador of God (that is, of the heavenly king), he is more qualified than Maurice to identify and interpret imperial obligations, particularly when those obligations touch upon matters related to the Church. As priest and servant of the heavenly kingdom, Gregory has not only the right but also the responsibility to critique a lapse in imperial obligation.[27] From a political perspective, we might say that this is a decidedly episcopal usurpation of imperial privilege. Although his tone is softer, Gregory's self-presentation as the figure in the best position to interpret theological matters on the emperor's behalf bears obvious traces of Gelasius's more acerbic statements in his famous letter to the emperor Anastasius in the 490s.[28]

Gregory's opposition to the imperial law barring soldiers from entering the monastic life and his criticism of the emperor's handling of the crisis over the ecumenical title both offer explicit testimony to our thesis that Gregory's administrative and diplomatic policies were largely informed by his theological and pastoral commitments. Whereas Gelasius had waged a protracted war against imperial authority in the midst of a dogmatic dispute and, as a consequence, fundamentally challenged the right of the emperor to involve himself in theological questions of the Church, Gregory's resistance to imperial authority was largely confined to those isolated affairs in which the emperor's policies were most at odds with Gregory's ascetic and pastoral ideals—namely that all Christians should be free to pursue the monastic life and that no priest can offer adequate pastoral leadership if he succumbs to pride.

Despite Gregory's willingness to challenge imperial policies on those issues that most directly contravened his theological commitments, there is little doubt that the pontiff considered himself a loyal son of the empire. In large part, this is because the Rome of Gregory's imagination was now a Christian Rome.

"Christian" Rome

It was precisely because Rome was now Christian that the legacy of ancient Rome had been transformed. Like Ambrose, Augustine, and Leo before him, Gregory devoted himself to the spread of Christianity and to creating a deeper commitment to Christianity among those already baptized. But whereas the prominent Latin theologians of the fourth and fifth centuries had to contend with local populations that were still devoted to pagan traditions, by the time of Gregory's election the majority of the urban population in Rome (and throughout other urban areas within the empire) was already ostensibly Christian.

Indeed, paganism of the Greco-Roman sort never appears to be a concern for Gregory in his public homilies. This indicates a stark contrast to Pope Leo, who had to remind the local population that the cult of St. Peter would be more beneficial than the cult of Romulus, or Pope Gelasius, who failed to prevent Roman aristocrats from patronizing a Lupercalia festival.[29] As we will see in subsequent chapters, Gregory worked hard to bring pagans among the Germanic tribes to Christianity and also to bring the heterodox Christians among them into the orthodox fold, but his extensive corpus leaves little evidence that he ever faced the challenge of convincing his local audience to accept baptism or abandon Greco-Roman cults.

The extent to which Rome's urban topography would have been filled with Christian shrines and basilicas no doubt added to Gregory's sense that his city was a Christian city—that his empire was a Christian one. The scholarship on Roman archeology and material culture from this period is particularly rich and often corrects scholarship that relies exclusively on the writings of Christian theologians for a sense of the transition from a pagan to a Christian Rome.[30] What is most significant for our purposes is that by the late sixth century, the city of Rome and its suburban neighborhoods had dozens of Christian basilicas and titular churches, many of which dated to the fourth and fifth centuries.[31] It also had dozens of smaller shrines (mostly dedicated to the cult of the martyrs) both inside and outside the city. Although many of those buildings would have been in need of repair, and although the local population was now too small to fill or use all of these shrines, the antiquity of these buildings would have reinforced Gregory's understanding that Rome had been a Christian city for a very long time.[32]

A careful examination of Gregory's *Homilies on the Gospels* reveals that he preached at a number of churches and shrines around the city. For the most part, this episcopal movement reflects a process that may have begun as early as the late fourth century during the tenure of Pope Damasus, in which the Roman bishop would travel to a particular church or martyr shrine to be seen leading the community's dedication to the particular saint.[33] With time, the Roman Lectionary—the biblical passages assigned to specific dates for all churches following Rome's liturgical authority—evolved to conform to the martyrological calendar of the city. The most important of these feasts, of course, was that of Sts. Peter and Paul on June 29, and it was Gregory who made it customary for all bishops in suburbican Italy to travel to Rome for the Feast of St. Peter, which would be commemorated in the basilica of St. Peter on Vatican Hill.[34]

Perhaps one of the most intriguing aspects of Gregory's thought is the way that his conception of a Christian Rome functioned alongside the secular pessimism of his apocalypticism.[35] Indeed, Gregory's understanding of the intersection of *Christianitas* and *Romanitas* is all the more arresting when we compare it to the triumphalism of Eusebius of Caesarea, who expected an ever-ascendant Christian empire in the wake of Constantine's conversion to Christianity.[36] In contrast, it is unlikely that many imperial loyalists living in late-sixth-century Italy could have shared Eusebius's optimism for the secular promise of a Christian empire. We will detail the extent of the imperial decline in Italy in the next chapter, but for now let us take note of the creative ways in which Gregory reinscribed the decline of the earthly kingdom as a gift of divine providence and a marker of God's privilege.

In his correspondence and in his biblical commentaries Gregory repeatedly refers to the traumatic events of his age (Lombard invasion, wars, plagues, earthquakes) as signs of the coming apocalypse.[37] At times he portrays this trauma as the consequence of human agency;[38] elsewhere he describes it as nothing more than a scene in the divine script for human history. In his *Homilies on the Prophet Ezekiel*, the pontiff states rather nonchalantly that his city—the great and mighty Rome—is nearly empty, a shadow of its former self.[39] Gregory delivered these homilies at the height of Lombard tension, when a host of Roman citizens were publicly carried into slavery. But those recent losses hardly speak to the massive decline in urban population that the city witnessed during the fifth and sixth centuries. Similar statements about the emptiness of the city pepper his *Homilies on the Gospels*.[40] For example, in the first homily

Gregory offers frequent confirmations of the fact that he is effectively living in a ghost town.[41] What is more, several of Gregory's naval metaphors (particularly those of the shipwreck) indicate a form of apocalyptic anxiety that was likely tied to his sense of secular decline.[42] Gregory may have very well believed himself to be living near the end of time.

Given Gregory's repeated predictions of future cataclysm and his rejection of a Eusebian vision for secular potential, how then are we to account for the fact that recent archeological evidence suggests that the city of Rome during the late sixth and early seventh century was not nearly as destitute as scholars have previously assumed? Indeed, materials recovered from the Crypta Balbi suggest that Rome remained a vibrant economic center of international trade, despite its depopulation, well into the seventh century.[43]

One of the great challenges to understanding the coherence in Gregory's thought and action is the apparent inconsistency in a man who repeatedly warns that the apocalypse is approaching but, at the very same time, seems to be doing everything possible to not only preserve but invest in the Rome of the future. Given the newly discovered archeological evidence, it would seem most appropriate, then, to interpret Gregory's apocalypticism for its theological and literary content rather than its historical value. Indeed, these findings suggest that Gregory's narrative of apocalyptic woe is more illuminating of his attempt to shape Christian behavior (especially to evoke renunciatory discipline) than it is source material for a historical account of the decline of Rome.

What is so intriguing about the idiosyncrasies of Gregory's apocalypticism is that he insists that Christians should rejoice when they view indications of earthly decline, precisely because it offers them lessons on how they should live. The "signs of the times" that Gregory identifies are a warning, delivered to Christians alone (only they can understand it properly), by a loving God who wishes that all prepare themselves for the coming judgment. For Gregory, of course, such preparation took on an ascetic and penitential character. In sum, the Christianization of Rome does not lead Gregory to envisage a triumphal empire as Eusebius had. Instead, the Christianization of Rome offers the careful exegete of Scripture a signal that he or she is in one of the last stages of human history.

"Barbarian Otherness" as a Literary and Rhetorical Tool

The final way that we will consider how *Romanitas* may have both bound and enabled Gregory's literary and rhetorical choices is through an assessment of his use of the category of "barbarian otherness" in his writings.[44] Given the size of Gregory's corpus and the extent to which he openly engaged the non-Roman rulers of his day, it is not surprising that "barbarians" appear frequently in his writing. His surviving correspondence includes dozens of letters to the Merovingians in Gaul, the Saxons in Kent, and, of course, the Lombards in Italy.[45] For the most part, these letters are convivial and deferential, and we find in them a late-ancient pontiff who is both steeped in the exercise of spiritual direction and experienced in the traditions of Roman statesmanship. In addition to corresponding with these leaders, Gregory frequently wrote about them in his letters to others. We might describe his account of the barbarians in his letters to ecclesiastical correspondents as balanced; although he often caricatures them as rustics who resist a complete commitment to the Christian life, Gregory never appears to waver from a belief that they will—eventually—become members of the body of Christ.[46]

By contrast, Gregory's portrayal of non-Romans in his letters to the imperial court is unequivocally negative. In these letters, Gregory stresses the difference between Roman and "barbarian," and his depiction of the Lombards in particular suggests both a real anxiety concerning the military threat that they pose to the city of Rome and hostility toward the Lombards as a people. Richards concluded from reading Gregory's imperial correspondence that the pontiff simply hated the Lombards.[47] Markus, similarly, postulated that Gregory preferred a dead Lombard to a live one.[48] I would propose that both Richards and Markus have overstated the case: they do not sufficiently consider that the pontiff may be emphasizing (even exaggerating) Roman and barbarian difference in order to prompt imperial action, precisely because he needs imperial action. For example, Gregory repeatedly warns Maurice that imperial armies are being defeated by barbarian forces because the emperor has failed to legislate in accordance with Gregory's expectations for imperial action within the Church.[49] In other words, "barbarian otherness" in these letters functions as a kind of rhetorical edge upon which Gregory sharpens his warnings about the need for a change in imperial policy. At the same time, it is likely that Gregory's stark contrast between Roman and barbarian in his imperial correspondence functions as a kind of self-defense against accusations that he had mishandled negotiations with the Lombards.[50] Put another way, when Gregory laments to Eastern correspondents that he has "become a bishop of Lombards," that he "sails a ship upon a sea of Lombard swords," and that "the only good Lombard is a dead Lombard," we might well consider whether or not Gregory was directing his rhetorical punch toward the imperial court and its policies (e.g., its failure to protect Rome and its unwillingness to follow Gregory's lead in ecclesial matters) rather than the Lombards themselves. But even if we can explain some of the reasons why Gregory might have exaggerated the distinction between Roman and barbarian in his imperial correspondence, there remains such a range of descriptions for the various Germanic tribes as a whole within his correspondence that it is challenging to gauge whether or not he possessed a single view of them as a group.[51]

It is with this difficulty in mind that I would like to consider the barbarian question from a different point of view, namely, how did Gregory turn the threat of barbarian violence and the challenge of barbarian otherness into a resource for the promotion of his ascetic, pastoral, and diplomatic goals? To help us with this question, we will turn to an often overlooked genre within his corpus, his hagiographic writings (i.e., the *Dialogues*), to see how our author transformed the threatening presence of barbarians in Italy into a literary tool for transmitting his theological and pastoral ideas. What is so intriguing about Gregory's *Dialogues* from the perspective of his understanding of Roman versus barbarian identity is the extent to which Goths and Lombards (and especially their leaders) serve the literary function of providing a vehicle through which Gregory's ascetic heroes reveal their sanctity. In other words, it is often against the violence, paganism, or heresy of Roman enemies that Gregory's saints demonstrate their greatness.

Gregory's *Dialogues* narrate at least twenty-six distinct encounters between Italian saints and the Goths or Lombards (there is also one story with the Vandals and another with the Visigoths).[52] Because we cannot survey all of these narratives, we will examine three different accounts that represent the whole, beginning with the lengthy account of St. Fortunatus contained in book 1. According to the text, a band of Goths had abducted two aristocratic boys whom they intended to keep as slaves.

St. Fortunatus appeals to the soldiers to release the boys, but the soldiers refuse Fortunatus's request. The next day, an unnamed Gothic leader visits the bishop before departing the city. Again, Fortunatus appeals for the boys' release, but to no avail. Foreseeing the future, the saint then warns the Gothic leader that he will meet with misfortune as a result of his denial of this request. As the Gothic ruler rides out of town, he passes by a church dedicated to St. Peter and suddenly is thrown from his horse, breaking one of his ribs in the fall. Realizing the ultimate cause of his injury, the Goth sends for the bishop's deacon and orders the boys to be released. Upon the safe return of the young men, Fortunatus sends holy water to the injured Goth so that he might quickly recover. Miraculously, the Goth is healed the moment he applies the holy water to his wound. Gregory's concluding comment notes simply that the Goth was forced to endure physical pain because he had failed to obey the bishop. Gregory's concern in the story about St. Fortunatus is the importance of spiritual authority and the consequence of disobedience, but it is significant that he employs the Goths and their leaders as the narrative placeholder for evil action, disbelief, and disobedience.

Book 2, which is Gregory's account of St. Benedict, develops similar themes. Chapters 14 and 15 include a series of encounters between Benedict and Totila, the notorious king of the Goths.[53] The first chronicles an attempt by Totila to test the saint's reputation for discernment. Totila sends a servant, dressed as himself, to learn whether or not the monk will comprehend the trick. Benedict, of course, spots the deception immediately, and the king's servants are so overcome by the saint's powers that they fall to the ground in fear of him.[54] Next, Gregory tells us, Totila decides to visit the monastery himself. As he approaches, Totila sees Benedict sitting in the distance and, like his servants in the previous story, falls to the ground, afraid to move any closer. Gregory writes, "Two or three times, Benedict asked him to rise. When Totila still hesitated, the servant of Christ walked to him and using his own hands helped him from the ground. Then he rebuked the king for his crimes and briefly foretold everything that was going to happen to him."[55] Following these prophecies, Gregory concludes his narration of the encounter by noting, "Terrified at these words, the king asked for a blessing and went away. From that time forward, he was less cruel."[56]

Like his account of St. Fortunatus, Gregory's *Life of Benedict* emphasizes the saint's ability to foretell the future and his willingness to bestow his blessings upon barbarian leaders. Perhaps more importantly, it stresses the fact that even the most vicious of the Goths is miraculously rendered passive when in the presence of the saints. It is intriguing that the encounters with sanctity (and the miracles that these encounters enable) do nothing to induce conversion or fully change the behavior in these Gothic leaders—they simply soften the threat that these men pose to the Roman population. The inevitability of barbarian violence is made explicit just two chapters later, when Benedict prophesies that his monastic community at Monte Cassino will be destroyed by barbarians.[57] This, of course, did happen: in 589, a few years prior to Gregory's authorship of the *Dialogues*, the Lombards, under the direction of Duke Zotto, devastated the Benedictine community there.[58] For some, the destruction of Monte Cassino could have been interpreted as a divine repudiation of Benedict's legacy. But Gregory seeks to confront this potential liability by proffering that Benedict had actually foreseen the destruction of his monastery.

A final example appears at the beginning of book 3 and chronicles a series of fanciful stories related to St. Paulinus of Nola. In the relevant portion of this lengthy narrative, Gregory tells us that in the midst of the Vandal invasion of Italy, a widow besought Paulinus to give her money so that she might ransom her son from the son-in-law of the Vandal king who had seized him.[59] Because Paulinus had already disbursed all of his resources for other captives, he offers himself as a slave to the Vandal warlord in exchange for the boy. After some time in this capacity, Paulinus informs his new master that the Vandal king will soon die and that he, the king's son-in-law, should prepare himself for how he will govern. At roughly the same time, the Vandal king has a dream in which he is judged for his misdeeds. When the king sees Paulinus for the first time, he trembles with fear because he realizes that Paulinus is one of judges from his dream. The king orders Paulinus to reveal his true identity and then sends him back to Italy alongside all of the other Romans who had been imprisoned by the Vandals.

While this final story involves the Vandals rather than Goths or Lombards, the patterns are consistent. A barbarian king is dumbfounded when he comes into the presence of holiness; he is made passive, but he does not convert to Christianity. Like St. Fortunatus, Paulinus's sanctity is revealed primarily through his ability to play an intercessory role between his Christian community and the barbarians who threaten it, specifically with respect to the ransoming of Roman prisoners. St. Paulinus is also able to accurately foretell a future in which a barbarian king will die. While Gregory set this narrative in a distant past (the Vandals vanquished Italy eighty-five years before Gregory's birth), he likely used it to speak directly to the concerns of his immediate audience, which was under the threat of the Lombards. Throughout the *Dialogues*, Gregory essentially collapses Vandals, Goths, and Lombards into a category of non-Roman "other."

Given Gregory's significant investment in the conversion of Saxons, Merovingians, and Lombards (detailed in chapter 13), the most perplexing aspect of the holy man/barbarian dichotomy in his *Dialogues* is that his saints rarely bring the barbarians they encounter into the Christian fold.[60] There is no conversion from paganism to Christianity, there is virtually no progression from heresy to orthodoxy—the Goths and Lombards always remain "other," always different, always a threat.[61] As such, the saints of the *Dialogues* and the communities of Christians they serve are decidedly not barbarian; they are Italian and they are imperial. Indeed, in each of the stories we surveyed, the ascetic hero either freed Romans from barbarian captivity or pacified a barbarian ruler such that he would be "less cruel" to the Romans in the future.[62] These themes are repeated in nearly all of the twenty-plus encounters in the text. As such, the barbarians of the *Dialogues* seem to function as a kind of proxy for a collective Roman fear, and it is against the threat of barbarian violence and a concomitant anxiety that the saints of the *Dialogues* reveal their sanctity. Not only do these saints perform miracles that astonish even the most menacing of barbarian warriors, they also bring Gothic and Lombard leaders themselves to the point of fear, which could be interpreted to mean that Gregory does not believe that these men are, in the end, as dangerous as his readers make them out to be.

By keeping the barbarians at a distance, and by suggesting that sanctity functions as a kind of antidote to violence, Gregory may seek to assuage the anxieties of his community, but the literary decisions he employs to do so ultimately reinforce barbarian otherness. The *Dialogues* do not compress barbarian and Roman identity as certain passages in his correspondence and theological works do; they exacerbate it, even when the holy man triumphs. While Gregory's ascetic heroes may be willing to help a barbarian who is suffering (as St. Fortunatus did for the Goth with the broken rib), there is no attempt to bring the barbarians into the Roman or Christian fold, no effort to bring them off the margins.

Equally intriguing about Gregory's connection between violence and the barbarian subject is the extent to which the pontiff embraces the discourse of barbarian violence in order to advance a particular theology of divine providence. In both the *Dialogues* and his correspondence, Gregory presents the increasing violence and chaos of his era within a narrative of divine *chronos*—God's eternal plan for the world.[63] However much suffering it may leave in its wake, the barbarian disruption of Italy functions for Gregory as an important signal of the coming end and is, therefore, a good. These events are simply a prelude to Christ's ultimate victory over death. Viewed from this perspective, the collapse of Italy that decorates the background of so many scenes in the *Dialogues* involving the barbarians was purposefully drawn by Gregory to illustrate the coming apocalypse.[64] The violence inflicted by the Lombards is a wake-up call—not to patriotic resistance,[65] nor to scrutiny of the imperial government that has failed to protect Italy, but for Christians to realize the necessity of an ascetic transformation of the individual.

The saints in these stories do not convert the barbarians because, for the *Dialogues*, Christianization is not the thesis—the thesis is the power of ascetic withdrawal.[66] While it may be that Gregory's ascetic heroes, owing to their greatness, are able to forestall barbarian violence, their ultimate testimony is to Christ's victory over death. On this point, it is worth identifying a transition that occurs between book 3 and book 4. Whereas the first three books offer numerous examples of barbarian violence, the final book offers very few. Indeed, book 4 shifts the focus from the miracles of the saints to the power of Christ over death, which Gregory narrates through a series of reflections on the soul after death. In this way, the barbarians and the violence that they inflict upon Roman populations can be seen to recede into the mystery of the eternal victory over death.

One final way to assess the literary function of the barbarian in the *Dialogues* is to view the holy man/barbarian juxtaposition as a proxy for the healthy and unhealthy soul. As we saw in chapter 1, Gregory frequently juxtaposed the spiritual life and the carnal life; the contemplative life and the active life; the holy man and the worldly man. Perhaps one way to understand the holy man/barbarian dichotomy is through the same kind of juxtaposition. Whereas the saints of Gregory's *Dialogues* are contemplative, ascetic, faithful, and compassionate, the barbarians are disruptive, carnal, superstitious, and violent. Even though they may temporarily recognize the sanctity of the holy men they encounter, and even though they may temporarily suspend their violent ways, the barbarians in these narratives are never brought to stillness; they are never brought to faith. As such, the barbarians represent a kind of carnal soul that is unable to reach its full potential. While the barbarians might be forced to their knees in the presence of holiness, they lack the tools (the stillness, the asceticism, and the proper faith) to imitate holiness. So too, in Gregory's theological imagination, the soul that is bound to a carnal life, a life of activity and pleasure, is unable to enjoy the liberation and insight provided by the spiritual life. The carnal soul might be able to recognize holiness in another, but it is unable to replicate it.

As noted, scholars have had difficulty situating the *Dialogues* within the Gregorian corpus because they have found it difficult to reconcile the outlandishness of some of these stories with the intellectual sophistication of Gregory's other works. But to question whether or not Gregory believed in the historicity of the tales he narrates is to miss the point of the *Dialogues*. The *Dialogues* offered Gregory an important medium to convey some of his most mature thoughts on the intersection of asceticism, service to others,[67] and the power of God to transform the lives of men who are confronted with otherwise impossible situations. It should not surprise us, therefore, that the Goths and Lombards feature prominently in these narratives. Indeed, the Goths and especially the Lombards represented for Gregory's audience the personification of impossible situations. Because that is the purpose of the barbarians in the text—that is, as a literary device within a narrative of ascetic and pastoral sanctity—the *Dialogues* may not really tell us what Gregory thought of the barbarians per se. However, they clearly attest to the fact that the barbarians were never far from Gregory's mind, and through them Gregory conveys his deepest ascetic and pastoral concerns.

As we complete the transition in our narration from Gregory's thought to his activity as a Roman leader, we might recall the ways in which Gregory and the Rome of his imagination were both similar to and distinct from some of the other well-known Latin theologians of the fourth and fifth centuries. Like Ambrose, Augustine, and Leo, Gregory inherited a rich intellectual Latin tradition that provided him with literary tools and intellectual categories that served him well in his many distinct roles as a Christian executive (theological, pastoral, and administrative).[68] Like them, Gregory took office at a time in which the traditions and ideology of empire remained very much alive, even if the reality of imperial activity in the West was not what had been. Like them, Gregory considered himself a patriotic Roman who was a servant of the emperor, even though he might feel compelled (as Ambrose, Leo, and Gelasius had) to "assist" the emperor in his recognition of orthodox policy and polity. Indeed, as Ambrose and Leo had maintained, it was the responsibility of episcopal leaders in the Roman world to "advise" and "assist" the imperial court so as to ensure that Rome would be a Christian Rome.

Perhaps the single greatest difference between Gregory's Rome and that of his predecessors was the degree to which the barbarian presence was not just a threat to Roman autonomy but a permanent and foreboding fixture that highlighted the difference between what Rome had been and what it had become. As we will see in the next chapter, the Lombard presence in Italy was a pervasive challenge to the completion of the simplest of administrative tasks. And yet Gregory attempted to make the most of the situation. As bishop of Rome, he experimented with a variety of initiatives (including Christian mission, pastoral attentiveness, and diplomatic pragmatism) to respond to the Lombard threat. But he also turned the barbarian presence in Italy into a powerful rhetorical symbol that he employed for his local ascetic communities and for his distant imperial correspondents so as to reinforce his core ascetic and pastoral principles.

CHAPTER TEN

Ever the *Praefect*

Gregory's "Secular" Responsibilities

As we began to discuss in the previous chapter, Gregory assumed the Roman pontificate at a time of disruption and decline for the Western empire and its ancient capital. For nearly fifty years the city of Rome had been under a persistent threat of siege, famine, and even plague. Of the aristocratic families that survived the Gothic wars, many had migrated to the East, either in search of fame and fortune or simply to escape the trauma of Italy. One of the most celebrated aspects of Gregory's story for his sympathetic biographers, of course, is the extent to which he stepped into this vacuum and attempted to preserve Rome from structural collapse and military devastation. But Rome's salvation, so to speak, was of a different order than the civic achievements of centuries past, for this time it had been undertaken by its bishop, not its senatorial elite, and it is therefore easy to see Gregory's actions (however one might interpret his motivations) as a watershed for papal history.

Many grand narratives of papal history point to Gregory's career as an important tipping point between the Rome that was (the former capital of a collapsing empire) and the Rome that would rise from its ancient ashes (the center of an ecclesial structure so powerful that it simply absorbed the responsibilities of secular government). Rather than speculate about whether or not Gregory's actions forced a rupture in the historical trajectory, we will content ourselves with an analysis of the ways that Gregory responded to the crises set before him and assess, as well as possible, the extent to which those responses were consonant with the ascetic and pastoral ideals of his sermons and commentaries.

Gregory, of course, was not the first late-ancient bishop to assume what are sometimes designated as "secular" responsibilities. In her masterful *Holy Bishops in Late Antiquity*, Claudia Rapp demonstrates and explains the gradual process by which the episcopate came to assume civic roles, which included relief for the poor, the ransoming of captives, the dissemination of imperial policies, the promotion of good order, and the adjudication of both civil and criminal legal suits. By the mid-sixth century, she notes, this elision of ecclesiastical and civic authority led to the increasing identification of the Church with the empire and the patronage of a bishop over his city.[1]

As noted in the previous chapter, the emperor Justinian played a critical role in the consolidation of the imperial and ecclesial spheres, a merger that had begun as early as the reign of Constantine. Justinian's *Novellae* are often cited as the prime locus for understanding the intersection of imperial and ecclesial law in the late Roman and early Byzantine world. Not only was Gregory familiar with the details of the Justinianic *Codex*,[2] but nearly every interpreter of Gregory's diplomatic and political activities, however they might construe those activities, understands the pontiff to have similarly held that the Church and State should work together for the common good. While not disputing that view, this chapter explores the ways in which (and the reasons why) Gregory undertook civic responsibilities, either in the absence of imperial authorities or when he felt that the imperial authorities assigned to those tasks were unable or unwilling to perform them suitably. The argument of the chapter lies in the notion that Gregory's balancing of civic and ecclesial concerns (what Richards and others have interpreted as a tension between his faith and his patriotism) was in fact an integrated project that drew from his theological commitment to the service of others.[3]

Assuming Civic Responsibility

When Gregory was elected to the Roman See in 590, imperial administrative leadership in Italy was completely centered in Ravenna, under the office of the exarch. Rome was protected by a small garrison of imperial troops, but the safety of the ancient capital was not a priority for the exarch or the armies who reported to him. At any given time, Lombard agitation could sever Rome's communication with Ravenna or Constantinople, or both, which in turn could lead to a breakdown in military coordination as well as disruption in the pay and resources expected by those troops who remained in the city. Lombard movements could also disrupt other resources destined for Rome, especially the ever-important grain shipments from Sicily. Indeed, by Gregory's tenure, the imperial grain supply to Rome had become increasingly unreliable and had, since the fifth century, needed to be supplemented or even replaced by the Roman Church's own charitable stocks.[4]

Gregory was, in many ways, well suited to face this series of challenges. Not only had he been raised in one of the few remaining Roman families with experience in property management, he had also served as the city prefect.[5] Added to these advantages, of course, are his years of experience in dealing with the imperial court. But, perhaps even more importantly, Gregory's theological vision included a deep commitment to service. As we will see, this commitment to service was more than a concern for the spiritual welfare of others. Indeed, Gregory presented it as a commitment to the well-being of others in all regards.

At the time of Gregory's election, the Roman Church owned property in Italy, Sicily, Gaul, Illyricum, North Africa, and elsewhere[6]—lands that it had been gathering since the fourth century through gifts and bequests.[7] During the sixth century, the size of St. Peter's patrimony (as it was called) had grown significantly.[8] Some patrimonial estates were more prosperous than others: production in Northern and Central Italy was hindered in Gregory's time by the Lombards, whereas the Sicilian holdings, which were the largest, thrived during this period. The Sicilian farms were so extensive (and important), in fact, that Gregory divided them into two distinct administrative units under the direction of separate *rectores*—an honorary title that Gregory bestowed upon his most valued patrimonial agents in Sicily, men who technically held the post of *defensores ecclesiae.*[9] It is worth noting the extent to which Gregory employed clerics to serve as his administrative agents (this is true for both his estate managers and other administrative roles).[10] And, because these men were clerics, Gregory characteristically sought administrators with ascetic and pastoral credentials.[11]

Both the significance of the patrimonies for Rome's survival and the extent to which Gregory took an active hand in their supervision are well attested by the pontiff's voluminous correspondence. Nearly one-fourth of Gregory's surviving letters were delivered to or from Sicily, and the majority of those were letters sent by the pope to his agents on the island, who simultaneously oversaw the estates and negotiated with Sicily's episcopal and imperial figures on Gregory's behalf.[12] Those unfamiliar with Gregory's correspondence might be surprised by the extent of the bishop's active role in the details of Sicilian property management.[13] His concerns included record keeping, rent negotiations, and tax levies. But as an indication of the integrated nature of Gregory's pastoral and pragmatic activity, many of these same letters reveal the pontiff's concerns for the living conditions and religious discipline of the peasants who worked the farms. The pontiff needed to guarantee that Sicilian grain shipments and rental revenue would make their way to Rome for the sake of the city's continued survival, but he urged his *rectores* to administer the Sicilian farms in such a way that the laborers would be drawn closer to the Church.[14]

As pope, Gregory had many additional civic responsibilities beyond food supplies and property management. For example, in the absence of civic leaders, it fell to the bishop to press for repairs to the system of aqueducts that brought fresh water to the city.[15] In a similar way, he took control of the rebuilding of the city's defensive walls, which had been damaged by warfare, neglect, and the pilfering of stone. More challenging was the need to ransom prisoners and deal with the large number of refugees who came to Rome from Northern and Central Italy in the wake of the Lombard wars.[16] On multiple occasions Gregory sought places to which he could relocate those displaced by war. For example, a large number of nuns (John the Deacon places the figure at three thousand[17]) remained as refugees in Rome and further strained the local church's financial resources. The pontiff frequently wrote to wealthy patrons in the East to solicit money to feed and clothe refugees.[18] When those gifts and his own resources were exhausted, he authorized the melting of church-plate (gold and silver chalices and other liturgical instruments) so that the funds could be used for the ransoming of captives.[19] By this time, the ransoming of prisoners had become such an important role for religious leaders that Gregory frames it as an exercise of sanctity in his *Dialogues*.[20] In short, by the close of the sixth century, the Roman Church had effectively supplanted the civic responsibilities once supported by local aristocratic patrons.[21] To a large extent, this was the consequence of geopolitical changes that had transformed both Italy and the empire as a whole. But it was also Gregory's theological commitment to serving others, detailed in part 1, that helps us to understand why he appears to have been among the most civically active bishops in the entire late-ancient period.

The accounts of Gregory's administrative competence are well known. What is perhaps less known and less expected is that a bishop of Gregory's ilk (i.e., ascetic and contemplative) would have been so involved in the recruitment, payment, and deployment of soldiers. For example, when the Lombard duke of Spoleto, Ariulf, made designs to invade points south in 591, Gregory took it upon himself to orchestrate the imperial defense by coordinating the efforts of three imperial generals, appointing an emergency mayor in the town of Nepi, and organizing Rome's own defenses, which he paid for from the papal treasury.[22] He took similar action for the protection of Naples.[23] And when these efforts proved unsuccessful, he depleted the Church's gold reserves to purchase peace with the Lombards.[24]

It is important to emphasize that Gregory's particular response to the civic crises of his tenure led to a near complete divestiture of the Roman Church's financial resources. The depletion stemmed not only from large-scale payments to the Lombards, but also the free distribution of grain to the city's poor. While it is true that this unrestricted spending would have been popular among its beneficiaries, perhaps the best way to understand why an administrator of Gregory's caliber would make such fiscally detrimental decisions is to consider that his theological and pastoral priorities might be framing his response to events. Indeed, Gregory appears far more concerned to protect the citizens of Rome from war and famine then he is interested in preserving or investing the Church's resources. It is also worth noting that not everyone in the Roman administration approved of Gregory's divestiture of the Church's resources. Indeed, when Sabinianus was elected as Gregory's successor in 604, he returned to a policy of selling the Church's Sicilian grain in Rome rather than distributing it freely.[25]

The "Bishop of Lombards"

To be sure, Gregory's civic activity was in large part necessitated by the persistent challenge posed by the Lombards. The imperial government had been wholly unprepared for the Lombard invasion of the Italian peninsula in the 570s, and the situation had only deteriorated from there.[26] By the time that Gregory became bishop in 590, imperial forces and treasure, such that remained, had been largely withdrawn to the provincial capital in Ravenna. The Roman Church—its clergy, grain, and financial resources—was responsible for keeping the ancient capital afloat in a sea of Lombard swords.

As noted in the previous chapter, it has been suggested that Gregory hated the Lombards—that he believed that a dead Lombard was preferable to a converted one. We have seen, I hope, the extent to which those calculations require revision and nuance. It remains to be seen, however, the extent to which Gregory actively engaged the Lombards and did so at the expense of his "duty" to the empire. We will concentrate our analysis of Gregory's activity (and the response that it prompted in imperial circles) to two moments of crisis—the siege of Ariulf in 592 and the siege of Agilulf in 593—as well as the contours of his correspondence with the Lombard queen.

In 591, two Lombard dukes, Ariulf of Spoleto and Arichis of Benevento, posed the greatest danger to the area around Rome. As Richards carefully details, the Lombard threat at this time was compounded by three factors: (1) the exarch in Ravenna, Romanus, preferred to protect the land route between Ravenna and Rome rather than the city of Rome itself; (2) the imperial troops in Rome went unpaid; and (3) plague had taken a considerable toll on imperial soldiers.[27] By 592 the situation had deteriorated further, as several Lombard dukes in Central Italy who had previously been in the employ of the empire went over to Ariulf because they had not been paid for so long. Fearful of the growing threat, Gregory wrote to Ravenna, pleading that the exarch make peace with the Lombards.[28] When the exarch proved unresponsive, Gregory took matters into his own hands and purchased peace with Ariulf.[29]

Whether it had been his plan all along or not, Romanus took advantage of the respite and attacked Ariulf, catching his forces by surprise. Having not been part of the negotiations between Gregory and Ariulf, Romanus, no doubt, did not recognize their treaty, and for a short time the exarch was able to seize the advantage. Romanus's attack, however, drew the ire of the Lombard king Agilulf, who had previously resisted open confrontation with the empire. Agilulf's forces, being more formidable than Ariulf's, moved south swiftly, and by 593 they laid siege to the area around Rome. From inside the city, Gregory watched with dismay as lines of captives were paraded below the city's walls on their way to Gaul, where they would be sold as slaves.[30] The situation was so dire that the pontiff broke off his commentary on the prophet Ezekiel because, he claimed, he could no longer find anyone willing to devote themselves to the study of Scripture.[31] When the grain ran out a few weeks later, Gregory met Agilulf at the Church of St. Peter (which, being on the western shore of the Tiber River, lay outside of the city's walls) and concluded a new truce with a hefty price—perhaps as much as five hundred pounds of gold.[32]

By 595 Romanus was pursuing his own treaty with Agilulf. Concerned that the exarch would mishandle this opportunity as well, Gregory played every card in his deck to secure a lasting peace.[33] Romanus, fearing that he was being undermined by Gregory's efforts, complained to the emperor that the pope was a fool and that his actions had bordered on the treasonous. The emperor, it would appear, shared the exarch's appraisal of Gregory's activity.[34]

A letter that Gregory wrote to one of Romanus's advisors at the height of the conflict offers a series of intriguing statements about the trilateral negotiations between the pope, the exarch, and the Lombard king.[35] Perhaps most revealing is the extent to which Gregory suggests that Agilulf understands the Roman Church and the imperial government to be independent entities and, as such, that he could be at peace with one and at war with the other. Gregory is quick to acknowledge that Agilulf's understanding of the situation is a false one (the Roman Church is very much a part of the empire), but the pontiff also seems ready to exploit this scenario, should Romanus prove unwilling to work for peace.[36]

Whether Gregory's appraisal of Agilulf's position is accurate or not, it testifies to the pontiff's ability to negotiate with the Lombards on behalf of the citizens of Rome, independent of Romanus's imperial efforts. The same letter partially justifies Romanus's claim that Gregory was undermining his ability to negotiate from a position of strength. But Romanus's conclusion that Gregory's actions would harm the interests of the empire is less certain. In fact, there is little reason to conclude (as both Romanus and Maurice did) that Gregory's efforts to secure a peace with the Lombards were divorced from an intelligent attempt to see the empire prosper. Based on surviving materials, there is little reason to doubt that the cessation of violence and imperial prosperity were mutually reinforcing (rather than mutually exclusive) enterprises. Gregory was so certain of this that he threatened to excommunicate anyone who undermined his efforts to arrive at peace.[37] Although the Lombards remained a persistent threat for the remainder of Gregory's tenure, particularly in Northern Italy, they never again posed the kind of danger to the city of Rome that Gregory experienced from 591 to 593.[38] In the end, it would seem, Gregory's pursuit of peace (and his willingness to pay for it with gold) was successful.

In a brief study of this affair, Peter Kaufman has emphasized a humorous phrase in one of Gregory's earliest letters that, in a very Kaufmanesque fashion, brilliantly captures the ambiguity and nuance of Gregory's predicament.[39] Writing to a well-placed court official in Constantinople just five months after he had been elected pope, Gregory laments that he has been made bishop "not of the Romans but of the Lombards whose promises are swords and whose gratitude is revenge."[40] In Kaufman's reading, whatever the pontiff may have meant by his witty missive to the East, Gregory determined that the best course for both his city and the Church was to engage the Lombards rather than ignore or resist them. And so, for the length of his papacy, Gregory pursued a three-pronged strategy designed to neuter the Lombard threat. This strategy included: (1) conversion from paganism and Arianism; (2) the healing of the Three Chapters schism, which was rampant among Catholics in Northern Italy; and (3) the military defense of Rome.[41]

Having sufficiently detailed Gregory's efforts to secure Rome's defenses, let us conclude, then, with a brief analysis of his efforts to pursue religious and pastoral solutions to political problems—namely that the security of Rome might be achieved by the conversion of the Lombards to Catholic Christianity. It is, in fact, rather surprising how little evidence survives in Gregory's correspondence for his missionary activities among the Lombards. Apart from a single epistle written early in his pontificate, the surviving letters offer no direct instruction to Italian bishops or monks about the conversion of Lombard populations (from either Arianism or paganism).[42] Richards concludes from this lack of documentary evidence that Gregory made little effort to evangelize the Lombard rank and file and concentrated, instead, on King Agilulf and, especially, his wife, Theodelinda.[43] While it is true that Gregory did pursue a careful (and partially successful) strategy with Theodelinda, Richards's presumptions may be misplaced.[44] Given Gregory's efforts to convert the local populations in Gaul, Sardinia, and Kent (as well as the leaders in those regions), it would seem out of character that he did not make equal efforts among the Lombards.[45] Indeed, it might be more likely that subsequent editors of Gregory's correspondence erased the record of Gregory's mission to the Lombards.[46]

Either way, we do have ample evidence of a careful, pastoral approach to Theodelinda, whom Gregory was courting on a number of fronts. At the time of the first exchange of letters between pope and queen, Theodelinda was a schismatic Catholic. (According to the disputes at the time, this would mean that she was Catholic rather than Arian, but that she opposed the condemnation of the Three Chapters.) Her husband, Agilulf, was an Arian Christian. As I have detailed elsewhere, Gregory took considerable care in presenting a carefully assembled collection of rhetorical arguments to convince the queen that she should abandon the Istrian separatists and join with Rome in the condemnation of the Three Chapters.[47] On this score we do have further confirmation of Gregory's efforts to reach out to the Three Chapters separatists.[48] In some respects, Gregory's pastoral strategy was successful.[49] In fact, it is likely that Theodelinda and Agilulf's decision to baptize their son in the Catholic faith in 603 would have been reckoned by Gregory as one his most satisfying diplomatic accomplishments.[50]

While Gregory's interaction with the Lombards, particularly the way in which that interaction caused friction between Gregory and the exarch, has long been a subject of scholarly attention, it is nevertheless interesting that his efforts to protect Rome from the Lombards went relatively unnoticed by Roman and papal biographers—even the *Liber*

Pontificalis attributes the Lombard retreat from Rome to the efforts of the exarch Romanus, rather than Gregory.[51] That oversight is all the more surprising when we compare Gregory's efforts to protect Rome to the apocryphal myths that sprung up concerning Pope Leo's involvement with Attila the Hun.[52]

A Theology of Service and the Rhetoric of Lament

Those familiar with Gregory's correspondence are, of course, well informed of the pontiff's laments about his involvement in civic affairs (something he repeatedly and pejoratively referred to as "worldly cares"). Writing to his former associates in Constantinople, he likened the Church of Rome to an "old and leaky ship" cast about by the waves of the world.[53] Having been placed at the helm of this ship, he is made "a slave to worldly cares while wearing the disguise of a bishop."[54] And he considers his life "ruined" by the responsibility of public service.[55] Upon learning that one of his episcopal friends had supported his election, he laments that the burden his friend has placed upon him is too great to bear, that it is breaking his back, and that it will be only a matter of time before he is "cast to the depths of this great tempest."[56] The ship of the world, it would seem, was sinking to the depths, and as some kind of cosmic joke, God was requiring Gregory to be the last to man the rudder.[57]

For all of Gregory's witty (and perhaps honest) laments about his civic responsibilities, he was in many respects an effective executive of public interests. How then are we to account for the apparent disconnect between Gregory's rhetoric of lament, particularly as it relates to his civic responsibilities, and his willingness to fulfill those responsibilities? The answer would seem to be found with the unique ascetic theology with which we began this study.

As noted in part 1, Gregory was deeply committed to a specific form of ascetic theology, one that conceived the summit of spiritual perfection to be found in the ascetic's sacrificial abandonment of personal spiritual joy for the purpose of providing guidance and care to those around him. It is, indeed, likely that Gregory would have viewed the ever-increasing civic responsibilities that accompanied episcopal office in his day as a natural extension of this very ideal.[58] In other words, just as the ascetic should be willing to suspend his personal contemplation in order to instruct others in the rudimentary aspects of prayer life, so too must a bishop be willing to put off his sacramental and educational duties to guarantee that his dependents are sufficiently clothed and fed. As Gregory was quick to discover, however, feeding and clothing the inhabitants of Rome so that they might devote themselves to scriptural study took a great deal more time and effort than he might otherwise have hoped: it meant overseeing an enormous corporate enterprise that included agricultural, municipal, diplomatic, and even defensive operations.

The disconnect between Gregory's tale of woe and his executive skill could therefore be understood as an amalgam of complementary and competing factors. There is little reason to dismiss the rhetorical lament as wholly fabricated and disingenuous, even if it did draw on both classical and Christian rhetorical precedents of a performance of unworthiness. Perhaps Gregory did miss the simplicity of the life of contemplation. He no doubt felt overwhelmed by the responsibility of office in the opening years of his pontificate, when the Lombard threat was the most acute, and as he grew into the realization of just how much of his time he would need to devote to public and civic rather than personal and spiritual purposes. But Gregory was as prepared for this role as anyone of his age—not only because of his civic expertise, but also because he was theologically committed to it. As Kaufman notes, more than anyone else, Gregory seems to have wanted to apologize to himself for being a skilled administrator.[59]

CHAPTER ELEVEN

Gregory's Ascetic Program and Its Opponents

However much time Gregory devoted to his civic responsibilities, his principal interests lay in the promotion of a particular kind of Christian life that emphasized moral reform and was predicated upon his ascetic commitments. Although we have devoted considerable attention to Gregory's ascetic theology and its role in his thinking about spiritual leadership, we have not yet had occasion to examine the specific ways in which he attempted to implement his theological program in the city of Rome, nor have we considered how that program may have challenged other clerical elites in the city. This is an especially pertinent avenue of investigation because, as one leading scholar has argued, the greatest threat to Gregory's authority was not the Lombards, imperial officials, or distant bishops, but rather an independent clerical faction within the city of Rome that did not share in the pontiff's ascetic inclinations and that had the most to lose from his reforming initiatives.[1]

Therefore, following a brief overview of the disparate nature of authority in the Roman Church in the period prior to Gregory's installation, we will examine a select group of city-bound initiatives that Gregory undertook during his tenure as bishop and assess the extent to which our sources offer evidence of internal opposition to the pontiff's ascetic program. While there is little doubt that Gregory's program was both unprecedented and wide-ranging—two facts that may have frustrated some Roman clerics—the surviving sources offer only partial support to the scholarly contention that Gregory faced the persistent threat of an opposing clerical party waiting in the wings to usurp his authority.[2]

The Church of Rome as Contested Space

We must resist our modern notions of the ecclesiastical structure of the Roman Catholic Church (wherein a city's bishop has direct oversight of all diocesan parishes and is responsible for appointing and disciplining the clerics who serve those parishes) when we think about the relationship between the bishop of Rome and the priests who served the various churches in Rome during the fourth, fifth, and sixth centuries. By the mid-fourth century, the city of Rome possessed a wide variety of spaces dedicated to Christian worship, including imperially funded basilicas, titular churches, martyr shrines, and private spaces within the *domus*, the household.[3] Nearly all of those religious sites developed through lay patronage, and the clerics who served them possessed a range of theological and factional interests. While it is true that the bishops of Rome would eventually gain control of all of these spaces and the clergy who officiated at them, that process of consolidation took centuries and was uneven in its achievement.[4]

In times of turmoil especially, the *tituli* churches and even the imperial basilicas became strongholds for factionalism and sites of extreme violence.[5] In some cases the divisions were based upon theological confession, but more often they lay in the unique and ever-shifting political alliances within and between the city's aristocratic and clerical circles.[6] The earliest contest for which we have ample evidence of the city's basilicas and shrines becoming embroiled in the partisan action of clerical factions is the contested papal election between Damasus and Ursinus in 366.[7] A century and a half later, during the protracted papal election between Symmachus and Laurentius from 498 to 506, Laurentius maintained control of every one of the city's basilicas except for St. Peter's (which lay outside of the city walls, across the Tiber), even though the secular ruler, Theodoric, had granted his support to Symmachus and multiple episcopal synods had declared Symmachus the rightful bishop.[8]

In a series of important essays in the 1970s, Peter Llewellyn documented the extent to which clerical factionalism had become a determinative factor for all ecclesiastic affairs within the city by the turn of the sixth century.[9] Although scholars occasionally present these factions as long-running cohesive groups based entirely upon clerical class[10] (e.g., the priests versus the deacons) or ideology (e.g., those in favor of pro-Eastern Christian policy and those against it[11]), we are probably on surer ground to understand that the various alliances between clergymen and their aristocratic supporters were forged and shifted according to a variety of factors, including imperial politics, the Ostrogothic court at Ravenna, and the individual personalities who either exacerbated or tempered hostility.[12] For example, the supposed "victory" synod of 502 that was intended to authorize, once and for all, the victory of Symmachus over Laurentius was barely able to muster half of the city's priests and deacons.[13] As we will see, current scholarly assumptions about clerical factionalism in Gregory's Rome presume the continuation of the bitter Symmachus/Laurentius divide.

Evidence of Gregory's Ascetic Program

Included in Gregory of Tours's *History of the Franks* is an otherwise undocumented account of the events surrounding Pope Gregory's election—namely that it occurred when the city of Rome was gripped by a plague that had included Pope Pelagius II, Gregory's predecessor, among its victims.[14] At a moment when Gregory had been elected and received imperial authorization for his election, but had not yet been formally installed, the soon-to-be pontiff initiated a citywide penitential procession designed to appease God's wrath and prepare the Christians of Rome for their impending judgment. The episode is not attested in Pope Gregory's own works.[15] Nevertheless, and even recognizing the hagiographic license with which Gregory of Tours presents the story, this account provides us with a glimpse of the ways in which Pope Gregory's ascetic and pastoral program would have been on public display throughout his pontificate.

The *History of Franks* presents a transcript of part of Gregory's rousing sermon of penitential encouragement. It also provides the specific details of an orchestrated parade of clerics and laity through the streets of Rome: the procession was to begin at a variety of religious sites throughout the city and then converge into a single march. According to the report, Gregory attempts to use the trauma of the plague as a catalyst for penitence and spiritual renewal: "May affliction open the door of conversion for us and may the punishment, which we are now suffering, dissolve the hardness of our heart."[16] But time was short, and so were the opportunities. The real fear, Gregory suggests, is not the physical death that the plague brings; rather, it is the fact that this illness strikes so quickly that its victims die before they have time to repent for their sins. How might Christians prepare for this? he asks rhetorically. They must enhance the fervor of their prayer through the merit of good works.[17]

To be sure, this message reflects the kind of penitential asceticism that Gregory advocates throughout his biblical commentaries, public sermons, and the *Pastoral Rule*. Rhetorically, the argument pivots on the theological relationship between physical and spiritual sickness. As we saw in part 1, Gregory understood physical sickness and death to be consequences of the spiritual sickness inaugurated for all of humanity through Adam and Eve. While a Christian's moral reform will not avert the eventuality of physical death, penitence and the spiritual reorientation that accompanies ascetic discipline offer the promise of eternal life. Thus, Gregory seeks to turn the fear of plague into an opportunity for spiritual renewal. To that end, Gregory's sermon unfolds as an enjoinder to a communal demonstration of faith in God.

For our purposes, what is significant about this episode is the extent to which the *History of the Franks* presents Gregory as able to marshal the entire population for this act of supplication. Indeed, we are offered many specific details of Pope Gregory's instructions. In anticipation of the event, the city's clerics offered three days of round-the-clock singing of the Psalms (a frequent marker of monastic spirituality). At the time of the procession, priests, abbots, and abbesses were assigned to lead specific groups of lay penitents from the city's various districts. Then, following a specific course through the city with prayer and lamentation (mostly cries of *kyrie eleison*—"Lord, have mercy"), the entire Christian population converged at the basilica of Santa Maria Maggiore, where they sang and beseeched the Lord in unison. The *History of the Franks* goes on to note that "the pope never stopped preaching to the people, nor did the people cease in their prayer," despite the fact that in a single hour eighty persons fell to the ground and died from the disease.[18] Obviously, our access to this event is limited by the highly sympathetic nature of the report. But the text testifies to the potential that a man such as Gregory had to harness the discourse of ascetic renunciation for a display of leadership that crossed any existing barrier between civic and ecclesiastical power.

In his study of authority and asceticism in late antiquity, Conrad Leyser latched onto this episode as an iconic event in Gregory's career.[19] For Leyser, the dramatic procession of supplicants is significant not because of its theological underpinnings or its communal character, but because it provided Gregory with an opportunity to emphasize (rather than allay) the trauma of the ravaged city and, in doing so, enabled him to upend the traditional power structures of Rome that would otherwise have opposed the pontiff's far-reaching ascetic program.[20] In the next section we will assess the extent to which Leyser is correct in assuming that Gregory's pontificate truly "upended" the power structures in Rome as well as the underlying assumption that Gregory's pontificate was always at risk of collapse because it had so many ready enemies among the city's clergy. But first, let us examine some of the additional ways that Gregory enacted this ascetic program through preaching, the promotion of ascetic allies to positions of power within the clerical administration, and the removal of clerics who did not meet his standards.

Although Gregory's surviving corpus is enormous by late-ancient standards, it is primarily from the *Homilies on the Gospels* that we gain the best sense for the style of his public preaching.[21] In part 1 we examined two of the forty surviving homilies to elucidate Gregory's theological commitment to asceticism and his efforts to impart those ideas to his listeners. In both cases Gregory was preaching at a particular martyr shrine rather than at the Lateran (the primary cathedral for the bishop of Rome, located inside the city's walls) or St. Peter's basilica (the symbolic headquarters for the papal promotion of the cult of St. Peter, located outside of the city). And it is, indeed, intriguing to see the ways in which the pontiff enlists the cycle of Roman martyr commemoration into his ascetic program.

Building upon the work of Antoine Chavasse, scholars are now able to identify ten cultic sites in Rome, mostly dedicated to Roman martyrs, at which Gregory preached many of these Gospel homilies.[22] As Leyser aptly notes, in most cases Gregory's sermons either ignore the life of the martyr altogether (focusing instead on the Gospel passage assigned for the day), or recalibrate the saint as a model of ascetic encouragement.[23]

Homily 37, delivered at the basilica of St. Sebastian, offers a fine case in point. Gregory's interpretation of the Lectionary reading for the day (Lk. 14:16–33) employs a series of rhetorical bursts designed to emphasize an ascetic reading of the biblical passage.[24] Throughout, he covers a great number of ascetic themes, including the abandonment of family, the temptations of physical desire, and the need to forsake material goods. He also recognizes the problem of false asceticism, bemoaning those who display the signs of renunciation but do so for the sake of vainglory rather than a genuine willingness to embrace the Christian life. Near its conclusion, the homily includes a lengthy aside about an ascetic bishop, Cassius of Narni (a figure who was included in book 4 of the *Dialogues*) so that Gregory can offer a saintly example by which his listeners might adopt the ascetic teaching of the Gospel passage.[25] What the homily does not include is any mention of St. Sebastian, the popular Roman martyr in whose honor the laity had assembled.

What is so intriguing about this omission of St. Sebastian in Homily 37 is that Gregory was at other instances engaged in the promotion of Sebastian's cult.[26] Despite the pontiff's frequent distribution of relics from the Roman martyrs and his repeated efforts to promote the cults of other Italian saints, his public preaching at the shrines of the martyrs appears to emphasize a particular kind of moral behavior and ascetic discipline that aligned with his own theological and pastoral commitments. As Leyser argues, this reflects a significant change of course with respect to the way that martyrs were enlisted by the bishops of Rome for the continued promotion of Christianity in the city. In sum, Gregory's *Homilies on the Gospels* demonstrate that he has co-opted the Roman martyr cults into a sophisticated promotion of his own program of ascetic and moral reform.

Shifting from Gregory's preaching of asceticism to his promotion of ascetics to positions of authority, we should acknowledge that nearly every modern assessment of Gregory's activity as bishop recognizes that the pontiff sought to elevate his own men (mostly monks from St. Andrews) to episcopal sees throughout the Western Church. We will detail the most important examples (including Maximian in Syracuse, Marinianus in Ravenna, and Constantius in Milan) in the next chapter.[27] But there is also reason to consider the types of men that formed Gregory's inner circle of nonepiscopal advisors and how that group, which would have been visible to observers within the city, might have both projected and carried out the pontiff's ascetic program.

According to John the Deacon, Gregory's earliest Roman biographer, the pontiff removed all laymen and chose only the "most prudent clerics" as his advisors, enabling the Roman Church to recreate the ascetic community of the era of the apostles.[28] In his detailed investigation of Gregory's administration, Jeffrey Richards connected the pro-monastic gloss provided by John the Deacon to an actual group of ascetically inclined individuals who formed Gregory's inner circle.[29] Although the pontiff performed relatively few ordinations (the *Liber Pontificalis* claims just five deacons during Gregory's fourteen-year tenure), Richards confirmed a monastic pedigree for three of them.[30] It is likely that Gregory's most trusted notaries (men entrusted with a range of administrative, judicial, and diplomatic efforts) were also men of ascetic inclination.

The administrative move that was likely the most significant, however, was the creation of two new posts that formed the core of Gregory's administrative team: a *vicedominus* and a *primicerius defensorum*. For Richards these moves were designed to recalibrate the power structures within the Church's administration. Specifically, Richards believes that they were designed to deprive preexisting career clerics of some of their authority.[31] While that may be true, it is noteworthy that the two candidates that Gregory chose to promote to these powerful positions were members of the already existing diaconal establishment.

As another example of the way that Gregory's ascetic program took shape in the city of Rome, let us look at the most intriguing illustration of Gregory's effort to integrate monastic spirituality, martyr cult, and clerical leadership in the city of Rome.[32] According to *Epistulae* 4.18, the basilica of St. Pancras had fallen into neglect due to the lack of pastoral attention provided by its priests.[33] After much consideration, Gregory tells us, he decided to remove the priests and attach a community of monks to the basilica in order that the Eucharistic service might continue and the Church thrive.

To be sure, the turn of events at St. Pancras offers clear evidence of a key component of Gregory's spiritual and pastoral strategies, analyzed in part 2, namely that he believed accomplished ascetics were in the best position to offer quality spiritual leadership. But what is so important about this particular example is the extent to which Gregory is folding the monastic and lay communities into a single body of Christians in the city of Rome. In other words, Gregory did not intend for this monastic "takeover" of St. Pancras to mean that basilica now belonged to the monks, and lay Christians in the neighborhood would have to look elsewhere to fulfill their sacramental needs. No, Gregory's plan was to establish a monastic outpost at St. Pancras for the explicit purpose of improving the lay community's access to the religious life. Indeed, Gregory's concern for the continuation of Eucharistic services at the site is explicit.[34] There may be no better example of the pontiff's holistic vision for the integration of ascetic spirituality into the practice of Christianity for lay believers.

Evidence of Opposition to Gregory's Policies?

What, we might ask, happened to the priests of St. Pancras that Gregory removed? Were they reassigned to another facility? Were they permanently dismissed? Perhaps even more importantly, what does this event say about Gregory's broader actions in Rome? Is St. Pancras the sole surviving example of a widespread priestly purge, or is it simply an isolated case of clerical incompetence that the pontiff addressed according to his administrative intuitions? Although answers to these questions are not easily forthcoming, it has become a historiographical commonplace since Gregory's Carolingian biographers to speak of a wholesale monastic "takeover" of the institutions of the Roman Church.[35]

As we have noted, many scholars understand Gregory's ascetic push to have played out across a city already deeply divided by clerical factions. But on what basis were those factions constituted during his pontificate? And how, exactly, did those factions pose a threat to Gregory's pontificate or his ascetic and moral initiatives?

One way of thinking about clerical factionalism in Rome during the late sixth century is to presume that the clerical colleges that were organized around professional ranks (deacons, priests, notaries, and *defensores*) were the basis of institutional turf wars.[36] Several papal historians, including Peter Llewellyn and Jeffrey Richards, have emphasized the extent to which these groups possessed a strong corporate consciousness and jealously guarded their administrative domains.[37] Another way to conceptualize possible factionalism in the Roman Church during Gregory's tenure is to presume the existence of fiercely guarded clerical rivalries that were affiliated according to groupings of clergy associated with individual churches—be they the *tituli* churches or the basilicas.[38] Viewed from this perspective, Gregory's removal of the priests of St. Pancras was more than an isolated act of clerical discipline; it also allotted control of the relics of St. Pancras to the new monastic community, thereby depriving the priestly community of the *titulus* of St. Chrysogonus of one of its prized religious treasures.[39]

Yet another way in which scholars conceptualize clerical factionalism during Gregory's pontificate, at least implicitly, is by suggesting that the Symmachian and Laurentian factions remained a constitutive element for clerical partisanship more than eighty years after the official resolution of the schism. For example, in his *Authority and Asceticism from Augustine to Gregory the Great*, Leyser contends that the Laurentian schism provides the primary context for understanding the fractious relationship between the ascetic Gregorians and their opponents in the Roman clergy.[40] Leyser is certainly correct to remind us that the Symmachian/Laurentian divide offers a powerful example of extreme, violent partisanship among the Roman clergy. But there is little direct evidence that those precise dividing lines continued to exist during Gregory's papacy. Even if specific papal biographies or texts such as the *Liber Pontificalis* perpetuated the aftereffects of those partisan battles, evidence of pro-Symmachian and pro-Laurentian factions during Gregory's pontificate is lacking.[41]

However we might wish to conceptualize the possibility of clerical factions opposed to Gregory's asceticizing initiatives, the question remains: what evidence is there of actual opposition to them? And should we understand Gregory's harnessing of the rhetoric of ascetic authority as a deliberate counteroffensive to that opposition?[42] Even though the idea of a Gregorian counterinitiative is plausible, there is little direct evidence of a contemporaneous anti-Gregorian clerical faction. In fact, there is little explicit evidence of organized resistance to any of his ascetic programs during his lifetime. So why do most accounts presume both to have been in existence?

We do know of at least one highly placed cleric who would have considered himself an enemy of Gregory: Laurentius, the archdeacon. The position of archdeacon was perhaps the single most influential post in the Roman Church other than pope. During the fifth and sixth centuries the office was often the final stepping-stone to a papal election. But when Gregory—as a junior deacon—was elected pontiff in 590, he essentially leapfrogged the heir apparent, Archdeacon Laurentius. Then, only one year into his office, Gregory summarily dismissed Laurentius from office on the grounds that Laurentius was guilty of "pride" and "evil deeds."[43] The apparent power play between Gregory and Laurentius is tantalizing. This is especially true because the only extant account also notes that the removal of Laurentius and the elevation of Honoratus as his replacement was done in the presence of the entire body of the city's clergy (priests, deacons, notaries, and subdeacons) in the Lateran basilica.[44] Perhaps it is not surprising that several scholars have assumed this episode reflects evidence of a conflict between Gregory's ascetic supporters and an anti-Gregorian clerical establishment.

But here again the historian is confronted with a problem. Was this an isolated case requiring Gregory's judicial action, or does it reflect a widespread pattern of clerical disenfranchisement? What is more, on what basis are we supposed to speculate about the reaction of other clerics to this move? Did Laurentius's removal fuel a fire of anti-Gregorian factionalism, or was this event largely forgotten in the months and years that followed? For Richards, the removal of Laurentius reflects more than a sui generis case of pastoral jurisprudence; it suggests a deliberate and thorough attempt by Gregory to remake the very power structures of the Roman clergy.[45] And it is precisely this project of ascetic remaking that Leyser, Llewellyn, and Richards believe to lie at the heart of a cohesive anti-Gregorian clerical faction. While both of those scholarly assumptions could reflect the historical situation in Rome during Gregory's pontificate, there is no direct evidence in the extant sources for either a wide-scale purge of the clerical establishment or a cohesive anti-Gregorian group.

In fact, we have only three examples in all of the contemporaneous sources that speak to the pontiff's efforts to remove staff in the city of

Rome: (1) the removal of the priests at St. Pancras, (2) the removal of the archdeacon Laurentius, and (3) the decision to bar laymen from serving as attendants in the papal *cubiculum* (bedchamber).[46] The two examples with the greatest potential to reflect clerical factionalism (i.e., St. Pancras and Laurentius) are both handled in the Gregorian sources as independent instances of clerical maleficence to which Gregory responds with his customary moral policing.

As it turns out, the scholarly contention that an anti-Gregorian clerical block consisting of the city's clerical establishment posed a real and persistent threat to Gregory's authority relies on a series of assumptions that is supported, almost exclusively, in post-Gregorian sources. Both Llewellyn and Richards argue that the string of pontiffs who succeeded Gregory—Sabinian, Boniface III, Boniface IV, Deusdedit, and Boniface V—reflect a seesaw battle between pro- and antimonastic sympathizers.[47] While there would appear to be little doubt that Gregory's legacy and, especially, his introduction of monastically trained personnel to the papal administration were a source of controversy for succeeding generations of Roman churchmen as they grasped for religious explanations for the further decline in the political and economic situation of Italy, this seventh-century evidence simply cannot demonstrate the existence of a cohesive anti-Gregorian or antimonastic party during the pontiff's actual tenure in office. It would appear, instead, that we are on steadier ground to see those expressions of inner-Roman clerical partisanship to be a debate about the value of Gregory's ideas and legacy rather than evidence of a contemporaneous and organized opposition to it.

We might even push this observation of historical anachronism a bit further still by considering whether or not John the Deacon's highly sympathetic account of Gregorian monastic innovation was not itself largely designed to respond the debates about the legitimacy of monastic qualifications for the Roman clergy of his own time. Such a reconsideration does not require us to look skeptically upon Gregory's ascetic commitments (there is ample, independently attested evidence for that), but it might give the historian pause before he or she uses John's testimony as an accurate witness to the presence of pro- and anti-ascetic clerical parties in Gregory's Rome, which was nearly three hundred years prior to his own writing.

As WE TURN now to consider how Gregory's theological commitments guided his actions and diplomatic posture in locales beyond the city of Rome, it is important to remember that his efforts to spur moral and ascetic reform abroad were almost certainly shaped by his experiments and experience with the same efforts at home. In this sense, Leyser's insight about the potential for the discourse of renunciation to engender real authority helps us to understand the means by which Gregory leveraged his own ascetic credentials to advance a potentially controversial program of ascetic renewal. But our assessment of Gregory's exercise of authority should not neglect the theological and pastoral concepts that served as the foundations of that program. For in doing so, we might lose sight of the fact that Gregory's initiatives were more than a mechanism by which he could assert and maintain his authority over a potentially divided city: they were the practical outcome of his entire theological project.

CHAPTER TWELVE

Prefect of the Roman Church

Throughout this volume, I have made a concerted effort to avoid the customary bifurcation between Greek East and Latin West that so often exaggerates late-ancient Christian difference and excavates anachronistic evidence for the birth of an eventual papal empire. We have seen the extent to which Gregory understood himself to be the subject of an empire centered in Constantinople, even if he did not always agree with imperial policies. We have also observed, if briefly, the extent to which Gregory's theological imagination was in concert with pastoral and ascetic traditions that were very much a part of the Eastern Church of his day. And while I remain fundamentally committed to that view, it is important to acknowledge that certain aspects of Gregory's career had a lasting impact on the structures of the Western Church in a way that did not affect the East. This chapter and the next will explore two such aspects. The first concerns the spread of the Roman Church's influence over episcopal sees in Northern Italy, Sicily, and the Balkans that were previously not part of Rome's superjurisdiction.[1] The second concerns Gregory's efforts to spread and deepen the Christian faith among the Merovingians and Saxons. What we find in both contexts is that here, too, Gregory was able to advance his ascetic and pastoral programs, in large part through the administrative pragmatism and efficiency that characterized his other endeavors.

Perhaps the most explicit way that a Roman bishop at the end of late antiquity could assert his influence over other churches was by the making and unmaking of the episcopal court. Although I will argue that Gregory's actions in this regard have, occasionally, been misinterpreted, there is little denying that he was very active in redrawing diocesan jurisdictions and reforming the qualifications for the men who would lead the Church in Northern Italy, Sicily, and Illyricum. Not only did he actively involve himself in a number of episcopal elections, he also censured and even removed those bishops whom he deemed unfit for leadership. Our analysis will also assess the limits of Gregory's ability to assert his authority. But in both cases—successful or unsuccessful—we will see the extent to which his efforts to effect change were always framed within a language that was consonant with his theological and pastoral convictions.

Northern Italy

As noted earlier, when Gregory assumed office in 590, the majority of the sees in Northern Italy had long been isolated from the Roman Church because of the controversy over the condemnation of the so-called Three Chapters at the Constantinopolitan synod of 553. In a bid to reconcile the Eastern churches under the banner of imperial orthodoxy, the emperor Justinian had pushed the condemnation in the hope of mollifying concerns from non-Chalcedonian circles that the council of 451 had been a capitulation to Nestorianism. In Italy, however, where there had never been similar concerns about the Fourth Ecumenical Council, the condemnation of the Three Chapters had been interpreted as backpedaling from the orthodox position and as imperial meddling in theological affairs. As we noted in chapter 10, by the time of Gregory's pontificate, this gulf between the See of Rome (which after the death of Pope Vigilius was consistently in support of the condemnation) and the Northern Italian churches was exploited by the Lombards, who hoped to disrupt Italian solidarity with the empire in all ways. Gregory's response to the situation was multifaceted and partially effective, but it was also unprecedented in a number of respects.[2]

Because the Lombard presence in Northern Italy compounded the problems caused by the Three Chapters schism, it is not surprising that his strategy sought to link the two. The linchpin in Gregory's endeavors in Northern Italy was the See of Ravenna. Since the late fourth century, the See of Ravenna had been under the authority of the Archbishop of Milan. But with the reestablishment of imperial rule in the wake of the Gothic Wars, and particularly with the centralizing of that rule through the office of the exarch, the See of Ravenna gained in stature. What is more, because Ravenna was so joined to the imperial government, the bishops of Ravenna had little choice but to endorse the condemnation of the Three Chapters, making Ravenna the only prominent Northern Italian city in communion with both the See of Rome and the See of Constantinople in the middle of the sixth century. The connection between Rome, Ravenna, and Constantinople became even more permanent in 578, when John was elected archbishop of the see. Whereas previous bishops had been appointed from Milan, John was a member of the Roman clergy and a friend of Gregory's. In fact, Gregory's famous *Book of Pastoral Rule* is dedicated to John of Ravenna.

Soon into his tenure, Gregory instructed John to address several Roman concerns simultaneously. John was to act as intermediary on Gregory's behalf according to the long-standing traditions of clients and patrons in the Roman world.[3] He was also to help promote the Roman See's efforts in Northern Italy.[4] For example, in April of 592, Gregory thanked John for his intervention in the affairs of the See of Rimini and announced that he was going to instruct all of the northern bishops to address their requests to John whenever travel to or communication with Rome was made impossible by the Lombards.[5] Cases that might otherwise be adjudicated in Rome would now be heard in Ravenna, under John's supervision.[6]

Gregory's relationship with the archbishop of Ravenna grew more complex, however, as events unfolded. The pope was delighted by John's zeal for condemning those bishops who refused to accept the Three Chapters condemnation. But he was aggrieved at John's apparent unwillingness to censure the exarch, even though the latter was, in Gregory's opinion, doing more harm than good with respect to the Lombards.[7] With time, the relationship between Gregory and John would cool further still, largely because John took to wearing the pallium—a liturgical vestment that signified his elevated rank—in nonliturgical settings, leading Gregory to conclude that the bishop of Ravenna had succumbed to pride.[8] As we have repeatedly seen, in Gregory's theological imagination, a bishop who had succumbed to pride lacked ascetic zeal and was incapable of serving as a genuine spiritual director.

When John died in 595, Gregory took special interest in the selection of his replacement. The exarch desired the election of the city's archdeacon, Donatus, who would have been a natural successor. Given that the exarch had just complained to the emperor that Gregory's actions with the Lombards were treasonous, Gregory, in turn, was unwilling to concede anything to Romanus. Thus, Donatus was unacceptable. Another candidate, John, was perceived by Gregory to be ignorant of the Psalms. (Because the chanting of Psalms was a common prayer discipline of ascetic communities at the time, this criticism is also a likely indication that John lacked the ascetic qualifications Gregory required.) Therefore, after some careful maneuvering, Gregory had one of his old companions from the monastery of St. Andrews, Marinianus, elected archbishop of Ravenna.[9] Not only did this continue the recent precedent of imposing a Roman candidate upon the Church of Ravenna, it was also the highest-ranking appointment to date for a graduate of Gregory's monastery, St. Andrews, other than the pope's own election. Although Gregory would eventually censure this new archbishop too, in most ways Gregory found a solid ally in Marinianus, who went on to promote Gregory's ascetic, theological, and political goals throughout Northern Italy.[10]

The other major archdiocese in Northern Italy, of course, was Milan, which had, until just before Gregory's pontificate, always been independent of Roman oversight. In fact, prior to the papacy of Leo I, it was the See of Milan, not Rome, that had the greatest influence over the churches in Northern Italy and Gaul.[11] At the Constantinopolitan council of 553, the archbishop of Milan, Datius, had been among the staunchest defenders of the Three Chapters. Not surprisingly, both he and his successor, Vitalis, sided with the archbishop of Aquileia against Rome and Constantinople.[12] In 569, a new archbishop, Honoratus, was forced to seek refuge from the Lombards in Genoa. But his successor, Laurentius, was persuaded to realign with Rome. Laurentius condemned the Three Chapters, in large part because he had become financially dependent upon his own church's estates on the island of Sicily and thus needed the support of both the empire and the See of Rome to guarantee that financial lifeline.[13] The financial and ecclesiastical quid pro quo between Rome and Milan was completed during Gregory's tenure as urban prefect, and upon his election as pope, Gregory wasted little time in assuring Laurentius (who remained exiled in Genoa) that these arrangements were still in place.[14]

Laurentius's death in 592 provided the first opportunity for the Roman See to exert its newfound authority over a Milanese election. Although Gregory was determined to see both an ally and an ascetic elected to the position, he executed his plan carefully so as to project himself as an interested observer rather than an overbearing partisan.[15] In the end, the archdiocese went to Constantius, yet another monastic colleague of Gregory's.[16] It was Constantius, in fact, who would assist Gregory in his wooing of the Lombard queen Theodelinda from the Three Chapters separatists.[17] But Gregory's appreciation for Constantius's assistance and even the archbishop's ascetic demeanor did not prevent the pontiff from subtly treating the See of Milan as though it was now part of Rome's superjurisdictional authority.[18] And, as a consequence of the new arrangement, Gregory issued frequent instructions according to his pastoral, ascetic, and administrative concerns.[19]

Sicily

Gregory's intervention in the northern churches was unprecedented and significant, but it paled in comparison with the efforts he made in Sicily, which by the time of his election had become a vital source of the Roman Church's wealth and authority. Leo I had been the first Roman bishop to claim jurisdictional supervision in Sicily, and by the middle of the sixth century the Sicilian clergy had largely acquiesced to that claim.[20] In large part, the spread of papal influence in Sicily can be explained by the accumulation of vast estates that had been gifted to the Roman See by the landowning aristocracy. As the papal landholding in Sicily grew, so too did papal influence over local ecclesiastical matters. Indeed, by

Gregory's tenure, the Roman Church owned approximately four hundred agricultural estates on the island—farms that provided vital income for the bishop of Rome and a steady supply of grain for the urban poor of the Western capital.[21]

As noted, nearly one-quarter of all of Gregory's surviving letters were sent to, or concerned, the island of Sicily—a fact that clearly indicates the importance of the Sicilian patrimony to the pontiff's broader plans.[22] As elsewhere, Gregory's administrative efficiencies transformed the traditional ways of doing business in overlapping contexts. For example, by formalizing a division of the Roman patrimony in Sicily into two administrative centers, Gregory effectively separated the governance of the Sicilian Church into two archdioceses (Syracuse and Palermo), both of which would be monitored from Rome.[23]

Prior to Gregory's tenure, the patrimonial administrators (often identified as *defensores ecclesiae*) were typically appointed from Rome, but they had often been local aristocrats or, in some cases, local bishops.[24] Beginning with Gregory, however, these administrators were always sent from Rome and held various clerical ranks.[25] The duties of Gregory's *rectores* were certainly legal and financial, but he, like some of his predecessors, entrusted his administrators with instituting his ecclesiastical policies as well.[26] The degree to which Gregory confided in his *rectores* varied, but the pontiff tried to ensure their cooperation by insisting that they swear an oath of allegiance at the tomb of St. Peter before embarking upon their commissions.[27]

Because Gregory's correspondence with Sicily is so extensive, it provides the most complete evidence of his attempts to effect clerical reform (what I have elsewhere described as his "asceticizing of spiritual direction"[28]) and the extent to which his policies were accepted or resisted by the local clergy.[29] For the most part, Gregory's direct interference in episcopal elections was confined to Syracuse (the senior of the two archdioceses). As elsewhere, he preferred candidates who possessed the ascetic qualifications that were so central to his pastoral theology. And even those candidates whose elections he helped to engineer would, eventually, be censured by him for failing to live up to his high expectations—Maximian of Syracuse offering a prime example.[30] Early in his pontificate, Gregory went so far as to license his *rector*, the subdeacon Peter, with the authority to scrutinize the qualifications of rural Sicilian priests and replace them with monks wherever it seemed appropriate.[31]

But Gregory's interference in the Sicilian Church was not as overbearing as some scholars have asserted.[32] For the most part, Gregory preferred that episcopal vacancies be filled by local candidates, so long as they met with his own ascetic predilections. This was true even in Palermo, which, as noted, rose to the stature of archdiocese during Gregory's tenure. If, however, a Sicilian cleric was charged with a serious moral or pastoral crime, he was to be brought to Rome to stand trial. During Gregory's tenure, papal *rectores* on the island brought a total of six of Sicily's thirteen bishops to trial. Even those clerics deemed innocent were forced into the humiliating position of swearing an oath at the tomb of St. Peter.[33]

In addition to his supervision of episcopal elections and his scrutiny of clerical misconduct, Gregory asserted his authority over the Church in Sicily in other ways. Perhaps the most symbolic way in which he did so was by requiring the Sicilian episcopate to gather annually on the Feast of St. Peter, June 29, under the supervision of the papal *rector*. Clearly the gathering functioned as a symbolic ritual designed to reinforce Rome's superjurisdictional rights, and by meeting on the Feast of St. Peter it reinforced the most exalted symbol of papal authority over regional bishops. But perhaps the most intriguing aspect of Gregory's use of the Petrine topos with the Sicilian Church is the extent to which he employed it so selectively. Whereas he repeatedly asserted his connection to Peter in his correspondence in the East and among the Lombards and Merovingians, Gregory never defended his jurisdictional claims in Sicily with a rhetoric of Petrine authority.[34]

Illyricum

Although the papal holdings in the Western Balkans were far less significant than those in Sicily, the Roman See had exercised jurisdictional authority over the churches in this region—albeit inconsistently—for centuries.[35] It is not surprising, therefore, that a significant portion of Gregory's international correspondence concerned the governance of the churches in Illyricum, nor is it surprising that the pontiff would chafe at the See of Constantinople's efforts to make inroads throughout the region.

As the steward of St. Peter's patrimony, the pontiff put his executive training to good use. As he had in Sicily, one of the first things Gregory did upon assuming office was to send a Roman administrator, the sub-deacon Antoninus, to Dalmatia as the new *rector* for papal lands.[36] The efforts of the previous officeholder, a local bishop, had been deemed un-satisfactory. As elsewhere, the patrimonial steward was tasked with mul-tiple responsibilities. Not only was he to turn the small patch of farms into an efficient and profitable enterprise, he was also to attend to all of Gregory's pastoral, ecclesiastical, and diplomatic interests in the region.[37]

Initially, the biggest obstacle to Gregory's efforts in Dalmatia was the local archbishop, Natalis, who seems to have been perfectly happy to act as though distant bishops had no real authority over his church. Particu-larly troublesome for Gregory was Natalis's penchant for punishing local ecclesiastics—and for seizing their property—without following canoni-cal statutes and without seeking the approval of Rome. We know of at least two such incidents.[38] The fact that Natalis had attempted to justify his reputation for lavish living by recourse to the Scriptures certainly did not make matters any better.[39] Gregory issued various instructions to An-toninus, including the removal of Natalis's pallium and the threat of ex-communication. Eventually, Gregory began official canonical proceedings against the archbishop for his pastoral and moral misconduct. But when Natalis suddenly took ill and died, Gregory had to contend with a rumor in Constantinople that he had poisoned the malcontented bishop.[40]

The selection of a suitable replacement for Natalis proved to be an even greater setback to the pontiff's efforts. Gregory favored the arch-deacon, Honoratus, who had previously been the victim of Natalis's ag-gression. Another candidate, Maximus, was favored by the See of Con-stantinople and had the backing of the imperial court.[41] To be sure, the Archdiocese of Salona lay at the crossroads of Roman and Constanti-nopolitan influence in the Balkans, and both ecclesiastical centers were keen to assert their authority in the region. From Gregory's perspective, the timing of a contested election in the Balkans could not have been worse—just as Maximus was installed on the arch-episcopal throne with the support of imperial troops, John of Constantinople began asserting himself as the Ecumenical Patriarch. Gregory's *rector*, who tried to prevent the ceremony, was forced to flee the region for fear of his life.[42]

Realizing that the Roman Church did not have a sufficient presence in Salona to alter the circumstances, Gregory initially threatened Maximus that if he would not travel to Rome and submit himself to an inspection of his candidacy, he would be barred from celebrating the sacraments and fall under the "anathema of God and St. Peter."[43] He also wrote to the emperor's wife, hoping that he might leverage his relationship with her to gain a diplomatic advantage.[44] But neither effort proved successful. In the end, Gregory could do nothing but accept the loss. Eventually, he came to acknowledge Maximus's legitimacy.[45] It was a telling sign of the rise of Constantinopolitan authority throughout the Balkans and the retrenchment of Roman influence to the western side of the Adriatic.

While it is clear that Gregory's actions in Dalmatia reflect a power struggle between bishops (between Rome and Salona primarily, but also indirectly between Rome and Constantinople), it is worth noting that the pontiff asserts his position within a discourse of episcopal authority with clearly defined ascetic and pastoral dimensions. Thus, when Gregory condemns Natalis's and Maximus's lack of humility, he is in effect asserting that neither man is able to offer adequate spiritual leadership because those who lack humility also lack ascetic self-discipline, and those who lack humility and ascetic discipline are incapable of offering effective spiritual leadership. Therefore, if Natalis and Maximus are too full of pride to submit themselves to Roman inspection as per the tradition of their predecessors, then they are unacceptable candidates for the episcopate.

For this reason, the sequence of events in Salona provides a telling example of why the traditional divide among Gregory scholars (i.e., between those who privilege his theological concerns and those who privilege his administrative and diplomatic prowess) is inadequate. Indeed, it is a false binary to assume that we must choose between Gregory the papal power broker and Gregory the ascetic and pastoral theologian. These two facets of Gregory's life are not mutually exclusive; they are mutually reinforcing. In this specific case, it would be foolhardy to insist that Gregory sought to dismiss Natalis and prevent Maximus either (a) because he genuinely believed they could not offer adequate spiritual leadership, or (b) because he was looking to extend his own authority in the Balkans. Rather, it is precisely because Gregory had spent so much time thinking about the ascetic and pastoral qualities that enabled sound spiritual leadership that he had the intellectual credentials and political acumen to extend his own authority outside of the traditional confines of the Roman episcopate through the censure of subordinate bishops who lacked those qualities.

As he had in Northern Italy and Sicily, Gregory invoked the rhetoric of ascetic detachment (most exemplified in the virtue of humility) to assert himself into matters of episcopal leadership in Dalmatia. Because the rhetoric of ascetic and pastoral qualifications was both so familiar and so powerful, Gregory was able to employ the topoi of ascetic virtue and spiritual leadership to assert his own authority. Although his letters could be ignored (and often were), by the late sixth century it would have been almost impossible for an ecclesiastical rival of Gregory's to argue that ascetic qualities and pastoral competence were insignificant in the selection and policing of subordinate clerics.

Religious Objects and Diplomatic Negotiation

To be sure, Gregory's intervention in the local churches of the West and for the papal farms specifically was not limited to Northern Italy, Sicily, and Illyricum. For example, there was a constant flow of letters from Gregory to the suffragan bishops of Central and Southern Italy (to Naples especially) and to his patrimonial administrators in Italy, Gaul, Sardinia, and elsewhere. A careful examination of these letters demonstrates a remarkable consistency in Gregory's approach to the tasks of estate management[46]—even when the Lombards caused disruptions in the agrarian cycle[47]—as well his promotion of a particular kind of spiritual leadership and his penchant for punishing those who did not live up to his moral standards.[48] Indeed, Gregory integrated the administrative and pastoral dimensions into a singular vision that he imposed upon the entire network of the Roman Church's sphere of influence. One aspect of Gregory's governance that we have not yet examined is the subtle way that he was able to distribute or withhold coveted religious artifacts as a tool of diplomacy.

We have already encountered some of the ways that the use and misuse of the pallium became an element of Gregory's negotiations with regional ecclesiastical leaders. The pallium was a liturgical garment that was reserved for those bishops—metropolitans or archbishops—who held a higher administrative rank than regular diocesan or suffragan bishops.[49] By Gregory's era, the possession of a pallium represented a special conferral of authority bestowed by the bishop of Rome upon those executives of "senior" episcopal sees (i.e., archdioceses) whom the pontiff had selected to lead other regional bishops on behalf of the See of Rome. Although anyone elected to one of these sees would have expected to receive a pallium in recognition of his rank, conferral was not automatic, and Gregory routinely treated its distribution as one element in a multifaceted relationship based on negotiated practices of patronage and service. Even when a pallium was distributed, the pontiff might threaten to withhold his blessing for its use whenever a recipient failed to adhere to Gregory's rigorous code of conduct.

As we have already seen, the reasons for which Gregory might withhold the pallium varied, but they almost always reflected in one way or another Gregory's concern that a person in authority must retain the virtue of humility. In other words, here, too, we find Gregory's diplomatic posture framed within the discursive network of ascetic virtue and pastoral expectation. For example, upon learning of the moral misconduct and pastoral failures of the archbishop of Salona, Gregory advised his *rector* to threaten to revoke the pallium from the bishop.[50] When it came to his attention that the archbishop of Ravenna was wearing his pallium outside of its customary liturgical use, Gregory chastised him for his arrogance and pride.[51] When he granted one to Marinianus upon his election to the same see a few years later, Gregory was explicit as to when the archbishop might and might not wear it.[52] In all, there is evidence in Gregory's letters of his distribution of pallia to several sees throughout those regions traditionally (and newly) within Rome's superjurisdiction, including Arles, Autun, Canterbury, Corinth, Justiniana Prima, Messina, Milan, Nicopolis, Palermo, Ravenna, Seville, Syracuse, Salona, and York.[53]

The conferral of a pallium on Syagrius, bishop of the See of Autun, offers an intriguing example of the way that Gregory could employ the liturgical artifact as a tool of negotiation. Syagrius was a suffragan bishop to the archbishop of Lyon, but he was closely connected to Brunhilde, the Merovingian queen. On his behalf, Brunhilde had requested that Gregory grant a pallium.[54] After a delay of an unspecified length, Gregory reported to the queen that he had agreed to her request, but only under a few conditions.[55] First, Syagrius was to make the request himself—it was against protocol for a civil authority to ask for one on his behalf. Second, both she and he were to commit themselves to purging simony from Gaul. Third, the practice of elevating laymen to the episcopate (without a requisite time in lower orders) would need to cease. Fourth, Brunhilde was to pressure any Three Chapters separatists in her realm to return to communion with Rome. And, fifth, both Brunhilde and Syagrius were to do what they could to end pagan rituals among the people.[56] It was, of course, quite unusual that a suffragan bishop would receive a pallium. Gregory implies that he had to seek the permission of the emperor, Maurice, in Constantinople before he could agree to issue one to Syagrius. While that claim may have been designed as an additional diplomatic mask rather than representing a limitation of Gregory's authority to issue a pallium, it further attests to the unprecedented nature of bestowing a pallium for the See of Autun.

At approximately the same time, Brunhilde's son, Childebert II, asked that Gregory bestow a pallium on Virgilius, the archbishop of Arles.[57] Because the archbishops of Arles had historically been granted the pallium and had served as papal vicars in Southern Gaul, this request was hardly unprecedented. But here, too, Gregory attempted to turn the desire for a pallium to his diplomatic advantage. He sent a long list of expectations for reform to both Childebert and Virgilius.[58] Thus, in both Autun and Arles, the pontiff used the honor of the pallium as leverage in his campaign to bring Christian leadership in Gaul more into conformity with his theological objectives.

To be sure, many of the directives that Gregory outlined as requirements for granting pallia in Gaul evince the ways that the pontiff's pastoral and ascetic concerns overlapped in his correspondence to secular rulers. For example, the demand that Brunhilde put an end to the promotion of laymen to the episcopate speaks directly to Gregory's oft-repeated concern that effective pastoral leadership demands that the candidate be experienced in the life of renunciation and trained in the life of the Church. What Gregory is particularly concerned about, however, is the rampant practice of simony in Merovingian Gaul. Gregory found simony to be a particularly loathsome practice, however common it may have been, because it fundamentally undermined his ideas about who was and was not worthy of pastoral leadership. In the end, Gregory's granting of pallia to Syagrius and Virgilius did little to bring the pontiff's reforms to fruition, but it demonstrates the extent to which he was willing to employ religious artifacts in the attempt to secure those objectives.

In addition to the distribution of pallia, the most common religious artifacts that Gregory distributed as acts of diplomatic negotiation were the relics of St. Peter. As we noted in part 1, Gregory believed that saints remained mysteriously active in the Church and performed miracles through their tombs and relics.[59] This not only helps to explain why he employed the tomb of St. Peter for the swearing of oaths, but also provides a theological rationale for the distribution of the saint's relics, a practice that Gregory repeatedly employed.[60]

Over the course of his tenure as pope, Gregory sent "relics" of St. Peter to a few more than a dozen persons, including Brunhilde, Childebert (her son), and Reccared (the Visigothic king of Spain).[61] These relics consisted of filings from the chains that had supposedly bound Peter during his imprisonment in Rome.[62] These filings were placed inside of a small key, symbolic of Christ's granting of the keys of heaven to St. Peter. As he distributed the relics to his select group of patrons and clients, Gregory issued various instructions concerning their care. Recipients were often told to wear the relic around their neck. Some were informed that it would cure illness, others that it had the power to release them from sin or offer protection. When Gregory sent such a relic to the exiled patriarch of Antioch, he instructed him that when the key is placed over the bodies of the sick, it often produces a brilliant miracle.[63] For his part, Childebert was instructed that "whenever he wears it around his neck he will be protected from all evils."[64] This distribution of relics was more than a transmission of sanctified objects; it was a targeted act of diplomacy, made possible by the papal connection to the Petrine "brand" and designed to achieve ecclesiastical goals for the Church of Rome.

It is, of course, significant that Gregory distributed the relics of Peter to three of most important Western leaders with whom he corresponded. Not only were these rulers powerful in their own right, but the exchange of relics also corresponded directly to Gregory's diplomatic efforts. For

Reccared, the Visigothic king, the relic functioned as a kind of reward for the king's renunciation of Arianism and conversion to the Catholic faith.[65] For Childebert, the relic was linked to Gregory's concerns for the Roman patrimony in Gaul and his desire to rid the Gallic Church of simony.

The relic for Brunhilde, like so many things in the pontiff's correspondence with the queen, did not follow normal patterns. Whereas Gregory's gifts to Reccared and Childebert came at the beginning of his correspondence with those kings, Gregory did not initially send one to Brunhilde. It was only after Brunhilde requested a relic (likely noticing that one had been granted to her son) that Gregory determined to send her one.[66] In the letter accompanying the gift, Gregory warned her vigorously about the need to care for the relic properly, lest it "be rendered useless and idle in the service of God."[67] Although he consented to share his spiritual treasure with the queen, he appears to have had little confidence that the exchange would affect the broader pastoral or diplomatic goals in a particular geographic region that normally accompanied the distribution of Petrine relics. Nevertheless, we see in this exchange the ways in which the encouragement of specific practices and the use of material objects could help to define and perpetuate the authority of the Roman See precisely because of Gregory's effort to strike a narrative posture in which he was serving as Brunhilde's spiritual advisor.[68]

CHAPTER THIRTEEN

Spreading Christianity
beyond the Roman World

In chapter 10 we described the ways in which Gregory's strategy for dealing with the threat of Lombard violence included efforts to bring pagan Lombards to Christianity and Arian Lombards to orthodox Christianity. As was the case with the Lombards, Gregory's missionary efforts among the Merovingians and Saxons reflect a combination of theological, economic, and political motives and further attest to the integrated nature of so many of his endeavors. In those regions where the Roman Church already had a presence through papal estates, such as in Gaul, Gregory worked primarily through his *rectores* to establish relationships with the secular hierarchy;[1] in those regions where he had less access, he turned to his episcopal colleagues or expanded the Roman presence through missionaries. In each situation, however, Gregory's management of the barbarian "other" functioned as a negotiation of difference rather than an erasure of it. In other words, drawing from well-developed and specific aspects of his pastoral theology, Gregory's missionary strategy did not require former pagans to abandon everything from their former religious experience; rather, it deliberately adopted and transformed pagan rituals, at least temporarily, in order to accommodate potential converts.

In their own investigations of Gregory's missionary activity, both Robert Markus and Jeffrey Richards argued that the connecting theme in Gregory's various missionary activities was a structured plan that emphasized the conversion of kings and queens, with the presumption that once the aristocracy had embraced Christianity their subjects would eventually follow.[2] There is ample evidence in Gregory's surviving letters to suggest that this was an important component of the pontiff's approach. His many letters to Brunhilde and Childebert among the Merovingians and to Aethelbert and Bertha in Kent demonstrate a determined effort to serve, personally, as a spiritual consultant for these rulers with the hope that through those relationships he might be able to leverage their support for a broader program of Christianization. Gregory's distribution of religious treasure (i.e., the pallia and the relics of St. Peter) to these rulers was accompanied by a combination of rhetorical strategies designed to encourage conversion. Those strategies ranged from flattery and the promise of being a "new Constantine" to the use of fear of the coming apocalypse.

But Markus's conclusion that Gregory's efforts rested solely on his courting of royal favor likely overstates the case. Indeed, there is a good deal of evidence that the pontiff engaged in multiple efforts for conversion simultaneously, beyond his courting of royal families. Most notably, Gregory relied largely on ecclesiastical agents (a combination of local clergy, papal *rectores*, and missionaries) to enact a series of strategies of accommodation so that both the baptized and the not-yet-baptized could be brought more fully into the community of God. To understand that all of these initiatives were acts of proselytism, we should not lose sight of the fact that a fundamental characteristic of Gregory's pastoral theology was the contention that "conversion" was a lifelong process that required persistent spiritual supervision—it was not achieved through baptism alone.[3] And, as in so many other ways, that aspect of Gregory's pastoral theology was intertwined with his ascetic commitments and experience.[4]

Gaul

Gregory's efforts in Gaul demonstrate well the multiple ways in which he sought to advance the Christian cause; they also reveal the deep-seated challenges that he faced. Although the Merovingian aristocracy had already converted to Christianity and had, since the reign of Clovis (466–511), largely abandoned Arianism, the perception in Gregory's Rome was that Christianity's inroads among the Franks were tenuous at best. The adoption of Christianity had done little to root out the deep-seated barbarian idealization of warrior cults, and Gregory's letters evince a persistent concern that the local populations continued to offer animal sacrifices to pagan deities.[5] In addition to those fundamental challenges, the Merovingian leadership—both secular and ecclesiastic—appeared to be irreversibly committed to making ecclesiastic appointments through nepotism, self-interest, and simony. From Gregory's perspective, if Rome was unable to inject a modicum of moral control over the selection of Gallic bishops, the prospects for advancing the Christian cause among the Franks would remain slim.

Thus, in 595, when the Lombard threat had begun to recede, Gregory inaugurated a multifaceted plan for the churches in Gaul. Spear-heading the charge was Candidus, a Roman priest whom Gregory assigned as *rector* of the papal lands near Arles. It had been generations since these farms had been actively managed from Rome, and, as else-where, the appointment of a Roman cleric offered multiple financial, diplomatic, and pastoral possibilities. Gregory's earliest surviving correspondence to the secular leaders of Gaul, in fact, served as letters of introduction for Candidus and his custodianship of the papal lands. Not knowing how a renewed Roman presence would be interpreted, Gregory was careful to underplay its significance, referring to the papal estates in the region as "tiny" and typically framing the Merovingian hospitality for Candidus as an act of kindness performed for St. Peter.[6] Gregory also took care in announcing Candidus's arrival to the local episcopacy.[7] There was good reason for Gregory to employ subtlety and to act carefully—the establishment of a Roman delegate in Gaul opened a beachhead in the region through which Gregory was able to channel his other efforts, and it officially ended the bishop of Arles's supervision of the Roman patrimony in the region.[8]

In Gregory's theological imagination, there were several indications that the Christian population of Gaul was spiritually immature. The continuation of pagan rituals, of course, was a clear sign that there was work to be done. So too was the rampant immorality among the rural clergy.[9] But other, less obvious customs also evinced the need for proselytism, spiritual growth, and pastoral supervision. One practice that Gregory found to be particularly problematic was the ownership by Jews of Christian slaves.[10] The willingness of the Merovingian aristocracy to permit this practice indicated, at least to Gregory's prejudice, the extent to which they were not yet prepared to rule according to the precepts of their faith in Christ.[11] Even more troublesome was the epidemic rate of nepotism and simony when it came to the appointment of bishops. Gregory wrote repeatedly to the senior clerics and the Merovingian court, hoping to put an end to the practice. But Gregory had little real leverage in this respect, and the aristocracy had little incentive to change the situation.

Gregory's letters to Brunhilde and Childebert, and to Theodoric and Theodebert (the sons of Childebert), indicate the seriousness with which the pontiff understood the Merovingian dynasty to be vital to each of his efforts in Gaul. Not only did he need them to permit Roman agents to do their work (including the collection of taxes on papal lands), he also needed Brunhilde, Childebert and their retainers to be active supporters of his pastoral initiatives. It is likely for this reason that Gregory was so eager to comply with the various requests sent to him by Brunhilde and Childebert. He granted the use of the pallium to their favored bishops, he bestowed relics of St. Peter upon them, and perhaps even more significantly he treated them with a measure of diplomatic respect that he otherwise reserved for the Eastern emperor. For example, in September of 595, writing for the first time to Brunhilde and Childebert, Gregory engaged in an extended exercise in royal flattery, praising the dignity, virtue, and, above all else, faith of the royal family.[12]

Tracing the letters in the years that followed, we gain a sense of Gregory's mounting frustration with the situation in Gaul in general and with the reigning dynasty in particular. By July of 599, Gregory wrote to Brunhilde decrying the fact that there had been so little progress on the practice of simony. He reminded the queen that his willingness to grant the pallium to Syagrius years earlier had come with the expectation that the she and her favored bishop would earn the dignity it represented. But by this point Gregory had all but acknowledged that this would be yet another failed endeavor. In all of his years of pandering to Brunhilde, the only thing he seems to have successfully received from her was some assistance with a further Christian mission to Kent in England.

Kent

Gregory's mission to Kent, of course, has drawn the greatest interest among English-speaking biographers.[13] In an important essay in 1994, Ian Wood cautioned scholars that they should not divorce the mission to Kent from Gregory's other Christianizing endeavors among the Franks. Gregory enlisted the assistance of Frankish aristocrats and their clergy, but it is also important to note that the queen of Kent, Bertha, was herself a Frankish (Catholic) Christian and already had a bishop available to her in Kent as a spiritual advisor.[14] Indeed, Gregory's mission to the English has become such an important moment in the medieval historical imagination that it is easy to lose sight of the fact that Christianity had been on the island for hundreds of years and was, at the time of the mission, actively practiced. These facts do not diminish the significance of Gregory's endeavor, but they help to put it into proper context.

For all of the attention that the mission has garnered, several key elements remain unknown. For example, we do not know exactly when Gregory initially dispatched Augustine to England, nor do we know the precise context in which the pontiff commissioned the expedition. The earliest indication in his surviving corpus that he knew of the Angli is a letter to Candidus, dated to September of 595: Gregory instructs Candidus to purchase English boys and raise them in a local monastery.[15] Near the end of his *Moralia*, which some believe that Gregory edited in 595, the pontiff mentions that a mission to England is "well underway."[16] But the first explanation for the mission—if we should understand it to be an explanation—within Gregory's correspondence stems from a letter issued jointly to Brunhilde's grandchildren, Theodoric and Theodebert, in July of 596.[17] After encouraging the young princes to hasten the conversion (*converti*) of their own people, Gregory notes, "It has come to our attention, that the nation of the Angli desires, through the grace of God, to be converted (*converti*) to the Christian faith, but that the clergy (*sacerdotes*) in the adjacent region neglect them and fail to match their desire with their own exhortations. On this account, we have determined to send to them the servant of God Augustine, the bearer of these presents, whose zeal and strength are well known to us, along with other servants of God."[18] A similar letter to Brunhilde written at approximately the same time confirms that the Angli wish to become Christian but have received little assistance from local priests. In fact, Gregory claims, perhaps rhetorically, that the local clergy have shown no interest whatsoever in bringing the Angli to Christianity.[19] Thus, for the benefit of the Frankish aristocracy, Gregory presents the mission to England as something that has been asked of him—it is not something he developed on his own. Given our limited evidence, it is impossible to know if such a request by the English was ever made prior to Augustine's mission; it may well be that Gregory fabricated the request in order to authorize the expedition.

In the same dispatch of letters, Gregory wrote to several bishops in Southern Gaul, requesting that they, too, assist Augustine with his passage through the area.[20] As a further indication of how integrated Gregory's activities were, many of these letters also announce the arrival of Candidus as *rector* of the papal patrimony. But even more intriguing in this batch of letters is one to Augustine, which indicates that several of the monks who had initially set out for England were now having second thoughts and that the entire mission was nearly abandoned.[21]

As best we can reconstruct from the surviving evidence, Augustine likely arrived in England in 597 and, following a careful negotiation with Aethelbert (and possibly the Christian leaders already present), he was permitted by the king to preach Roman Christianity in the area around Canterbury. In July of 598 Gregory wrote to Eulogius of Alexandria, boasting that Augustine had baptized ten thousand souls on Christmas of the previous year.[22] It is generally assumed that Aethelbert, king of Kent, was among those baptized.[23] The oldest surviving letters to the Christians in England date to the summer of 601. The pontiff wrote to Aethelbert, Bertha (his wife), and Augustine. Gregory is pleased that so many of the Angli have converted to Christianity—he warns Augustine that he not fall victim to pride through his success—but he remains concerned that these initial achievements are superficial and that neither Bertha nor Aethelbert has done enough to support the endeavor.[24]

For our purposes, the mission to England is most relevant because it offers an important testimony to the ways in which the pontiff put his pastoral theology into practice. Employing the principles of *condescensio*, a temporary relaxation of prescribed rules, and understanding conversion to be a long-term process, Gregory encouraged Augustine to make a series of pastoral concessions so as to coax the local population into the Christian fold. Perhaps the most famous of these was the pontiff's instruction that Augustine should transform the pagan shrines (*fana*— note, not *templa*) into churches after the idols inside of them were destroyed: "Let holy water be prepared and sprinkled in these shrines, and altars constructed, and relics deposited, because, as long as the shrines are well built, it is necessary that they should be transformed from the cult of demons to the service of God."[25] In other words, Gregory presumed that because religious custom brought the indigenous population to these shrines for worship it would be beneficial, in the long run, to smooth the transition to Christianity by appropriating a familiar site for Christian use. Although some scholars have opined that Gregory's decision with respect to pagan shrines amounts to a reversal of policy, I have previously argued that the dual instructions to Augustine (via Mellitus) and Aethelbert (who was told to destroy the pagan temples in his realm) were complementary instructions designed to hasten the adoption of a more complete Christianity by both the king and his people.[26]

But the conversion of pagan shrines into Christian churches was not the only form of religious accommodation that Gregory encouraged in Kent. Although there are some complications with the manuscript tradition, there survives a long letter, the *Libellus responsionum*, which purports to be a series of pastoral questions and answers between Augustine and Gregory.[27] The finer points of the textual details need not concern us, apart from the fact that the majority of scholars now believe that the core of the text is authentic, even if a few of the questions and answers contained in the surviving manuscripts were later additions.[28] According to Bede, Augustine had asked Gregory's advice on twelve different pastoral matters. In nearly every case, Gregory encourages Augustine to adopt a model of spiritual supervision that is accommodative to recent converts. For example, he permits the marriage of second cousins, reduces the impediments to receiving the Eucharist, and even allows bovine sacrifice to continue, so long as it is now offered to God.[29] In doing so, Gregory explains the necessity of employing *condescensio* so as to achieve the greater pastoral good. In other words, Gregory reasons, common sense dictates that the Angli should receive pastoral concessions because they are not yet sufficiently strong in the faith to endure the spiritual rigors demanded by

tradition. In both cases (i.e., the use of the pagan shrines and the willingness to reduce various regulations), Gregory shows himself to be accommodative of the indigenous population in the hopes that, with time, they
might mature in the faith. And, as elsewhere, the operative assumption is
that the Christians in Kent would increasingly adopt the disciplines of ascetic renunciation as they matured in the faith.

Barbarian Kings and Roman Emperors in
Gregory's Negotiation of Conversion

One final aspect of Gregory's efforts to bring the non-Roman tribes
to Christianity for consideration is the rhetorical posture Gregory takes
when writing to their kings and queens, particularly with respect to his
negotiation of the dichotomy between their kingdoms and Rome's empire. We have already examined the extent to which Gregory viewed
himself as a loyal son of the empire, and we have sufficiently dismissed
Ullmann's contention that the pontiff's turn to the Germanic tribes was
an effort to insulate the See of Rome from Byzantine domination. What
remains to be considered is the way that Gregory subtly establishes a hierarchy of secular leadership (which places kings below emperors) but
simultaneously narrates Christian faith as an important criterion of
differentiation between the two. To gain an appreciation for this aspect
of Gregory's diplomatic efforts, two examples should suffice.

The first example stems from a brief passage in a letter to Brunhilde
that we encountered in the context of Gregory's distribution of religious
treasure. In response to Brunhilde's request for a pallium for her favored
bishop, Gregory articulates an elaborate, if subtle, hierarchical structure of
authority. God, of course, is both the "Ruler" (*dominator*) and the source
of ruling.[30] Although Gregory presents the divine authority as the source
of Brunhilde's leadership among her subjects, the pontiff asserts that
there is another human authority greater than she. The pope is able to
grant her request, he writes, only because he has learned from his deacon
who is stationed in the imperial palace in Constantinople that the "most
serene one" (i.e., the emperor) "wishes that this [request] be granted."[31]
Whether or not Gregory would have needed the emperor's permission to

grant a pallium is unclear (there is no similar acknowledgment elsewhere in the surviving sources), but what is clear is that Gregory is willing to concede in this letter to a Frankish queen that the pious and Christian emperor of the East has a powerful role in the appointment or election of individual leaders throughout the Church. What is so intriguing about this assertion of Maurice's role in ecclesiastical matters is that Gregory asserts it in the very same letter in which he chastens Brunhilde for her inability to halt the rampant simony and nepotism that characterize the leadership of the Gallic church. Clearly, Gregory wishes to alert Brunhilde, if indirectly, to the fact that she and her son do not possess the authority of the Roman emperor.

The second example is even more direct and stems from Gregory's letter to Aethelbert in the summer of 601. Hoping to inspire him to take more seriously his responsibility for the conversion of their subjects, the pontiff enlists the example of Constantine, who, according to Gregory, was the ultimate model for civic leadership because through his efforts the Roman Empire had adopted Christianity. As a consequence, "he surpassed the fame of the ancient emperors with praises and excelled beyond his predecessors in both fame and good works."[32] If Aethelbert will take seriously his responsibility to assist in the conversion of his people, then he too might aspire to the dignity of the mighty Constantine.[33] In a compendium letter to Bertha, Gregory similarly employed St. Helen (Constantine's mother) as a model of saintly inspiration.[34]

In short, Gregory presumed that the Frankish and Saxon rulers with whom he corresponded would desire to be as powerful and significant as the rulers of Rome. When it suited his purposes to do so, Gregory could suggest that all a king or queen needed to do to become emperor-like was to imitate the Christian faithfulness of the emperor Constantine — namely, to employ his or her position of leadership for the good. But Gregory could also use the gap between kingship and imperial leadership to remind Western rulers that they were not, at least not yet, the peers of their distant Roman counterparts. Perhaps, if they behaved more appropriately, such comparisons might be possible, but in the meantime Brunhilde and others in her family would need to get approvals from Rome and Constantinople if they wanted their bishops to have special privileges.

As THE PRECEDING chapters have shown, Gregory's administration of the Roman Church was of a sort that defies modern distinctions between secular and religious authority. Whether responding to the Lombard invasion, governing the Church of Sicily, or negotiating with the Merovingian dynasty, Gregory's methods reflect an integrated and comprehensive model of governance that was inspired simultaneously by theological conviction and civic responsibility. To be sure, we find a similar intersection of what we might today call the "sacred" and "secular" in his engagement with leaders (both imperial and ecclesiastical) in the East—his activity during the crisis of the ecumenical title offering a prime example. Indeed, it probably never would have occurred to Gregory that his responsibility for the spiritual welfare of the people of Rome was in any way separated from his responsibility for the survival of the city itself. In fact, he would have likely understood his supervision of the papal estates and his negotiation with foreign leaders to have been very much a part of his responsibility as bishop, his responsibility as the *praefectus* of the Roman Church. And it is precisely for these reasons that his stewardship of the Church—even into the realms that we might today identify as diplomatic or economic—always drew from his experience as a spiritual leader and was guided by an ascetic theology that understood the summit of spiritual perfection to be located in the messiness of worldly affairs.

CHAPTER FOURTEEN

The Steward of Peter's Tomb

As we bring our investigation of Gregory's leadership of the Roman Church and its people to a close, we will take a brief look at the various ways in which the figure of St. Peter defined, justified, and enabled the pontiff's self-understanding of his stewardship of the Roman See. Since the fourth century, Roman bishops had been exploiting the cult of St. Peter to their personal advantage, whether for justifying their legitimacy against rival claimants to Peter's throne (as in the disputed elections of 366 and 498) or asserting their doctrinal authority in international debates (such as the Christological controversies in the era of Chalcedon). In many cases, the papal escalation in rhetorical claims to ecclesiastical authority by means of Petrine rhetoric was actually precipitated by public humiliations for these bishops in one form or another.[1] For Pope Gregory, however, the appropriation of Petrine themes and the implementation of the Petrine topos was often quite different than it had been for his predecessors. While it is certainly true that Gregory leveraged the cult of St. Peter—and especially the physical space of his tombs and relics—to his advantage, the ways in which he employed Peter in his ecclesiastical and political diplomacy further attest to the nuance of his thought and action. To gain a sense for Gregory's stewardship of Peter's authority, we will briefly examine the pontiff's appropriation of both the physical and rhetorical aspects of the apostle's cult.

Peter's Tomb and Relics

When Damasus was elected to the See of Rome in 366, there were two sites in the suburbs of the city that had a claim to be the location of St. Peter's tomb: a cemetery on Vatican Hill that received a Constantinian basilica[2] (in effect granting imperial sanction to the site as the proper place for the commemoration of St. Peter) and a second location in the catacombs on the Via Appia (underneath the present basilica of St. Sebastian), where commemoration of St. Peter (and St. Paul) went back, at least, to the middle of the third century.[3] We need not concern ourselves with the scholarly quagmire that seeks to adjudicate the antiquity of these rival sites; we simply need to note that one of Damasus's most famous epigrams acknowledges that the catacombs on the Via Appia remained a popular pilgrimage site for St. Peter, even if it no longer possessed any of the saint's relics.[4] It is also interesting to note that during Damasus's tenure and for a significant period afterwards, Roman bishops did not have the financial means to compete with imperial and aristocratic patrons for the embellishment of Peter's shrine on Vatican Hill. Beginning in the later fifth century, however, Roman bishops began to possess greater resources than they previously had and started to spend lavishly at the basilica in order to link themselves more directly to Peter's cult and his authority. Interestingly, some of the pontiffs most responsible for the expansion of the facilities at the Vatican were precisely those who came under the greatest scrutiny of rival clerical factions in Rome—Pope Symmachus offering the most obvious case in point.[5]

Although scholarly investigations of Gregory's building activity at St. Peter's has been confined almost exclusively to the domain of archeological studies, the pontiff did embark upon a series of important refurbishments of the site that were replicated in other churches in Rome and elsewhere.[6] Specifically, during Gregory's tenure as bishop of Rome the underground tomb was enhanced to accommodate a steady flow of pilgrims. Pilgrims could progress into a room adjacent to the reliquary. Looking through a window, they could see the chamber where the relics and tomb were housed, but they could not see the actual relics or tomb.[7]

This semicircular chamber was large enough to enable the pilgrims to pray in close proximity to remains of the saint, which naturally enabled an expansion of Petrine pilgrimage to Rome.[8] What is more, during Gregory's tenure the altar was repositioned in the church above the shrine so that it sat directly above St. Peter's body. This not only enhanced the relationship between Peter's cult and the Eucharistic celebration, but also allowed liturgy and pilgrimage to occur simultaneously.

CONSIDERING THE SCOPE of the cult of the martyrs in Rome in earlier centuries, which is well documented in a series of texts known collectively as the *Gesta Martyrium*, Gregory's seeming ignorance of that textual tradition has puzzled scholars for more than a century. In 598 Gregory received a request from the patriarch of Alexandria for manuscripts contained in Rome about lives of martyrs.[9] Gregory responded that the Roman Church kept a record of the names and dates of a list of Roman martyrs but that there were very few actual biographies known to him about the details of the martyrs' lives and passions. In a recent examination of Gregory's *Homilies on the Gospels* (many of which were delivered on the occasion of martyr feasts), Guy Philippart has demonstrated that Gregory's encomium for St. Felicity wove together details of the saint's life from a myriad of known and unknown sources in a way that conformed to his particular pastoral concerns. Philippart argues that the pontiff's sanitized presentation of St. Felicity conformed to the pseudo-Gelasian decretals, which sought to censor the biographies of many of the Roman martyrs for fear of heterodox sympathies but also sought to bring the cult of martyrs under papal supervision.[10]

What Philippart and other scholars have not addressed is the extent to which Gregory's continuation of the cult of Roman martyrs, while active, was superseded by his promotion of the cult of St. Peter, the preeminent Roman martyr. To be sure, the reorganization of Roman martyr cult into a hierarchical structure centered on Peter and Paul stretched back to the fifth century. But it was through physical enhancements to the site, and especially through a series of new ritualized embellishments, that Gregory effectively transformed the cult of St. Peter in Rome from its late-ancient to its medieval form.

Among other things, Gregory is the first pontiff on record to require his administrators, particularly those deployed outside of Rome, to swear an oath of loyalty at Peter's tomb prior to their commission. The importance of this stage in the Petrine story should not be underestimated. Not only was it a powerful symbolic mechanism by which Gregory (and subsequent popes) could demand obedience from his agents (at times he reminded them of their oaths), but employing the physical space of Peter's tomb also represented an important expansion of the way that the Petrine discourse enabled papal control and exclusion.[11] Whereas Popes Leo and Gelasius had loaded their Petrine arsenals with mostly rhetorical weapons, Gregory added the ritualistic exercise of public submission at the very locus of papal power—the tomb of St. Peter. A second, similar, way in which Gregory emphasized the connection between Peter's authority and his own was to make those clerics who had been brought to Rome for trial to swear an oath of innocence in Gregory's presence at the tomb of St. Peter. Even those bishops deemed innocent were forced to humble themselves in this way. Indeed, when it suited his purposes to do so, Gregory might remind a correspondent of one of these public submissions (via Peter) to papal authority.[12]

A further expansion of Petrine authority via the tomb of St. Peter that we have already encountered concerns the way in which Gregory began to distribute Petrine relics to various ecclesiastical and political correspondents. Although he might not have been the first pontiff to disseminate Petrine relics, he was the first to employ religious treasure as a central component of his ecclesiastical diplomacy. The particular physical qualities of the sacred material (filings of chains, inserted into a key, which were to be worn around the neck) offered a series of symbolic attributes that drew the recipient to the heroic acts of the apostle and, more importantly, to the See of Rome as the locus of St. Peter's temporal and spiritual authority.

It is noteworthy that Gregory's distribution of relics, in some ways, seems at odds with his other efforts to curtail the relic trade. Especially noteworthy is a letter he sent to the wife of the emperor, denying her request to send a portion of the relics of St. Paul to Constantinople on the premise that it was not the custom of the Roman Church to dismember and distribute the relics of the saints (something the Eastern Church did routinely).[13] The distinction between Gregory's practice and what he censures is a rather fine one—recall that Gregory is not sending the actual bones of Peter; he is sending filings of Peter's chains—but one that allows Gregory to simultaneously keep sole control of Peter's bones and yet distribute Petrine power. Indeed, we might say that Gregory's deference for and use of Peter's tomb and relics offers a considerable insight into the Christian understanding of religious sites and artifacts at the transition from the late-ancient to the medieval world.

We might also observe the extent to which Gregory's appropriation of Peter's tomb and relics fits within his broader theological and pastoral program. As we noted in part 1, Gregory—like most of his contemporaries—assumed that the saints had the potential to remain active in the world long after their deaths. Their tombs and relics especially could serve as loci for divine power. In part 2 we detailed some of the ways that Gregory, following in a long tradition of ascetic literature, employed the topos of a saintly exemplar as a way to encourage individuals to embrace more fully the life of renunciation and faith. When we bring these aspects of Gregory's theology to bear upon his use of Peter's cult to exert his personal authority, we see further the extent to which his ideological commitments enabled and sustained a comprehensive program of activity that could be simultaneously theologically well-intentioned and practically self-serving. Gregory was at once a sophisticated theologian and an exacting corporate executive of the Roman Church.

Gregory and the Discourse of Petrine Authority

Gregory's engagement with the Petrine tradition, of course, was much more extensive than the ritualized acts and diplomatic endeavors centering on St. Peter's tomb and relics. The pontiff was a careful interpreter of the biblical Peter, whom he could enlist in a variety of contexts to serve a range of exegetical needs. Like Leo and Gelasius before him, Gregory could assert Roman ecclesiastical privilege (in terms of both appellate jurisdiction and censoring other bishops) whenever he needed to do so by turning to well-worn scriptural and canonical precedents rooted in the belief that Peter's authority among the apostles transferred to the bishop of Rome's privilege among other bishops. But unlike his papal predecessors, who almost never acknowledged the biblical Peter's mistakes (especially his denial of Christ), Gregory routinely examined the apostle's flaws in order to advance his pastoral and ascetic ideas. Having extensively analyzed the Petrine topos in Gregory's career and writing elsewhere, I will confine my discussion here to a few relevant summary observations.[14]

First, Gregory's biblical commentaries frequently employ Peter as a theological and pastoral resource. In Gregory's hands, the biblical Peter serves as a model of humility and repentance precisely because of his imperfections. In the *Moralia* alone, Gregory reflects nearly a dozen times on Peter's errors—the most common being the denial of Christ during the Passion, the altercation with Paul over circumcision, and the failure to interpret properly the significance of the Transfiguration—in order to encourage humility among his clerics and repentance among the laity. Perhaps surprisingly, there is no analysis of Matthew 16 (the primary scriptural reference for Petrine authority) in Gregory's surviving *Homilies on the Gospels*, nor does he reflect upon the passage in any significant way in his other theological works.[15] What is more, pontiff's *Book of Pastoral Rule* offers scant reflection on the biblical Peter and never does so to assert Roman ecclesiastical privilege. As in the biblical commentaries, the references to Peter in the *Book of Pastoral Rule* are designed to reinforce humility and repentance.

Second, Gregory typically does not avail himself of the traditional staples of papal authority, rooted in the Petrine legacy, in the vast majority of his correspondence with bishops and secular rulers. This is even true for most instances in which Gregory actively asserts his authority, such as the censuring of malcontent bishops. Never, for example, in the two hundred letters sent to Sicily does Gregory appeal to the biblical justifications for Peter's privileged status or to the link between Peter and the See of Rome when he seeks to expand Roman interests on the island. Such restraint (if we should call it that) is a contrast to Popes Leo I and Gelasius I, who consistently appealed to the authority of Peter whenever and wherever their own authority or that of the See of Rome was in question.[16]

Third, this is not to say that Gregory's letters never mention St. Peter or appeal to him as a marker of Gregory's own authority. We have already seen, for example, several ways in which the pontiff might describe a kindness offered to the See of Rome as a sign of love "for St. Peter" (such as when Constantinopolitan aristocrats send funds for the refugees in Rome or when the Merovingians grant hospitality to Gregory's agents).

Indeed, Gregory frequently inserts the name of Peter in letters when the pontiff is actually referring to himself. He similarly refers to the tomb of St. Peter when he might actually mean to imply the city of Rome more broadly.[17] While these literary substitutions convey an important rhetorical connection linking Gregory and Rome to Peter's apostolic authority and, by extension, his primacy among the apostles, these statements are typically divorced from the vitriolic assertions of Peter's authority that mark some of Leo's and Gelasius's most desperate correspondence.

The lone significant exception to this occurs in the controversy over the ecumenical title. We have already examined this altercation in some detail. For the purposes of understanding Gregory's appropriation of the Petrine topos, recall the extent to which the pontiff's increasing frustration with the situation in the East seems to have been mirrored by his escalation of the claim to Petrine authority. Not only did he rehearse the traditional appeals to biblical and canonical precedents for Roman privilege, he also sought creative new ways to enlist potential allies under the umbrella of a common Petrine appeal that differentiated Antioch, Alexandria, and Rome (apostolic sees, according to Gregory) from Constantinople (an imperial see).

Although Gregory's appropriation of the Petrine topos was idiosyncratic, he stood in a long line of papal actors who successfully harnessed the legacy of the apostle to his own ends. To the extent that the development and control of discourse can be seen as a key to social power, Gregory's expansion and promotion of the Petrine discourse can be seen as one of the crucial factors of a legacy that contributed to the papacy's ascendancy over other power structures in Western Europe in the later Middle Ages.

Conclusion

The Apostolic Steward

As we come to the close of this examination, it is appropriate to reflect upon some of the ways in which the themes central to Gregory's thought and practice reflect broader changes in the Christian imagination at the dawn of the Middle Ages. As we saw in part 1, Gregory's theological vision was intrinsically an ascetic one. The implications of this were both theoretical and practical. On a theoretical level, Gregory's ascetic commitments affected nearly every aspect of his theological vision, including his understanding of the Fall, the potential for human cooperation in the process of salvation, and the mystery of the sacraments. Perhaps the most distinctive aspect of his ascetic theology is the extent to which he recalibrated late-ancient ideas about ascetic perfection so that the summit of the Christian life was no longer to be understood in a mystical encounter of the divine that required detachment, but found rather in the ascetic who was willing to suspend temporarily his personal enjoyment of the spiritual life so as to assist others. For Gregory, Christian perfection involved a willingness to engage a polluted world in which sin was virtually inevitable. As a result, he presented a spirited theoretical justification for the practical needs of his papal administration—namely the recruitment of like-minded ascetics. And, as we saw in part 2, the intersection of Gregory's ascetic and pastoral theology found its most pronounced expression in his articulation of the life of the spiritual director.

But it is in part 3 that we examined the fullest expression of Gregory's ideas in action. It is noteworthy that this integration both continued and transformed earlier ideas and practices of leadership. Among other things, in Gregory's administration of the Roman See we find a coalescing of the ancient Roman office of the *praefectus urbi* and the late-ancient Christian conception of episcopal stewardship.[1] Like the civic authorities of previous periods, the Roman bishops of late antiquity were figures of dual authority and, thus, had two distinctive sites of responsibility, to their private households and to their city. To be sure, many late-ancient bishops drew upon classical models of leadership in their articulation of the way that clerics should respond to these dual roles—Gregory Nazianzen and Ambrose of Milan offer probably the best previous examples. But what distinguishes Gregory's vision of leadership from those of previous theologians and, especially, of Rome's previous civic leaders was his unprecedented vision of spiritual leadership that demanded social activity.

Indeed, the extent to which Gregory assumed civic responsibilities for the city of Rome in the absence of imperial support evinces an unprecedented blurring of the boundary between civic and ecclesial leadership. Not only was Gregory an active participant in the day-to-day administration of Roman affairs, but his theological treatises and hagiographic works reframed the very conception of Christian leadership at the dawn of the Middle Ages. And while scholarship since Jeffrey Richards has largely recognized the *Romanitas/Christianitas* dynamic of Gregory's public administration, the extensive foregrounding of Gregory's ascetic and pastoral commitments in the present study has sought a more thorough and careful analysis of the connection between the specific characteristics of his religious conviction and the examples of his stewardship of the Roman community. Whereas a previous generation of scholars had largely opted to explore either the contemplative and ascetic side of Gregory's theology *or* the pragmatism of his international action, this study argues for a new interpretive paradigm by insisting that the "problem of the two Gregorys" is not a problem at all. Simply put, Gregory's ascetic and pastoral theology informed and structured his administrative practice.

Let us conclude, then, by noting that while Gregory's appropriation of the Petrine topos was less aggressive—albeit no less significant—than that of some of his predecessors, it is easy to lose sight of the extent to which Petrine authority was a key feature of the vision of Christian leadership in the West that Gregory bequeathed to subsequent generations. Indeed, one of the most important legacies of Gregory's pontificate was the way in which key traditions of ancient Rome and ancient Christianity came together in the narrative of apostolic authority. This combination enabled a new trajectory for leadership for the Christian Middle Ages. That legacy is much broader than the simple exercise of papal authority over the Western Church: it also touches upon aspects of the medieval religious imagination and ritual that are as seemingly distinctive as biblical interpretation, the cult of relics, pilgrimage, and patronage. Although Gregory may have only rarely needed to justify his personal authority on the basis of his connection to St. Peter via Matthew 16, his elaboration of the cult of St. Peter in Rome and his dissemination of Petrine relics throughout Western Europe perhaps did as much to perpetuate the connection between Peter, Rome, and the Roman bishop as any of Leo's or Gelasius's rhetorical harangues. Indeed, Gregory's vision of the bishop of Rome as an ascetic and apostolic steward of the ancient imperial capital is one of the most important, if subtle, of his contributions to the religious imagination of the Middle Ages.

ABBREVIATIONS

Series

CCSL	Corpus Christianorum, Series Latina
CSEL	Corpus Scriptorum Ecclesiasticorum Latinorum
FC	The Fathers of the Church
MGH	Monumenta Germaniae Historica
PL	Patrologiae Latina
SC	Sources chrétiennes

Works of Gregory the Great

Dia.	*Dialogues [Dialogorum libri IV]*
Ep.	*Letters [Epistulae]*
Hom. Evang.	*Homilies on the Gospels [Homiliae in Evangelia]*
Hom. Ez.	*Homilies on Ezekiel [Homiliae in Hiezechihelem]*
Mor.	*Morals on the Book of Job [Moralia in Iob libri]*
PR	*Book of Pastoral Rule [Liber regulae pastoralis]*

NOTES

Introduction

1. Gregory says that Pope Felix (without identifying which Felix) had been a relative of his. Gregory, *Homilies on the Gospels [Homiliae in Evangelia]*, crit. ed., ed. Raymond Étaix (CCSL 141), 38; hereafter *Hom. Evang.* Charles Pietri raised doubts about Gregory's family relation to Felix III because it is reconstructed largely through inscriptions; see "Aristocratie et société cléricale dans l'Italie chrétienne au temps d'Odoacre et de Théodoric," *Mélanges de l'École française de Rome. Antiquité* 93 (1981): 435n84.

2. Gregory mentions them in the same sermon (38) in which he refers to Pope Felix as a relative.

3. The connection between Gordianus and the Roman Church relies upon the testimony of John the Deacon (1.1 and 4.83), a ninth-century biographer of Gregory, who claims that Gordianus was a *regionarius*. It is more likely, however, that Gordianus was a *defensor*, as the rank of *regionarius* was a later designation. John the Deacon, *Vita Sancti Gregorii Magni* (PL, 75). F. Homes Dudden speculated more than one hundred years ago that Gordianus was responsible for administering the property in the neighborhood of the basilica of St. Peter's, which was outside of the city's walls, on the western shore of the Tiber River. F. Homes Dudden, *Gregory the Great: His Place in History and Thought*, 2 vols. (New York: Russell and Russell, 1905), 1:6–7.

4. On the location of Gregory's childhood home, see John the Deacon, *Vita* 1.6; on his education, see Gregory of Tours, *History of the Franks [Historia Francorum]*, crit. ed., ed. Rudolf Buchner (Berlin: Rutten & Loening, 1955), 10.1.

5. Modern assessments of the educational program in Rome at this time are inconclusive. It has been suggested that Roman students no longer studied

Greek authors by the middle of the sixth century, even though there is some evidence to the contrary. Either way, it is likely that the majority of his studies included Cicero, Seneca, and Virgil. Pierre Riché identifies Gregory's reliance upon Scripture (rather than classical authors) as a marker for the transformation from a late antique to a medieval literary culture. Pierre Riché, *Écoles et enseignement dans le Haut Moyen Age* (Paris: Aubier Montaigne, 1979), 17–18.

6. The principal source for Justinian's military expeditions in Italy is Procopius, *The Wars [De bellis]*, crit. ed., ed. Jakob Haury (Leipzig: Teubner, 1905–1913; revised by G. Wirth, 1976).

7. Dudden, *Gregory the Great*, 1:33–35. For a more recent account of Gregory's youth and the impact of the Justinianic wars, see Barbara Müller, *Führung im Denken und Handeln Gregors des Grossen* (Tübingen: Mohr Siebeck, 2009), 8–14.

8. The population decline in the city of Rome began long before the Gothic Wars of the sixth century. Some estimates place the population of Rome during Gregory's life at only one-fifth of its former peak.

9. While it is obviously difficult to gauge the population levels of the ancient world, Michel Rouche has estimated that the city of Rome declined from a population of 700,000 in the fourth century to 200,000 during Gregory's life. Michel Rouche, "Grégoire le Grand face à la situation économique de son temps," in *Grégoire le Grand*, ed. Jacques Fontaine, Robert Gillet, and Stan Pellistrandi (Paris: Colloques Internationaux du CNRS, 1986), 41–58. See also A. H. M. Jones, *The Later Roman Empire: 284–602*, 2 vols. (1964; repr., Baltimore: Johns Hopkins University Press, 1986), 2:1040–45.

10. Concerning Gregory's apocalypticism, see Claude Dagens, "La fin des temps et l'église selon saint Grégoire le Grand," *Recherches de Science religieuse* 58 (1970): 273–88. See also Carole Straw, *Gregory the Great: Perfection in Imperfection* (Berkeley: University of California Press, 1988), esp. 2, 14–15 and 25–26.

11. Müller, *Führung im Denken*, 14–18.

12. For a detailed list of prefecture privileges and responsibilities, see Dudden, *Gregory the Great*, 1:101–3; and A. H. M. Jones, *Later Roman Empire*, 1:523–62.

13. Dudden, *Gregory the Great*, 1:105. The Lombard threat to the city at this time may have been exaggerated by Dudden, but there is little doubt that the Lombards were increasingly disrupting imperial control of the peninsula.

14. The vacancy was ten months. Although our sources do not explain the reason for the lapse between candidates, it is conceivable that the breakdown in communications with imperial court in Constantinople could have delayed the approval process. See the entry for John III in the *Liber Pontificalis*, 2d ed., ed. Louis Duchesne (Paris: E. de Boccard, 1955), 1:305–07.

15. On the integration of civil and military authority in sixth-century Italy, see T. S. Brown, *Gentlemen and Officers: Imperial Administration and Aristocratic Power in Byzantine Italy, A.D. 554–800* (Rome: British School at Rome, 1984), esp. 8–20.

16. "My cares began to threaten me so much that I was in danger of being overcome, not only in outward activity, but what is more serious in my soul." Gregory, *Letters [Epistulae]*, crit. ed., ed. Dag Norberg (CCSL 140–140A), 5.53; hereafter *Ep.* This letter is the prefatory address to Leander of Seville, to whom Gregory sent the first copy of the *Moralia in Iob.* I have followed the numbering for Gregory's letters in Norberg's critical edition. Dagens notes the linguistic parallels between Gregory's narration of his "conversion" from civic life to monastic life and Augustine's own narration of his conversion in the *Confessions.* Claude Dagens, "La 'Conversion' de saint Grégoire le Grand," *Revue des Études Augustiniennes* 15 (1969): 149–62.

17. Gregory of Tours, *History of the Franks*, 10.1. Although the story of Gregory's monastic conversion is not included in the *Liber Pontificalis*, it was expanded by later papal biographers, especially Paul the Deacon, *Vita Sancti Gregorii Magni*, 2 vols., crit. ed., ed. Sabina Tuzzo (Pisa: Scuola normale superiore, 2002), 3; and John the Deacon, *Vita.* Müller offers a plausible account for Gregory's life at St. Andrew's. Müller, *Führung im Denken*, 40–52.

18. See, for example, Gregory of Tours, *History of the Franks*, 10.1.

19. Gregory summarizes his life in Constantinople, if vaguely, in a letter to his friend Leander of Seville that accompanied the pontiff's sending of the *Moralia in Iob* years after their time together in the Eastern capital. Gregory, *Moralia in Iob libri [Morals on the Book of Job]*, crit. ed., ed. Marci Adriaen (CCSL 143, 143A, 143B), *ad Leandrum* 1; hereafter *Mor.*

20. Gregory's official residence was in the *domus Placidiae* near two churches (each with double patrons) that followed a Latin rite, Sts. Sergius and Bacchus and Sts. Peter and Paul. For an extended (and somewhat speculative) account of how Gregory filled his time in Constantinople, see Dudden, *Gregory the Great*, 1:123–57. A more grounded assessment of Gregory's experience is offered by Müller, *Führung im Denken*, 66–110.

21. The emperor Maurice, in fact, asked Gregory to serve as the godfather for his oldest son and heir, Theodosius, in 584. Gregory's Eastern correspondence is filled with letters to members of the imperial family or illustrious men of court whom he came to know during his tenure in the capital. Similarly, Gregory also befriended other up-and-coming ecclesiastics, including Leander of Seville and the future patriarch of Constantinople, John IV (sometimes known as John the Faster).

22. Peter Kaufman, *Church, Book, and Bishop: Conflict and Authority in Early Latin Christianity* (Boulder, CO: Westview Press, 1996), 120.

23. Gregory of Tours, *History of the Franks*, 10.1.

24. It has long been a commonplace to understand Gregory's introduction of monastics to the papal administration as having a detrimental effect on Rome's entrenched clerical ranks. That position has been successfully challenged by Pietrina Pellegrini, who shows that a careful understanding of Gregory's terminology and practice does not support such a conclusion. Pietrina Pellegrini, *Militia Clericatus Monachici Ordines: Istituzioni Ecclesiastiche e Società in Gregorio Magno*, 2d ed. (Catania: Edizioni del Prisma, 2008), esp. 298–99.

25. See Ernst Pitz, *Papstreskripte im frühen Mittelalter: Diplomatische und rechtsgeschichtliche Studien zum Brief-Corpus Gregors des Grossen* (Sigmaringen: Thorbecke, 1990), 30–35, 252–52, and 280–86.

26. On the potential for editorial erasure to serve as a powerful tool in the creation of ecclesiastical memory, see the collective essays in Kate Cooper and Julia Hillner, eds., *Religion, Dynasty, and Patronage in Early Christian Rome, 300–900* (Cambridge: Cambridge University Press, 2007), especially the introduction (1–18) and the essay "Memory and Authority in Sixth-Century Rome: The Liber Pontificalis and the Collectio Avellana," by Kate Blair-Dixon (59–76).

27. There is, of course, an anonymous biography produced by a monk at Whitby that likely dates to the early eighth century. Although its author is clearly concerned about ecclesiastical affairs in Britain, the Whitby life was known in Rome in the ninth century.

28. Straw, *Perfection in Imperfection*.

29. Straw, *Perfection in Imperfection*, 17. While Straw's insight is creative and her knowledge of Gregory's exegetical works is exhaustive, her analysis implies a level of consistency in thought and action that are not entirely borne out by the sources, especially the hundreds of routine and pragmatic letters that attend to the administrative tasks that occupied Gregory's time as steward of the Roman Church's patrimony. A more balanced reading of Gregory's theological insights and his enormous correspondence (his is the largest surviving correspondence of the ancient world) might suggest that Gregory was more of an occasional thinker than a systematic one.

30. While Straw never seeks to differentiate between Gregory's "thought" and his theology, she does venture twice into distinctly theological categories. The most prolonged is Gregory's Christological vision (*Perfection in Imperfection*, 147–78), which on her analysis maps well onto the thesis of Gregorian paradox. The second concerns her analysis of original sin (122–25), which I will critique in part 1.

31. Claude Dagens, *Saint Grégoire le Grand. Cultre et experience chrétiennes* (Paris: Études Augustiennes, 1977).

32. Dagens, *Saint Grégoire le Grand*, 272.

33. Greschat, *Die* Moralia in Job *Gregors des Großen: Ein christologisch-ekklesiologischer Kommentar* (Tübingen: Mohr Siebeck, 2005).

34. Rade Kisić, *Patria Caelestis: Die eschatologische Dimension der Theologie Gregors des Großen* (Tübingen: Mohr Siebeck, 2011).

35. Note also Robert Wilken's study of Gregory's use of allegorical interpretation in the *Moralia*, which serves as a kind of apologetic for the sophistication of the work. Robert Wilken, "Interpreting Job Allegorically: The *Moralia* of Gregory the Great," *Pro Ecclesia* 10 (2001): 213–26.

36. Robert Markus, *Gregory the Great and His World* (Cambridge: Cambridge University Press, 1997).

37. The *Libellus responsionum* is a list of pastoral instructions that Gregory sent to Augustine of Canterbury in the summer of 601.

38. In the introduction, Müller acknowledges her decision to omit the evidence from the *Moralia*, although she does not provide a suitable justification for doing so. Müller, *Führung im Denken*, 7.

39. The only significant discussion of the text occurs during her narrative of Gregory's tenure in Constantinople. Here Müller emphasizes the setting and potential audience of Constantinopolitan elite who may have attended Gregory's lectures. Müller, *Führung im Denken*, 99–106.

40. Gregory's *Moralia* also offers his most detailed reflections upon the necessity of ascetic experience as a prerequisite to spiritual authority. Surprisingly, Müller chooses not to explore this aspect of Gregory's thinking about leadership or the *Moralia* more generally.

41. In short, whereas one might characterize Müller's biography as a historical biography, the present volume is more a work of historical theology that not only considers theological questions but also supplements traditional historical-critical methods with the insights provided by discourse analysis.

42. Bronwen Neil and Matthew Dal Santo, eds., *A Companion to Gregory the Great* (Leiden: Brill, 2013).

Part One

1. In the nineteenth century, Edward Gibbon got the ball rolling by decrying Gregory's naiveté for believing in the miraculous power of relics and his endorsement of the fanciful myths concerning the Italian saints. Edward Gibbon, *The Decline and Fall of the Roman Empire* (London, 1806), 6:162–71. See also Adolf von Harnack's condemnation that Gregory's work indicates a decline of

civilization into superstition. Adolf von Harnack, *History of Dogma*, trans. Neil Buchanan (New York: Dover, 1961), 5:262. See Sofia Boesch Gajano, "Dislivelli culturali e mediazioni ecclesiastiche nei *Dialogi* di Gregorio Magno," *Quaderni storici* 14 (1979): 398–415.

2. Robert Markus, *Gregory the Great and His World* (Cambridge: Cambridge University Press, 1997), 40. Although Straw notes Gregory's debt to John Cassian and eagerly seeks to demonstrate Gregory's creativity and nuance, she typically follows the Markus trajectory in seeing the distinctions between Gregory's and Augustine's thought as being swept up in a broad cultural shift that separates the thought-world of the fourth century from that of the sixth. See Straw, *Perfection in Imperfection*, 9–10.

3. As we will see, the fanciful nature of the miracles included in the *Dialogues* has troubled a number of scholars. One misguided solution to the conundrum is to insist simply that Gregory did not author the *Dialogues*, on the basis of a perceived gap between the sophistication of his exegetical works and the superstition of his hagiographical works. Chief among the skeptics of Gregorian authorship is Francis Clark, *The Pseudo-Gregorian Dialogues* (Leiden: Brill, 1987). For a more recent response to Clark, see Matthew Dal Santo, "The Shadow of a Doubt?: A Note on the *Dialogues* and *Registrum Epistolarum* of Gregory the Great," *Journal of Ecclesiastical History* 61 (2010): 3–17. Earlier criticisms of Clark may be found in Paul Meyvaert, "The Enigma of Gregory the Great's *Dialogues*: A Response to Francis Clark," *Journal of Ecclesiastical History* 39 (1988): 335–81; and Robert Godding, "Les *Dialogues* . . . de Grégoire le Grand. A propos d'un livre recent," *Analecta Bollandiana* 106 (1988): 201–29.

4. Note, especially, the essays by Loreno Saraceno, Giuseppe Cremascoli, and Guy Philippart in *Gregorio Magno e L'Agiografia fra IV e VII Secolo*, ed. Antonella Degl'Innocenti, Antonio De Prisco and Emore Paoli (Firenze: Edizioni del Galluzzo, 2007). For an overview of the reception of the *Dialogues*, see Müller, *Führung im Denken*, 214–18.

5. Sofia Boesch Gajano makes something of a similar point in her 2004 biography, *Gregorio Magno: Alle origini del Medioveo* (Rome: Viella, 2004), arguing that although Gregory's *Dialogues* in many ways reflect the popular religious imagination of the Middle Ages, they simultaneously contain several sophisticated rhetorical and structural elements.

6. While this represents both an inheritance and a modification of the ascetic writers who preceded him (especially Evagrius and John Cassian), my purpose will be to illuminate Gregory's thought rather than to examine its continuities and discontinuities with others' work.

7. I first proposed this category in an essay entitled "The Soteriology of St. Gregory the Great: A Case against the Augustinian Interpretation," *American*

Benedictine Review 54 (2003): 312–28. Previously, Straw had explored the reciprocal and complementary relationship between grace and human agency in Gregory's thought. Straw, *Perfection in Imperfection*, 160–61 and 177–78.

8. By "mystical characteristics" I refer to those aspects of the divine–human relationship that Gregory understood to be hidden or veiled. As we will see, Gregory believed that God's interaction in the world (particularly the mysterious ways in which grace interacted with and spurred the will) were largely incomprehensible to the postlapsarian mind.

Chapter 1. A Theology of Asceticism

1. "Our external possessions, no matter how few, are sufficient for the Lord. He examines the heart, not the substance, and does not consider the amount we sacrifice for him but rather the means by which we offer it to him." Gregory, *Hom. Evang.* 5.2.

2. Gregory, *Hom. Evang.* 5.3.

3. Gregory, *Hom. Evang.* 5.4.

4. Although the homily does not name the martyr, modern scholars have identified St. Pancras as the site and feast for the occasion. See Conrad Leyser, "Temptations of Cult: Roman Martyr Piety in the Age of Gregory the Great," *Early Medieval Europe* 9 (2000): 289–307, at 296n33.

5. *Hom. Evang.* 27 begins with Christ's declaration to the apostles to love one another as he has loved them.

6. Gregory, *Hom. Evang.* 27.2.

7. Gregory, *Hom. Evang.* 27.4.

8. Gregory, *Hom. Evang.* 27.9.

9. Portions of this section appeared in a different form in Demacopoulos, "Gregory the Great," in *The Spiritual Senses in the Western Christian Tradition*, ed. Paul Gavrilyuk and Sarah Coakley (Cambridge: Cambridge University Press, 2012), 71–85.

10. Elizabeth Clark, *Reading Renunciation: Asceticism and Scripture in Early Christianity* (Princeton: Princeton University Press, 1999), 4.

11. Clark, *Reading Renunciation*, 9. Drawing theoretical inspiration from Derrida, Foucault, and Said, Clark understands these Christian interpreters to produce "new meaning" that effectively "displaced" the biblical text through commentaries on it. Clark, *Reading Renunciation*, 6–10.

12. Indeed, in Gregory's rendering, the prophet Ezekiel provides a prototype for a monastic prophet, emphatically castigating those who lack renunciatory practices and leading those who possess them into a mystical contempla-

tion of the divine. Job, likewise, serves as the quintessential preacher, whose service to the world is nicely complemented by his ability to offer the necessarily distinctive pastoral messages to his children, wife, and friends.

13. Gregory, *Homilies on Ezekiel [Homiliae in Hiezechihelem]*, critical ed, ed. Marcus Adriaen (CCSL 142), 1.5.1; hereafter *Hom. Ez.*

14. Gregory, *Hom. Ez.* 1.10.1–3. The drink symbolizes that which is easiest for human understanding; food is a metaphor for that which is the more obscure.

15. In his *Book of Pastoral Rule [Liber regulae pastoralis]*, crit. ed., ed. Floribert Rommel (SC 381–82) (hereafter *PR*), 2.11, Gregory argued that a pastor must continuously return to the Scriptures in private meditation whenever he feels that his secular responsibilities have diluted his focus. Only this can protect him and reinvigorate him for his work in the secular world.

16. In *Hom. Ez.* 1.8.33, Gregory argues that the Scriptures are "veiled in mysteries" (*obvolutum mysteriis*). In *Hom. Ez.* 2.5.3, he notes that although "the whole of Scripture was indeed written for us," it cannot be fully "understood (*intelligitur*) by us."

17. Gregory, *Hom. Ez.* 2.5.4. Gregory's notion that not all readers can comprehend the words of Scripture seems to reflect Origen, who introduced three levels of interpretation (for beginners, intermediates, and experts) in his *De Principiis* 4.11. According to Gregory, the more difficult passages of Scripture require the interpretive lens of allegory and metaphor, but, for those who have achieved spiritual advancement through asceticism, these passages contain discernable divine truths. Earlier in the same commentary Gregory had argued that the reason that "holy preachers" (one of his more frequent phrases for an accomplished ascetic who had taken on pastoral leadership) were able to comprehend the Scriptures more effectively than others was that they were able to discern when a passage should be interpreted "historically" versus in a spiritual or allegorical sense (*Hom. Ez.* 1.3.4). Sometimes, he argues, the Scriptures require a historical reading; sometimes only an allegorical reading is appropriate; occasionally, both will prove fruitful. Through the Scriptures, the holy preacher who possesses the proper hermeneutical discernment is able to gain true knowledge of God (*Hom. Ez.* 1.12.20–21). On the relationship in Gregory's thinking between ascetic progress and the criteria for spiritual authority, see George Demacopoulos, *Five Models of Spiritual Direction* (Notre Dame, IN: Universtiy of Notre Dame Press, 2007), 130–39.

18. Following the lead of John Cassian and other ascetic authors, Gregory held that *discretio* was bestowed by God primarily upon those spiritual leaders who had successfully combined ascetic experience with humility. See Demacopoulos, *Five Models*, 112–13 and 131–37.

19. To be clear, Gregory does not believe that this is the only way to gain knowledge—it can also be obtained in contemplation and through listening to others—but discernment is that quality that enables a proper reading of Scripture.

20. Gregory, *Hom. Ez.* 1.5.3.

21. See, for example, his allegorical interpretation of Leviticus 21, which removed the "bleary-eyed" from ancient Jewish priesthood. Gregory understands the bleary-eyed to symbolize those who "naturally spring toward knowledge of the truth (*ingenium ad cognitionem veritatis emicat*)" but whose carnal deeds obscure that truth. Gregory, *PR* 1.11.

22. Gregory, *PR* 1.11. See *Five Models*, 132.

23. For example, he argues in his commentary on the Prophet Job that humanity's greatest attribute is its rational soul (*anima rationalis*), which allows holy men and women, such as Job, to resist evil by the power of their reasoning faculties (*Mor.* 14.15.17). Later in the same text, he argues that we are able to employ the mind to comprehend spiritual things that we are unable to apprehend through our physical senses, especially our eyes (*Mor.* 23.19.35). Similarly, in his commentary on Ezekiel, Gregory describes the saints as being able to ponder the ineffable wisdom of God, without the clamor of words ("sine strepitu verborum") (*Hom. Ez.* 1.8.17).

24. For example, in his *Book of Pastoral Rule*, the pontiff argues that one either knows or does not know who he is through humility. The person who lacks humility will "forget" who he is; the person who possesses humility will learn through no other effort who he is. Gregory, *PR* 1.3.

25. Gregory, *Hom. Ez.* 2.6.2–4.

26. See Straw, *Perfection in Imperfection*, 248–49.

27. Cf. 1 Jn. 4.8, 20–21.

28. The fact that it is so easy for someone such as Straw or Dagens to jump from the biblical commentaries to the *Dialogues* or *Pastoral Rule* indicates that Gregory's hermeneutical practices were in lockstep with his other theological and practical considerations.

29. For Gregory's most explicit explanation of his three-part exegetical analysis, see *Mor.* 1.prol.3.

30. See, for example, *Mor.* 8.10.19; *Hom. Evang.* 16.2–3; *Dialogues [Dialogorum libri IV]*, crit. ed., ed. Adalbert de Vogüé (SC 251, 260, 265), 4.praef; hereafter *Dia.* See also Bernard McGinn, "Contemplation in Gregory the Great," in *Gregory the Great: A Symposium*, ed. John Cavadini (Notre Dame, IN: University of Notre Dame Press, 1995), 146–47.

31. The following examples, far from exhaustive, provide a broad survey of the many different ways that ascetic considerations informed his interpretation

of Scripture: Gregory, *Hom. Ez.* 1.7.6; *Hom. Ez.* 2.1.7; *Hom. Ez.* 2.3.21; *Hom. Ez.* 2.5.2; *Mor.* 4.26.47; *Mor.* 5.3.4; and *Mor.* 14.53.64–65.

32. Gregory, *Hom. Ez.* 1.2.9–10.

33. Gregory, *Hom. Ez.* 2.3.3–7.

34. Gregory, *Hom. Ez.* 1.12.26–28. See also *Hom. Ez.* 1.7.22.

35. E.g., Gregory, *Mor.* 2.15.37.

36. Gregory, *Mor.* 3.33.64.

37. Gregory, *Mor.* 9.55.84.

38. Gregory, *Mor.* 31.2.2. In *Mor.* 26.17.27–31, Gregory produces a list of various animals that represent specific vices to which "holy men" are not subject due to their discipline and lack of carnality. Most of book 31 of the *Moralia* is an extended allegory and moralizing of a host of animals, which reveal quite well Gregory's asceticizing hermeneutic. See Katharina Greschat, "Die Verwendung des Physiologus bei Gregor dem Grossen: Paulus als gezähmtes Einhorn in *Moralia in Job XXI*," *Studia Patristica* 43: 381–86. See also Straw, *Perfection in Imperfection*, 52n31.

39. See, for example, Gregory, *Hom. Ez.* 1.8.8.

40. The Christian ascetic tradition was not unlike the classical philosophical schools that sought to develop routines in the way of life that could orient the practitioner in such a way as to achieve self-mastery. For more on the classical philosophical traditions in this respect, see the collective works of Pierre Hadot.

41. For broader discussion of this, see Demacopoulos, *Five Models*, 12–13 and 117–21.

42. I have located only a few exceptions to this pattern, where Gregory does employ the classical model of the four cardinal virtues: Gregory, *Hom. Ez.* 1.3.8; *Mor.* 2.49.76; *Mor.* 22.1.2; *Mor.* 29.31.72; and *Mor.* 35.8.15. In a few of these examples, especially *Mor.* 2.49.76 and *Mor.* 22.1.2, Gregory's discussion of cardinal virtues transitions to an examination of the seven ascetic virtues.

43. For more on the development of the seven deadly sins in medieval thought, see Richard Newhauser and Susan Ridyard, eds., *Sin in Medieval and Early Modern Culture: The Tradition of the Seven Deadly Sins* (York: York Medieval Press, 2013). Note especially the introduction, which surveys recent literature.

44. The ability to preach effectively, of course, is also critical.

45. Gregory, *Mor.* 31.45.87–31.45.91. Gregory is typically understood to be the author who "edited" the lists of vices to seven, removing pride from that list and placing it as the source of all others. One of Gregory's most important sources, Cassian, had previously reconceptualized Evagrius's list of eight *logismoi* (or evil thoughts) as vice (*vitium*). For more on Gregory's understanding of pride as a gateway to vice and sin, see Straw, *Perfection in Imperfection*, 241–47.

46. See, for example, *Mor.* 30.18.58–62 on gluttony.

47. Here, prime examples include Gregory, *Hom. Ez.* 1.11.24; *Mor.* 1.8.10–11; *Mor.* 7.28.34–35; *Mor.* 10.11.20; and *Mor.* 25.9.24. See also the same concern expressed throughout book 3 of the *PR*.

48. Not surprisingly, the theme is particularly acute in book 2 of the *Moralia*, where Gregory discusses the devil's temptation of Job. See *Mor.* 2.18.32; *Mor.* 2.40.65; *Mor.* 2.45.70; and *Mor.* 46.72–73. Gregory argues that God permits the devil to tempt us so that we will learn humility through our falls into sin. In *Hom. Evang.* 33, Gregory briefly notes that the seven demons that Christ casts out of Mary Magdalene represent the seven vices.

49. See Straw, *Perfection in Imperfection*, 125–26 and 137.

50. Examples of how Gregory believes that the vices attack people in different ways include *Mor.* 4.30.57; *Mor.* 6.16.22; and *Mor.* 8.6.9.

51. See, for example, Gregory, *Hom. Ez.* 1.5.3; *Hom. Ez.* 1.5.4; *Hom. Ez.* 1.7.2; and *Mor.* 3.33.65–3.36.69.

52. See Gregory, *Hom. Ez.* 1.8.7; *Hom. Ez.*1.8.8; and *Mor.* 9.25.37.

53. See, for example, Gregory, *Hom. Ez.* 1.5.2; *Mor.* 1.27.38; *Mor.* 22.1.3; *Mor.* 26.28.53; and *Hom. Evang.* 32.

54. Gregory, *Hom. Ez.* 1.10.32–36.

55. Indeed, power itself is problematic in Gregory's eyes because the obedience of others made a human godlike. For a lengthy treatment of the problem of pride and authority, see Gregory, *PR* 1.8–9.

56. This is especially true of John of Constantinople, who appropriated the title "Ecumenical Patriarch," which Gregory thought to be the height of pride. It is also reflected in Gregory's confrontation with the imperial exarch in Ravenna. See George Demacopoulos, "Gregory the Great and the Sixth-Century Dispute over the Ecumenical Title," *Journal of Theological Studies* 70 (2009): 600–21.

57. Gregory's criticism of simony appears in more than fifty of his letters but is especially prevalent in his letters to the civil leaders of Gaul. As we will see in part 3, Gregory occasionally refers to simony as a heresy. See George Demacopoulos, "Gregory the Great and the Pagan Shrines of Kent," *Journal of Late Antiquity* 1 (2008): 353–69.

58. Gregory, *Mor.* 31.1.1.

59. A point well developed by Straw; see *Perfection in Imperfection*, 239–51. A key text not identified by Straw is *PR* 3.17.

60. Among others, Straw offers a detailed analysis of humility as the conceptual partner and antidote to pride. See especially 242–56.

61. "L'humilité est pour lui la première des vertus, la qualité indispensable à tout prédicateur. Si bien que la charge pastorale est définie comme un veritable *magisterium humilitatis*." Dagens, *Saint Grégoire le Grand*, 93. Interestingly, William McReady thinks that the most important virtue for Gregory is charity. Ob-

viously, both virtues have long traditions within ascetic literature, and both reflect Gregory's pastoral (i.e., service-oriented) concerns. See William McReady, *Signs of Sanctity: Miracles in the Thought of Gregory the Great* (Toronto: Pontifical Institute of Medieval Studies, 1989), 69–70.

62. Conrad Leyser, *Authority and Asceticism from Augustine to Gregory the Great* (Oxford: Oxford University Press, 2000), esp. 160–87. For Leyser's extended discussion of the ways in which Gregory's Job reflects authentic humility in contrast to his friends, whose humility is false, see 172–75.

63. For the connection between Cassian and Gregory, see Leyser, "Expertise and Authority in Pope Gregory the Great: The Social Function of *Peritia*," in *Gregory the Great: A Symposium*, ed. John Cavadini (Notre Dame, IN: University of Notre Dame Press, 1995), 38–61; and Demacopoulos, *Five Models*, 137–38. Evagrius's link to Gregory was more indirect and likely came via Cassian.

64. Some of the most substantial treatments include book 23 of the *Moralia*, which offers an extended excursus on the danger of pride, the susceptibility of preachers to it, and the absolute need for preachers to be vigilant against it. *Mor.* 34.23.48–56 offers a lengthy examination as to why pride is so much more dangerous than any of the other vices, how it attacks rulers differently than subjects, and how learning its sources makes the possibility of humility all the stronger. See also *Mor.* 6.16.23–6.18.32 and *Hom. Evang.* 20.

65. Gregory, *Mor.* praef., 9.19; *Mor.* 25.12.29. Many scholars have commented on Gregory's concern for pride, particularly in his discussions of successful pastoral ministry. See, for example, Greschat, *Die* Moralia *in Job Gregors des Großen*, 85–88; Müller, *Führung im Denken*, 135; and Straw, *Perfection in Imperfection*, 239–51.

66. Gregory, *Mor.* 2.1.1.

67. See, for example, Gregory, *Hom. Ez.* 1.4.7 (about David, Paul, and Peter); *Hom. Ez.* 1.7.14 (about David and Peter); *Hom. Ez.* 1.8.2 (about Peter and Mary Magdalene); and *Hom. Ez.* 2.3.6 (about Peter).

68. See George Demacopoulos, *The Invention of Peter* (Philadelphia: University of Pennsylvania Press, 2013), 137–39.

69. For Paul, see Gregory, *Hom. Ez.* 1.4.7; for Benedict, see *Dia.* 2.2; for Job, see *Mor.* 8.1.1.

70. Gregory, *Hom. Evang.* 20.

71. Even though Evagrius and Cassian were both writing for communities of ascetics, they did not stress the "social" dimension of the commandment to love one's neighbor. For a typical expression of Cassian's understanding of humility, see his *Institutes [Institutiones]*, crit. ed., ed. Michael Petschenig (CSEL 17), 12.6–15.

72. Gregory, *Hom. Ez.* 1.9.13.

73. Gregory, *Mor.* 5.37.67; *Mor.* 9.25.39.

74. See Susan Holman, *The Hungry are Dying: Beggars and Bishops in Roman Cappadocia* (Oxford: Oxford University Press, 2001).

75. This is the case because Cassian's final installment of the *Conferences* deemphasizes the importance of the eremitical life and begins to speak positively about providing spiritual assistance to one's neighbor. John Cassian, *Conferences [Conlationes]*, critical ed., ed. Michael Petschenig, CSEL 13. See Demacopoulos, *Five Models*, 124–25. See also Philip Rousseau, *Ascetics, Authority, and the Church in the Age of Jerome and Cassian* (Oxford: Oxford University Press, 1978), 199; and Columba Stewart, *Cassian the Monk* (Oxford: Oxford University Press, 1998), 131–32. For the view that Cassian was disinterested in the outside world, see Peter Munz, "John Cassian," *Journal of Ecclesiastical History* 11 (1960): 1–22, esp. 2–4; and Owen Chadwick, *John Cassian: A Study in Primitive Monasticism* (Cambridge: Cambridge University Press, 1950), esp. 105.

76. Carole Straw, Barbara Müller, and Pietrina Pellegrini all address, each in her own way, what I previously termed as Gregory's "active contemplative."

77. The concept runs through much of Straw's biography of Gregory, *Perfection in Imperfection*, but see especially 248–56.

78. Perhaps the single greatest distinction between my study and Straw's is the attempt to analyze Gregory's activity as bishop through the lens of his theological ideas.

79. In *Mor.* 5.4.5–6, Gregory argues that those who seek a perfect heart through contemplation and mortification are nonetheless called to serve their neighbors. Even though they will personally lose something in the process, it is better for the common good that they do so. What is more, Gregory argues that if contemplative ascetics selfishly guard their time, they will actually miss their own goals because of that selfishness.

80. Gregory, *Hom. Ez.* 1.5.7.

81. Gregory, *Hom. Ez.* 1.7.23.

82. Gregory, *Mor.* 6.34.53.

83. Gregory, *Mor.* 7.24.28.

84. Gregory, *Dia.* 3.15. According to Gregory, the eremitical brother became so accustomed to his performing miracles that he took them for granted and fell into pride.

85. According to Gregory, Benedict did not need a spiritual mentor; he did not spend any time in a monastic "training ground," but instead was a fully functioning renunciant in his youth, perfectly capable of performing miracles. *Dia.* 2.1. See Demacopoulos, *Five Models*, 158–63.

86. In book 4 of the *Dialogues*, the importance of spiritual supervision is taken a step further still, when Gregory extolls the salvific power of the Eucharistic sacrifice, which is, of course, administered by the priest or preacher.

Chapter 2. Fall, Redemption, and the Ascetic's Filter

Portions of the section "Original Sin and the Fall of Adam" in this chapter appeared in a different form in George Demacopoulos, "The Soteriology of St. Gregory the Great: A Case against the Augustinian Interpretation," *American Benedictine Review* 54 (2003): 312–28.

1. Straw, *Perfection in Imperfection*, 128–46.

2. In this context, I would suggest that Straw both neglects to consider other possible interpretations of the Fall that would have been available to Gregory and limits her evidence for this "Augustinian" reading to Gregory's so-called *Responsa*—a series of questions and answers purportedly exchanged between Gregory and his missionaries in Kent, which has come under scrutiny regarding its authenticity. In her preceding chapter (*Perfection in Imperfection*, 107–27), Straw does offer a more nuanced interpretation of Gregory's view of the Fall, indicating some points that differentiate him from Augustine, but retaining Augustinian categories as the determinative possibilities. Concerning Straw's use of the *Responsa* in this context, see 135–36. For the prevailing scholarly view of the status of the authenticity of the *Responsa*, see Paul Meyvaert, "Bede's Text of the *Libellus Responsionum* of Gregory the Great to Augustine of Canterbury," in *England before the Conquest*, ed. Peter Clemoes and Kathleen Hughes (Cambridge: Cambridge University Press, 1971), 15–33; and Ian Wood, "Some Historical Re-identifications and the Christianization of Kent," in *Christianizing Peoples and Converting Individuals*, ed. Guyda Armstrong and Ian Wood (Turnhout: Brepols Press, 2000), 27–35.

3. In her *Die* Moralia in Job *Gregors des Großen* (esp. 79–99), Greschat interprets Gregory's understanding of the Fall and human sin within the general Augustinian framework. More recently, she has argued that Gregory followed Augustine's understanding of the limited potential for secular leadership because of humanity's fallen condition. Katharina Greschat, "Feines Weizenmehl und ungenießbare Spelzen: Gregors des Großen Wertschätzung augustinischer Theologie," *Zeitschrift für antiques Christentum* 11 (2007): 57–72. For additional examples one might look to Dagens's assessment of Loofs's charge of Gregory's supposed "semi-Pelagianism," in which Dagens takes the Augustinian view to be the normative one. Dagens, *Saint Grégoire le Grand*, 272f, 446f; and Friedrich Loofs, *Leitfaden zum Studium der Dogmengeschichte* (Halle-Saale: Niemeyer, 1906).

4. On the possible connection between Augustine's bleak interpretation of the human condition and his Manichean past, see Demacopoulos, *Five Models*, 96–98.

5. Interestingly, Straw argues throughout the section that Gregory was not bound to Augustine's view and that in many ways he followed Cassian's view of the relationship between grace and free will (see esp. *Perfection in Imperfection*, 140). But she consistently projects onto Gregory an Augustinian view of the body. For her, the difference between Gregory and Augustine is located not in their anthropological starting points, but in the "solution" to the human dilemma—Gregory's solution involving ascetic detachment, whereas Augustine's lies in a mysterious healing through grace (see esp. 136).

6. Concerning Gregory's relatively positive assessment (at least in contrast to other late-ancient ascetic authors) of the postlapsarian body, see Gregory, *Hom. Ez.* 2.7.19 and *Mor.* 20.14.28. A more pessimistic note is struck at *Mor.* 8.6.8. For Straw's acknowledgement of these passages in Gregory, see *Perfection in Imperfection*, 126–27 and 141–46.

7. See, among others, Reinhold Seeberg, *Lehrbuch der Dogmengeschichte III: Die Dogmengeschichte des Mittelalters* (Leipzig: A. Deichertsche Verlagsbuchhandlung D. Werner Scholl, 1930), 43; Dudden, *Gregory the Great*, 2:294; Dagens, *Saint Grégoire le Grand*, 271; and Karlmann Beyschlag, *Grundriß der Dogmengeschichte*, vol. 2, *Gott und Mensch*, part 2, *Die abendländische Epoche* (Darmstadt: Wissenschaftliche Buchgesellschaft, 2000), 124f.

8. For an overview of my interpretation of Augustine's thinking on these subjects, see *Five Models*, 100–03; and "Soteriology."

9. Concerning Gregory's identification of death as the punishment of sin, see Ephesians 7:31: "For we say that the first man died in soul in the day that he sinned and that through him the whole human race is condemned in this penalty of death and corruption." See also Gregory, *Mor.* 4.27.54, where he argues that Adam was capable of maintaining immortality but, because of his sin, he and his descendants became subject to death. In *Mor.* 9.33.50, Gregory notes that humanity longs to escape the sentence of death; and in *Mor.* 11.42.58–11.43.59, he described the consequences of the Fall as "the soul being banished from the light of truth, finding itself in darkness." Finally, in *Mor.* 25.3.4, he argues that humanity inherits mortality from Adam: "since we spring from his stock, it is as a shoot to a root."

10. "When we hunger, we eat without sin, though it has come of the sin of the first man that we do hunger. Moreover, the menstruation of women is not at all a sin in itself owing to the fact that it occurs naturally." Gregory, *Responsa*, 8. The *Responsa*—the question-and-answer correspondence between Gregory and Augustine of Canterbury—does not appear in the oldest manuscripts of Gregory's correspondence. For this reason, Dag Norberg did not include them in the critical edition of Gregory's letters. The *Responsa* does survive in Bede, *Ecclesiastical History of the English People [Historia ecclesiatica gentis anglorum]*, crit. ed.,

ed. Bertram Colgrave (Oxford: Clarendon Press, 1969), 1.27. See also *Hom. Ez.* 2.7.19 and *Mor.* 20.14.28.

11. Although Gregory's large corpus contains an array of different (sometimes contradictory) statements about the possible link between procreative sex and sin via lust, his most substantial treatment occurs in *PR* 3.27. Therein, he essentially argues that spiritual directors should try to lead their married disciples to life without sexual activity, even though procreative sex is not in itself sinful. In this context, even though he remains concerned about lust, he advises spiritual directors to emphasize the proper use of sex within marriage. This position, of course, is at odds with Augustine's more pronounced view that procreative sex did entail venial sin and was the trigger for the transmission of original sin from parent to child.

12. "In forsaking the love of God, the true strength of his dignity, man does not remain in himself either because of the desires of the slippery condition of his mutability. . . . And now, in that he is not secured by the steadfastness of his creation, he is ever being made to vary by the fit of alternating desire, so that at rest he longs for action and when busied he pants for rest." Gregory, *Mor.* 8.10.19. See also *Mor.* 26.44.79, *Mor.* 29.8.18, and *Mor.* 34.21.40.

13. Gregory, *Mor.* 34.21.40.

14. See Straw, *Perfection in Imperfection*, 110–11.

15. See Greschat, *Die* Moralia in Job *Gregors des Großen*, esp. 79–99.

16. Gregory, *Mor.* 5.34.61.

17. Gregory, *Hom. Evang.* 16.2–3.

18. Gregory, *Mor.* 8.6.9.

19. Gregory, *Hom. Evang.* 36.

20. He employed it three times in a single paragraph in the *Moralia* (15.51.57) and twice in a letter to Secundius (*Ep.* 9.148).

21. For Augustine, no such distinction was possible because "from the moment, then when 'by one man sin entered into the world, and death by sin, and so death passed upon all men in whom all sinned'[Rom. 5:8] the entire mass of our nature was ruined beyond doubt and fell into the possession of its destroyer." Augustine, *On Original Sin*, 2.34.

22. According to Gregory, infants were damned, not only because they lacked the sacrament of baptism but, more important, because their lives were cut short before they were able to participate in their salvation through good works. "Indeed, not a few are withdrawn from the present light before they demonstrate the good or evil merits of an active life. And because they are not freed (*liberant*) from original sin (*culpa originis*) by the sacrament of salvation nor discharged by their own actions (*et hic ex proprio nil egerunt*), they are brought to torment." Gregory, *Mor.* 9.21.32. In other words, infants die before they are able

to atone for Adam's *culpa* in the manner that the saints of the Old Testament did before the institution of baptism.

23. Augustine, Epistle 6, in the collection of recently discovered letters published as "New Letters," crit. ed., ed. Johannes Divjak (CSEL 88); see also Augustine, *On Marriage and Concupiscence [De nuptiis et concupiscentia]*, crit. ed., ed. C. F. Urba (CSEL 42), 1.20ff. et al. It was the concupiscence associated with the sexual act that transmitted original sin from parent to offspring.

24. Gregory, *PR* 3.27; *Mor.* 32.20.39; *Responsa*, 9. In the *Responsa*, Gregory entertains a question as to whether or not the man who has copulated with his wife must temporarily suspend his reception of the sacraments. Gregory's pastoral response is that priests should not issue strict rules but rather leave it to the judgement of individuals whether or not their sexual relationships were motivated by excessive lust.

25. "When the married have intercourse incontinently [i.e., without procreative intent], they escape a lapse into sin (*lapsus scelerum*), and are saved through mercy. For they find, as it were, a little city wherein they are protected from the fire; since indeed the married life is not known for virtue but is nonetheless secure from punishment." Gregory, *PR* 3.27. In *Mor.* 32.20.39, Gregory is less willing to concede that non-procreative sex is free of sin. Augustine, of course, had argued that non-procreative sex within marriage carried the weight of a venial sin. Augustine, *On Marriage* 1.16–17, 1.27.

26. Gregory, *Mor.* 15.51.57, presents something of a convoluted position on the link between children and their parents. While Gregory says nothing about the physical act of sex being a mechanism for the transmission of guilt, he does hold that that children inherit the "guilt of their parents," a guilt that can only be remedied through baptism. Later in the same paragraph, however, he backpedals by noting that "whoever does not follow in the wickedness of his parents is free of their offences."

27. For an excellent and up-to-date account of the many factors involved, see Alexander Hwang, Brian Matz, and Augustine Casiday, eds., *Grace for Grace: After Augustine and Pelagius* (Washington DC: Catholic University Press, 2012).

28. Demacopoulos, "Soteriology."

29. Gregory, *Hom. Evang.* 3.3.

30. Gregory, *Mor.* 16.25.30. See also *Mor.* 24.10.24, where Gregory puts his participationist position into the mouth of Paul.

31. A small sampling of references includes Gregory, *Hom. Evang.* 11; *Hom. Evang.* 4; *Hom. Ez.* 1.1.15; *Hom. Ez.* 1.3.18; *Hom. Ez.* 1.4.4; *Hom. Ez.* 1.9.2; *Mor.* 25.7.14; *Mor.* 33.17.38–40; and *Dia.* 3.20. In each of these there is a certain reciprocity in view: God gives grace that humans return as free will and

good works. As Straw summarizes, God is, in a sense, ultimately rewarding his own gifts. Straw, *Perfection in Imperfection*, 140, 160.

32. Gregory, *Mor.* 5.36.66.

33. Gregory, *Mor.* 5.36.66. He goes on to suggest that "when we are lifted up in great contemplation we attain a knowledge of the eternal One."

34. In addition to the *Dialogues*, Gregory employed the genre of hagiography in his *Homilies on the Gospels* (e.g., *Hom. Evang.* 39 and 40) and his letters, including *Ep.* 3.50 and 4.30.

35. Gregory, *Hom. Evang.* 31.1; *Mor.* 35.14.28–33.

36. Gregory, *Mor.* 35.14.28.

37. See Demacopoulos, *Five Models*, 144–46.

38. The whole of book 3 of the *PR* presents pastoral guidelines for the instruction of subordinates.

39. Gregory, *Mor.* 24.4.7–8, offers a concise summary of Gregory's outlook on this matter. Here, the pontiff presents the Fall as the event that forces separation between humanity and God by introducing both mortality and carnality. Through the grace of the incarnation and the cultivation of ascetic discipline that it enables, however, humans are able to reunite with God and thereby overcome both carnality and mortality.

Chapter 3. Ecclesiology and the Rhetoric of Episcopal Equality

1. As a consequence, the reader of Gregory's corpus must be ever mindful that the majority of his ecclesiastical statements were crafted for specific rhetorical and narrative purposes and thus introduce the possibility of a gap between what he "wrote" in these specific instances and what he might have "thought" about the same questions in a more abstract way.

2. By *administrative authority* I refer to three aspects of episcopal duty: (1) the selection of clergy, (2) the building and maintaining of churches and their property, and (3) the supervision of the diocesan finances.

3. See Demacopoulos, *Invention of Peter*, esp. ch. 5.

4. Gregory, *Hom. Evang.* 26.5.

5. Cf. Mt. 16:19 and Jn. 20:23.

6. It may, indeed, be for precisely this reason that Caspar's monumental study of the development of the papal idea largely ignored the career of the late-ancient pope with the largest surviving corpus. Eric Caspar, *Geschichte des Papsttums*, 2 vols. (Tubingen: J. C. B. Mohr, 1930–33).

7. Gregory, *Dial.* 1.4.

8. Gregory, *Dial.* 1.4.

9. Interestingly, Gregory partially blames the papal mistake on the distractions of service—a theme frequently repeated in his personal tales of woe.

10. Gregory, *Dial.* 4.42.

11. For a summary of the schism and lasting effects it had on the "instruments" of papal memory, see Demacopoulos, *Invention of Peter*, ch. 3.

12. Gregory, *Dial.* 4.42.

13. That Symmachus was "unanimously" accepted by both parties is an irenic fiction, possibly of Gregory's making, since it is not contained in *Liber Pontificalis* or in any of the other surviving propagandist tracts from the period.

14. To be sure, Gregory seeks to emphasize the power of prayer and alms—Paschasius's mistake was one of ignorance, which can be easily overcome, so much so that the good deeds and the prayers of others can lead to miracles.

15. Gregory, *Dial.* 4.42.

16. Indeed, is Paschasius's crime that he failed to recognize Symmachus or that he failed to recognize the authority of the electors who, according to Gregory, ultimately selected Symmachus unanimously?

17. Concerning the former, Gregory repeatedly defended the rights of monasteries to select their own abbots, preserve their property against episcopal seizure, and refuse an episcopal chair in their churches. See, for example, Gregory, *Ep.* 5.49, 6.24, 6.46, 7.12, 7.40, 8.32, and 13.10. Indeed, of the more than fifty occasions when Gregory adjudicated a matter that pitted an ascetic community against clerical or lay rivals, he found in favor of the ascetic community in every case. See Demacopoulos, *Five Models*, 150–53.

18. Although Gregory believed that Roman jurisdiction in the area to have been ancient and consistent (see *Ep.* 5.39), its history is more complicated. See Brian Daley, "Position and Patronage in the Early Church: The Original Meaning of the 'Primacy of Honour,'" *Journal of Theological Studies* 44 (1993): 429–53, at 539.

19. See Jeffrey Richards, *Popes and the Papacy in the Early Middle Ages* (London: Routledge and Kegan Paul, 1979), 317–18.

20. Gregory, *Ep.* 5.6, 5.39. See also Demacopoulos, "Ecumenical Title," esp. 606–7.

21. See Gregory, *Ep.* 5.6, 5.39, 6.3, and 6.25. See also Demacopoulos, "Ecumenical Title."

22. Gregory, *Ep.* 6.3. Dogmatically speaking, simony is not a heresy; it is a breach of moral conduct that undermines the integrity of the hierarchal structure of the Church.

23. Gregory, *Ep.* 6.25.

24. Gregory, *Ep.* 6.26.

25. Gregory, *Ep.* 6.25.

26. Gregory, *Ep.* 5.27 and 6.25.

27. For more on the way in which Gregory employed the topos of Petrine authority as leverage in his diplomatic efforts, see Demacopoulos, *Invention of Peter*, ch. 5.

28. See, especially, Demacopoulos, "Ecumenical Title." See also Demacopoulos, *Invention of Peter*, ch. 4, and "Gregory the Great and a Post-Imperial Discourse," in *Power and Authority in the Eastern Christian Experience*, ed. Fevronia K. Soumakis (New York: Theotokos Press, 2011), 120–37.

29. See Demacopoulos, "Ecumenical Title."

30. Note, for example, Gregory's assertion to the emperor (*Ep.* 5.37) that John is claiming the honor of all priests for himself ("sed absit a christianis cordibus nomen istud blasphemiae in quo omnium sacerdotum honor adimitur, dum ab uno sibi dementer arrogatur").

31. Gregory, *Ep.* 5.44.

32. Gregory, *Ep.* 5.44.

33. See, especially, Gregory, *Ep.* 5.41, 6.61, 7.24, and 7.37. Gregory was more effective with Eulogius of Alexandria than he was with Anastasius of Antioch, who essentially told Gregory that the title was a non-issue and it would be best if he just dropped the matter entirely. See *Ep.* 7.24.

34. Gregory, *Ep.* 5.37, 5.39, 5.41, 5.44, and 7.24.

35. Gregory, *Ep.* 5.37.

36. Gregory, *Ep.* 7.37.

37. To be sure, Gregory offers other arguments as well (e.g., that John is imitating the devil in his pride or that security of the empire rests upon the good conduct of leading bishops) but those arguments offer even less insight into Gregory's ecclesiological convictions.

38. Near the beginning of Gregory's tenure as pope, two Eastern clerics — John, a priest from Chalcedon, and Athanasius, a priest-monk from Isauria — were found guilty of heresy by another local synod in Constantinople. Both clerics traveled to Rome to appeal their case before Gregory. He agreed to intervene and, through his legate in Constantinople, Sabinianus, attempted to solicit from John the acts of the trial and an explanation of what had transpired. John responded to Gregory's inquiries by claiming that he had no knowledge of the case — an assertion that was not well received in Rome. So, in July 593, Gregory reproached John's intransigence. According to Gregory, John was either ignorant of what was taking place in his own church, or he was dismissing the request in a bid to assert his sovereignty. If the former was true, then the patriarch was unfit for office; if the latter was true, which is what Gregory suspected, it confirmed the pope's suspicions that his friend had let the corruptive power of

episcopal office get the better of him. From Gregory's perspective, the accused clerics deserved a fresh trial; if John was not going to provide one, then it was within the pope's jurisdiction to conduct it himself in Rome. See Demacopoulos, "Ecumenical Title," 604–6.

39. One could, of course, argue that his involvement in Sicily and his interference in an episcopal election in Milan were both de facto expansions of Roman authority.

Chapter 4. Some Mystical Attributes of Gregory's Ascetic Theology

1. However much God revealed himself through Scripture, he and his activity were only partially known and rarely understood. That God was active in the world was clear to Gregory, but he firmly believed that divine activity was often encoded through symbols and in need of interpretation. See Demacopoulos, "Gregory the Great," in *Spiritual Senses*.

2. Concerning the criticism of Gregory, see discussion above as it relates to the criticisms of Harnack, Gibbon, Dudden, Clark, and others. Of course, not all Gregory scholars have condemned the *Dialogues*. The two most positive interpreters of the twentieth century were Straw and, especially, McReady.

3. Too many scholars have either bracketed the *Dialogues* in their appraisal of Gregory's thought or lowered their estimation of Gregory's sophistication on the basis of their scrutiny of the *Dialogues*. While the *Dialogues* may not conform to typical standards of post-Enlightenment theological discourse, it is simply irresponsible to discount them as irrelevant or unsophisticated. A few notable exceptions to this trend would be Matthew Dal Santo, "Gregory the Great and Eustrathios of Constantinople: The *Dialogues on the Miracles of the Italian Fathers* as an Apology for the Cult of the Saints," *Journal of Early Christian Studies* 17 (2009): 421–57; Lorenzo Saraceno, "*Scriptura crescit cum legente:* Un Paradigma anche per l'agiografo? Una rilettura del II libro dei *Dialoghi* di Gregorio Magno," in *Gregorio Magno e L'Agiografia fra IV e VII Secolo*, ed. Antonella Degl'Innocenti, Antonio De Prisco, and Emore Paoli, 229–43; and Guy Philippart, "Grégoire le Grand et les *gesta martyrum*," in *Gregorio Magno e L'Agiografia fra IV e VII Secolo*, ed. Degl'Innocenti, De Prisco, and Paoli, 257–83.

4. The fact that many of these narratives are repeated in the *Homilies on the Gospels* and even in his correspondence further attests to their prominence within Gregory's outlook.

5. In his *Athanasius and the Politics of Asceticism* (Repr.: Baltimore: Johns Hopkins Press, 1998), David Brakke demonstrates how Athanasius was able to use the life of Anthony as a vehicle for the bishop's own theological and ideological concerns. In Gregory's case, let us not forget that the *Dialogues* and the

Moralia (presumably the most sophisticated treatise in Gregory's corpus) were narrated for similar monastic audiences.

6. In the opening pages of his treatment, McReady groups Gregorian scholars into two categories: those who read the *Dialogues* at face value and therefore question the ultimate sophistication of their author, and those who discount Gregory's claim's to factual veracity and instead see him emphasizing the moral and spiritual significance of the tales. See McReady, *Signs*, 2. Several examples (Gibbon, Harnack, Wallace-Hadrill, etc.) of the first category were noted in the opening pages of the chapter. Added to these could be Batiffol, who suggested that the *Dialogues* were a *City of God* "written for the simple," and Dudden, who is utterly perplexed by someone who could so ably manage the papal estates but simultaneously perpetuate such superstition. Pierre Batiffol, *Saint Gregory the Great*, trans. John Stoddard (London, 1929), 181–82; Dudden, *Gregory the Great*, 1:295 and 356. For an example of the second category, see W. F. Bolton, "The Super-Historical Sense in the Dialogues of Gregory I," *Aevum* 33 (1959): 206–13. Concerning McReady's defense of Gregory's belief in miracles, see especially 110–76, where he considers twenty-three different episodes in the *Dialogues* that might constitute a literary invention on Gregory's part, before launching into a protracted investigation of whether or not Gregory would have understood the creation of a pious fiction to constitute a lie.

7. To be fair, McReady does recognize the pedagogical value of miracles in Gregory's discussion of them and distinguishes Gregory's use of them, by way of comparison, to John Cassian (who notes in the opening lines of the *Institutes* that he is going to pass over the miracles attributed to the Egyptian fathers so as to emphasize their teaching with respect to monastic discipline). McReady, *Signs*, 102; cf. Cassian, *Institutiones*, pref.

8. For an alternative interpretative approach, see Saraceno, who interprets book 2 of the *Dialogues* (the *Life of Benedict*) as an extended exegetic exercise. Saraceno, "*Scriptura crescit cum Legente*."

9. Gregory, *Dial.* 1.1. Gregory narrates the story of a young man who lived with his parents in a mountainous region of Italy. Through a miracle, the man is able to obtain fish (otherwise unavailable) so that he can fast from the meat that his parents serve to their dinner guests.

10. Specifically, it ridicules the saint's parents, who think it foolish that he refuses to eat meat.

11. Gregory, *Dial.* 1.4 attests to a miracle that enabled a monk to free himself from lust; *Dial.* 3.16 places a miracle in the service of protecting a monk's chastity; and *Dial.* 3.33 offers a rare autobiographical account in which Gregory claims that he was the recipient of a miracle that enabled him to fast more rigorously than his weak health would have otherwise enabled in the days before Easter.

12. The two (i.e., asceticism and spiritual growth) are not mutually exclusive but rather mutually reinforcing. For an examination of the similarities between Pope Gregory's use of the miraculous and that of Gregory of Tours, see Giuseppi Cremascoli, "Il Miracolo Nell'agriografia di Gregorio Magno e di Gregorio di Tours," in *Gregorio Magno e L'Agiografia fra IV e VII Secolo*, ed. Degl'Innocenti, De Prisco, and Paoli, 246–56.

13. On the ambivalent presentation of the Lombards in the Dialogues, see Gregory, *Dial.* 3.27, 3.28, 3.37, and 4.22–24.

14. Indeed, many of the stories recounted in book 4 of the *Dialogues* detail the various ways in which the saints visit people after their death. In Gregory's presentation, holy men and women who are still living can frequently converse with reposed saints through miraculous visions. One possible implication of this literary presentation is that the loss of divine contemplation and communion that occurred with the Fall is overcome by the life of sanctity, which is rooted in the purity of heart.

15. See Gregory, *Ep.* 8.29. Of course, Gregory also warned Augustine that he not let the ability to perform miracles become a source of pride. See *Ep.* 11.36.

16. See, for example, Gregory, *Hom. Evang.* 29.4; *Mor.* 27.11.20–21; *Mor.* 30.2.6; and *Hom. Evang.* 4.3. See also McReady, *Signs*, 35–37.

17. Some examples of apostolic miracles in Gregory's *Moralia* include *Mor.* 9.10.11, 27.18.36, and 31.2.2.

18. Gregory, *Hom. Evang.* 29.4.

19. Gregory, *Hom. Evang.* 29.4.

20. Gregory, *Mor.* 30.2.6.

21. Gregory has an important discussion in *Dial.* 1.4 about the link between the ability to perform miracles, the purity of a saint's life, and the saint's preaching of the gospel. Gregory argues, in fact, that both the purity and the preaching are more important than the ability to perform miracles. It is these qualities, Gregory reasons, and not "signs" (i.e., miracles) that enable the saints to govern the souls of others so well. The same idea is repeated at the end of *Dial.* 1.12.

22. See McReady, *Signs*, 67–68.

23. See Demacopoulos, *Five Models*, 123–24.

24. Gregory, *Dial.* 1.pref.

25. Gregory, *Dial.* 1.pref.

26. Sulpicius Severus, *Vita S. Martini* 1.6–9 (SC 133:252–54); Palladius, *Historia Lausiaca*, crit. ed, ed. Cuthbert Butler (Cambridge: Cambridge University Press, 1904), prologue; etc.

27. Gregory, *Hom. Ez.* 1.10.31–39. Here, too, Gregory holds that the study of the saints teaches humility because we inevitably compare ourselves to them and, in doing so, learn of our deficiencies. See also *Hom. Ez.* 2.5.21.

28. Gregory, *Dial.* 1.9. See also *Mor.* Praef.6.14 and *Mor.* Praef.7.16, where Job is presented as a type of "redeemer" on the model of Christ.

29. In book 1 Gregory submits that even though Peter performed many more miracles than Paul, they are "brothers in the apostolic college" and "have an equal share in the rewards of heaven." *Dial.* 1.12.

30. This is particularly surprising because it was during the sixth century, especially, that papal biography became one of the primary vehicles by which papal actors and their supporters advanced their particular causes. See Demacopoulos, *Invention of Peter*, esp. ch. 4. The *Dialogues* offer brief accounts of three popes (Felix III, John I, and Agapetus), and the miracles associated with two of them are attributed to the intercession of St. Peter. See *Dial.* 4.17, 3.2, and 3.3 respectively. What is more, the *Dialogues* also include the case of St. Equitius, who is said to have been persecuted by members of the papal administration, and Gregory's narration implies that the pope at the time was susceptible to pride. Gregory, *Dial.* 1.4. See McReady, *Signs*, 88. See also Adalbert de Vogüé, "Le pape qui persécuta saint Equitius. Essai d'identification," *Annolecta Bollandiana* 100 (1982): 319–25; and Joan Petersen, *The Dialogues of Gregory the Great in their Late Antique Cultural Background* (Toronto: Pontifical Institute for Medieval Studies, 1984), 79 (she maintains that the pope in question is John III, whereas de Vogüé believes that it was Agapetus).

31. Müller notes Gregory's willingness to speak of Peter's weakness in the *Homilies on the Gospels* as strategy of pastoral encouragement, but she does not connect it to any specific theological commitment or examples elsewhere in Gregory's corpus. See Müller, *Führung im Denken*, 157–58.

32. On this score we have literally dozens of examples. Some of the more noteworthy ones include Gregory, *Hom. Ez.* 1.4.7; *Hom. Ez.* 2.8.21; *Mor.* 3.20.38; *Hom. Evang.* 9.3; *Hom. Evang.* 21.4; *Hom. Evang.* 25.9–10; *Hom. Evang.* 26.7; and *Hom. Evang.* 33.

33. See, especially, Gregory, *Hom. Evang.* 25.9–10, which is primarily concerned with the example of Mary Magdalene's repentance, but includes the additional examples of Peter, David, and the thief.

34. According to Gregory, this is because Thomas's return to faith (after doubt) offers consolation to the mind that doubts—thereby supporting belief in a way that pious example alone cannot. Gregory, *Hom. Evang.* 26.7.

35. See, for example, Gregory, *Hom. Evang.* 24. The more thorough account of Gregory's understanding of relics belongs to John McCulloh, "The Cult of Relics in the Letters and 'Dialogues' of Pope Gregory the Great," *Traditio* 32 (1976): 145–84. See also Straw, *Perfection in Imperfection*, 54–58.

36. See Demacopoulos, *Invention of Peter*, ch. 5.

37. See Demacopoulos, *Invention of Peter*, ch. 5.

38. In a sense, the remains of the saints both represent and point toward the purpose of the physical world. For a thorough analysis of Gregory's eschatology, see Kisić, *Patria Caelestis.*

39. Gregory offers several accounts of negative consequences of tampering with or not sufficiently respecting the relics or shrines of the saints. See, for example, Gregory, *Dial.* 1.4, 1.10, and 3.22.

40. Gregory's distributions of Petrine relics were not actual bones of St. Peter. Instead, they typically consisted of pieces of cloth that came into contact with Peter's shrine or the supposed "filings" of metal chains that had bound St. Peter. Both the cloth and the filings were often inserted into small keys and distributed as talismans, which were to be worn by their owner. See, for example, *Ep.* 6.6. In June of 594 Gregory wrote to the Roman empress, Constantina, denying her request for the head of St. Paul (or some other body part from the saint). According to Gregory, he is afraid to approach the body of St. Paul in this way because it has performed so many miracles, even miracles designed to keep patrons away from their shrines. Gregory instructs the empress that it is not the custom of Roman Christians to dismember and distribute the bones of the saints. Gregory, *Ep.* 4.30.

41. Dal Santo, "Gregory the Great and Eustrathios of Constantinople."

42. Dal Santo, "Gregory the Great and Eustrathios of Constantinople." See, especially, 440–42.

43. Dal Santo, "Gregory the Great and Eustrathios of Constantinople," 435.

44. Gregory, *Dial.* 3.3.

45. Gregory, *Dial.* 3.17.

46. Gregory, *Dial.* 3.30.

47. Gregory, *Dial.* 1.10. It is worth noting that Gregory's *Responsa* suggests that, while it is not ideal, it is not sinful to receive the Eucharist the morning after intercourse. Even allowing for the "pastoral" and "economic" nature of the *Responsa,* it is difficult to see how the two accounts can be reconciled.

48. Gregory, *Dial.* 4.57–59.

49. Gregory, *Mor.* Praef.8.17–18.

50. Gregory, *Mor.* 2.35.57.

Part Two

1. Gregory, *PR*, prol. Müller considers the intriguing possibility that the text was addressed to John of Constantinople ("John the Faster") rather than John of Ravenna, an idea initially proposed by Erich Caspar. Müller, *Führung im Denken,* 119–23; and Caspar, *Geschichte des Papsttums,* 365.

2. Gregory, *Ep.* 5.53.

3. More than six hundred manuscripts (an astonishing number) survive in libraries from Madrid to Moscow. Not only did Gregory's blueprint set the foundation for the medieval understanding of spiritual direction, it was also cited as a model for civic leadership in the ninth century by Alfred the Great, who was responsible for the translation and circulation of the text in England. See Demacopoulos, *Five Models*, 130–39 and 165–67.

4. Gregory served as godfather to the emperor's oldest son, Theodosius, when the child was baptized in 584, six years prior to Gregory's election as pope.

5. In the modern setting, "pastoral care" is typically understood to mean the act of offering comfort (whether emotional, physical, or spiritual) through acts of listening, advising, and simply being present for others in their times of need. In contrast, "spiritual direction" refers to active guidance in the progress toward spiritual enlightenment and is typically reflective of an ongoing spiritual teacher–spiritual student relationship.

6. Indeed, Gregory repeatedly uses the Latin phrase *cura pastoralis*, "care of souls," when referring to the act of spiritual direction. See, for example, *Ep.* 5.53a, where he laments the difficulty associated with leadership of others.

7. For a brief analysis of the continuities and discontinuities between Gregory's text and those that preceded it, see Demacopoulos, introduction to *St. Gregory the Great: The Book of Pastoral Rule*, trans. Demacopoulos (Crestwood, NY: St. Vladimir's Seminary Press, 2007).

8. For a detailed analysis of the *Pastoral Rule*, particularly the extent to which it encapsulates Gregory's ascetic interests, see Demacopoulos, *Five Models*, 130–39.

9. For his part, Leyser refers to the text as offering a baseline that is "as close as we may come to Gregory's centre of gravity as a writer and thinker." But, characteristic to his concerns, Leyser focuses exclusively on the extent to which the text offers a formulation of Gregory's view of authority; he does not engage the pastoral and theological aspects of the text in their own right. Leyser, *Authority and Asceticism*, 140.

10. For the most extensive assessment of the pastoral considerations of the *Moralia*, see Greschat, *Die* Moralia in Job *Gregors des Großen*.

11. See, for example, books 28, 29, and 30. Here, as elsewhere, Gregory's ideas, concerns, and examples reflect his ascetic theology and his desire to recruit experienced and administratively competent ascetics into the offices of "preaching," "teaching," and "ruling."

12. Gregory, *Hom. Ez.* 1.12.10 offers a prime example of a recurring pattern in Gregory's commentary in which he argues that the prophets say x so that preachers will do y. In this particular example, Gregory argues that "preachers"

will know what to say in order to correct the behavior of their disciples. Another example, which similarly identifies the words of Scripture as a source for preachers to correct their disciples, is provided at *Hom. Ez.* 2.1.10.

13. *Sacerdos* is used nineteen times, *praedicator* twenty-one times, and *pastor* nineteen times.

14. See, especially, Wilhelm Gessel, "Reform am Haupt: Die Pastoralregel Gregors des Grossen und die Besetzung von Bischofsstühlen," in *Papsttum und Kirchenreform: Historische Beiträge. Festschrift für Georg Schwaiger zum 65. Geburtstag*, ed. Manfred Weitlauff and Karl Hausberger (St. Ottilien: EOS Verlag, 1990), 17–36. See also Robert Markus, "Gregory the Great's 'rector' and its Genesis," in *Grégoire le Grand*, ed. Jacques Fontaine, Robert Gillet, and Stan Pellistrandi (Paris: Éditions du Centre National de la Recherche Scientifique, 1986), 137–45.

15. Although Müller has a more accurate sense for the flexibility in Gregory's terminology, as well as his sense for the variety of persons who might engage in spiritual leadership, she also understands the *Pastoral Rule* to be a bishop's manual for executive leadership. See Müller, *Führung im Denken*, especially 2, 58, and 125–29.

16. Among other things, Gregory first developed the long list of personality traits set in opposition to one another, which is the subject of part 3 of the *Pastoral Rule*, during his preparation of the *Moralia*. In general, it is impossible to know what elements of the *Moralia* were original to Constantinople and what was added through the editorial process after Gregory had become bishop of Rome.

17. Examples include *Ep.* 10.18 and 11.54, which offer specific suggestions for the incorporation of additional monastic houses under the authority of the abbots to whom the letters are addressed. In most cases these acts were precipitated by monastic desertion caused by war. Some examples of Gregory's rebuke of an abbot's pastoral decisions include *Ep.* 1.12, 6.44, and 10.9.

18. The first line of Gregory's *Pastoral Rule* defines spiritual direction as an "art" (*ars*). *PR* 1.1. The passage, no doubt, is reminiscent of Gregory Nazianzen's *Orationes* 2, which defines spiritual direction as the "art of arts."

Chapter 5. The Importance of Spiritual Leadership

1. Near the end of his life, Michel Foucault became fascinated with the idea of truth telling and the practice in the ancient world in which truth telling was facilitated by the speaking of truth about oneself to another (whether that other was a teacher, a guide, a friend, or some other companion). Foucault's final lectures provide considerable (albeit occasionally imprecise) detail about this ancient

practice. See Michel Foucault, *The Hermeneutics of the Subject: Lectures at the Collège de France 1981–1982*, trans. Graham Burchell (New York: Picador, 2005); *The Government of Self and Others: Lectures at the Collège de France 1982–1983*, trans. Graham Burchell (New York: Picador, 2010); and *The Courage of Truth: Lectures at the Collège de France 1983–1984*, trans. Graham Burchell (New York: Picador, 2011).

2. As Pierre Hadot has observed, the philosophical dialogue that occurred in the Socratic schools (and elsewhere) was a "spiritual exercise" intended for the improvement of the self. The philosopher, according to Hadot, would harness all of his rhetorical resources, not so much to supply an exhaustive explanation of reality as to enable his disciples to orient themselves to their world in a way that would bring assurance and peace to the soul. See, for example, Pierre Hadot, "Forms of Life and Forms of Discourse in Ancient Philosophy," *Philosophy as a Way of Life: Spiritual Exercises from Socrates to Foucault*, trans. Michael Chase (Oxford: Blackwell, 1995), 49–77, esp. 63–64.

3. As all students of Christian history are aware, the consolidation of authority in the episcopate and even the episcopate's gradual centralization were two of the most important ecclesiological developments of the early Christian era.

4. For an alternative account, see Aelred Niespolo, who proffers that Gregory's commitment to service was derived from his theological interpretations of the incarnation and the Fall. Not only does Niespolo ignore the Greco-Roman traditions of public service, he also fails to account for the ascetic dimensions of Gregory's commitment to service. Aelred Niespolo, "Authority and Service in Gregory the Great," *Downside Review* 122 (2004): 113–28.

5. A monk's advisor was not always his abbot, and by the sixth century it was still quite possible that he would not have been a member of the clergy. Typically, advisor and advisee communicated regularly; the novice confessed his sins to his mentor, while the mentor encouraged, taught, and reprimanded the novice as necessary. A fuller discussion of this phenomenon exists in Demacopoulos, *Five Models*, 9–13. The premier study of the role of the spiritual father in ascetic culture is still Irénée Hausherr, *Spiritual Direction in the Early Christian East*, trans. Anthony Gythiel (Kalamazoo, MI: Cistercian Publications, 1990). See also John Chryssavgis, *Soul Mending: The Art of Spiritual Direction* (Brookline, MA: Holy Cross Orthodox Press, 2000), esp. 49–58.

6. I believe that Müller misdirects her investigation of the link between Gregory's *Pastoral Rule* and the monastic rules of her day. By focusing almost exclusively on whether or not Gregory perceived his *Pastoral Rule* to be a kind of monastic rule for the lay church, she does not sufficiently reflect upon the numerous similarities of style and ideology between Gregory's text and the ascetic traditions of his age. Müller, *Führung im Denken*, 142–44.

7. On the link between Cicero and episcopal activity, Ambrose of Milan likely served as an important precedent. Ambrose's *De Officiis* directly sought to recast Cicero's public servant as a bishop

8. Here, too, there are both classical and Christian precedents. The pioneering work of Hadot, who teaches us that classical "philosophy was a way of life," is the starting point for any comparison between the classical and Christian traditions.

9. Gregory, *Mor.* 22.7.16. Not surprisingly, as the analogy develops Gregory emphasizes the importance of ascetic works and the damage that can be done by pride.

10. Gregory, *Hom. Ez.* 2.2.3.

11. Any spiritual progress, in fact, will likely induce pride. See, for example, his treatment in *PR* 3.19 of the way that a priest should counsel those who frequently fast.

12. Examples abound, but see Gregory, *PR* 1.2; *Hom. Ez.* 1.12.30–33; and *Dial.* 4.37.

13. See, for example, Gregory, *Mor.* 1.14.20. Whereas most ascetically-inclined authors of late antiquity differentiate between celibates and married or monks and lay, Gregory envisions a world of three "orders of faithful" (*tres ordines fidelium*): spiritual leaders, celibates, and married—with the first being the most challenging, deflating, and important. For her own assessment of how Gregory handles this three-tiered taxonomy, see Pellegrini, *Militia Clericatus Monachici Ordines*, 41–48. See also Georges Folliet, "Les Trois categories de chrétiens, survie d'un theme augustinien," *L'Année théologique augustinienne* 14 (1954): 81–96.

14. The passage stems from Gregory's prefatory to the *Moralia*, which he sent to Leander of Seville in 595. The letter has been transmitted both as a prologue to the *Moralia* and as *Ep.* 5.53a (not to be confused with *Ep.* 5.53, which is the cover letter for Gregory's sending of the *Pastoral Rule* to Leander).

15. Gregory, *Ep.* 5.53a.

16. Gregory, *Ep.* 5.53a. In the letter, Gregory speaks of the active prayer life of his ascetic companions as a kind of lifeline that allowed him to complete his secular responsibilities without abandoning his spiritual pursuits.

17. Although she does not consider this possibility, Greschat does offer a helpful framework for Gregory's situation in Constantinople. Greschat, *Die Moralia in Job Gregors des Großen*, 23–30.

18. Again, see Gregory, *Ep.* 5.53a, especially section 1. For her part, Greschat has argued that Job served as a perfect vehicle for Gregory to emphasize simultaneously the monastic desire to flee from the world and the pastoral responsibility

to work within it. Greschat, "Feines Weizenmehl und ungenießbare Spelzen." In her broader examination of the same themes in her monograph, *Die* Moralia in Job *Gregors des Großen*, Greschat emphasizes the extent to which Gregory allegorizes Job's life to the life of Christ in order to provide a model for preachers to develop a proper active/contemplative balance.

19. For an extended explanation of why the order of preachers is necessary, see Gregory, *Mor.* 9.4.6–9.8.8.

20. Gregory, *Mor.* 6.37.56. Gregory supplements his arguments with a long list of biblical examples, including Abraham, Moses, Peter, and Paul.

21. Some of the lengthier references include Gregory, *Mor.* 1.14.20; *Mor.* 25.16.39–40; *Mor.* 32.20.35; *Hom. Ez.* 2.4.5; and *Hom. Ez.* 2.7.3.

22. That it does not come into effect until the apostles, see Gregory, *Mor.* 1.14.20. In this particular instance, the three categories are shepherds (*pastor*), celibates, and married.

23. For example, in *Mor.* 1.14.20 Gregory uses *pastor*, but in *Hom. Ez.* 2.4.5 he uses *praedicator*. In both cases the celibates are designated as *continentium* and the married as *coniugum*.

24. For more on Gregory's restrictions against a married priesthood, see Demacopoulos, *Five Models*, 145–46.

25. Gregory, *Hom. Ez.* 2.4.5. See also *Hom. Ez.* 2.7.3. Leyser, drawing on Folliet, argues that Gregory appropriated the three-tiered taxonomy from Augustine for the very purpose of replacing it with a bifurcation between preachers (*ordo praedicantium*) and listeners (*multitude audientium*). Leyser, *Authority and Asceticism*, 156–57.

26. Even though that text clearly reflects its author's contention that a priest who willingly suspends his own contemplation for the sake of his neighbor is superior to the ascetic who selfishly protects his own spiritual interests. See Gregory, *PR* 1.5–6.

Chapter 6. The Recruitment of Leaders

1. Gregory presents both men as able to perform ascetic feats in their youth. Then, without any personal training, the two saints build monasteries, perform miracles, and shepherd a large number of monks who come to them for spiritual guidance. The story of St. Honoratus is contained in *Dial.* 1.1; the life of St. Benedict occupies the entirety of book 2.

2. Gregory, *Dial.* 1.1.

3. For Plato, the only one who can be trusted to be king is the one who does not want to be king, because anyone who wants to be king will govern in

such a way as to secure his own position rather than in a way that is best for the community. Thus, for Plato, only the philosopher should be king, because the philosopher desires only what is true and good.

4. I have analyzed the ascetic dimensions of Gregory's *Pastoral Rule* elsewhere, including *Five Models*, 131–34; and *Pastoral Rule*, 14–17.

5. Gregory, *PR* 1.10.

6. Gregory, *PR* 1.11.

7. Gregory, *PR* 1.11.

8. Note, for example, the prevalence of the discussion in John Cassian's *Conferences* (especially book 10) and *Institutes* (especially book 5).

9. See Demacopoulos, *Five Models* 7–9, 132. See also Cassian, *Conference* 2; Benedict, *Rule* 2.

10. Gregory, *Dial.* 1.4 and 2.4.

11. Gregory, *Dial.* 1.2.

12. In many ways, Gregory's presentation of Job is, in fact, an extended excursus on this theme. Of course, he also presents other ascetic-credentialed biblical figures as paragons of leadership, such as St. Paul. See *Mor.* 18.54.89–90.

13. Gregory, *Mor.* 1.34.48–1.35.49. We might compare this passage to any number of the letters of the Egyptian ascetic Ammonas.

14. Gregory, *Mor.* 5.4.5.

15. Gregory, *Mor.* 14.35.42ff offers an example of Gregory's acknowledgment that not all who possess the title "priest" (*sacerdotes*) rightly possess the qualifications needed for effective leadership.

16. In other words, Gregory frequently presents humility as something that accompanies successful preaching (e.g., *Mor.* 19.23.37) and pride as something that will prevent it (*Mor.* 23.11.20–21). The holy man who mixes with sinners for the benefit of leading them to sanctity will gradually eradicate pride in others without learning it for himself (*Mor.* 24.22.49–24.23.50).

17. Gregory, *Mor.* 24.23.50.

18. Gregory, *Mor.* 21.20.32.

19. Gregory, *PR* 1.5.

20. Gregory, *PR* 1.5.

21. Gregory, *PR* 1.5.

22. See Demacopoulos, *Five Models*, 133. Relying almost exclusively on the *Dialogues* and correspondence, Pellegrini argues that Gregory understood there to be a rather firm dividing line between the clergy who served the administrative church and the monks who lived under the rule of a monastic community. Only under certain situations and for sacramental necessity were monks permitted into the ranks of the clergy, and even then they were only permitted to cele-

brate the sacraments within the monastic community. This is an important observation of the way that Gregory's terminology functions in these two texts, but it is significant to note that monks were routinely called by Gregory into the clerical orders in order to serve the broader community of Christians. Pellegrini, *Milita Clericatus Monachici Ordines*, esp. 298.

23. Gregory, *PR* 1.6.

24. Gregory, *Mor.* 6.34.53.

25. Gregory, *Mor.* 30.13.48. Pursuing a slightly different approach earlier in the *Moralia*, Gregory notes that even those ascetics who do not wish to be involved in ministry will sometimes be mysteriously directed by God to serve others against their own will. Gregory, *Mor.* 5.4.5–6.

26. Gregory, *Mor.* 6.38.61.

27. Gregory, *Hom. Ez.* 1.3.9–13.

28. Gregory, *Hom. Ez.* 2.2.9–10.

29. Gregory, *Hom. Ez.* 2.2.10.

30. See, for example, *Mor.* 5.4.5, where Gregory suggests that ascetics who sacrifice their contemplation for earthly endeavors offer an example of humility; and *Mor.* 19.25.45, which reflects the pontiff's vision that the combination of activity and contemplation produces a positive result.

31. See, for example, Gregory, *Hom. Ez.* 1.5.7; *Hom. Ez.* 1.7.23; *Hom. Ez.* 1.9.4; and *Hom. Evang.* 6, which argues that it is selfish to withhold the gifts that God has bestowed.

32. Gregory, *Hom. Ez.* 2.1.7; *Hom. Ez.* 2.7.5.

33. As noted, dating for the *Moralia* is complicated. The original sermons were delivered prior to Gregory's election, but his distribution of the text to colleagues seems to have occurred in 595.

34. Gregory, *Hom. Ez.* 1.10.31.

35. Gregory, *Hom. Ez.* 2.7.12.

36. Gregory, *Hom. Ez.* 2.9.20. This would seem to contradict the first paragraph of the *Pastoral Rule*, in which Gregory suggests that no one is able to teach an art that he has not previously mastered through study. *PR* 1.1.

37. In most cases, of course, ascetic hagiography was designed to project a particular vision of ascetic behavior or ascetic theology. But saints' lives, even of the desert ascetics, could be crafted with other purposes as well. See, for example, David Brakke's important discussion of Athanasius's portrayal of Anthony as reinforcing the bishop's specific theological and ecclesiological concerns. Brakke, *Athanasius and the Politics of Asceticism*, esp. ch. 4.

38. Although she does not address this particular aspect of Gregory's concern or its presence in his narrative of Benedict, Müller also believes that the

Dialogues reveal a great deal about Gregory's ideas and ideals concerning leadership. Müller, *Führung im Denken*, 228–48.

39. See, for example, Gregory, *Dial.* 1.1 and *Dial.* 3.15.

40. See, for example, Gregory, *Mor.* 27.24.44–45 and *Mor.* 30.2.8.

Chapter 7. The Tasks of the Spiritual Leader

1. On the comparison to Nazianzen and Augustine, see Demacopoulos, *Five Models*, 168.

2. Only *rector* (crudely translated as "ruler") is used more frequently. See Demacopoulos, *Five Models*, 130.

3. See Müller, *Führung im Denken*, 123–29; and Gessel, "Reform am Haupt."

4. Demacopoulos, *Five Models*, 142.

5. Gregory, *Dial.* 3.17. In this context, Gregory argues that the miracle that brought about Paul's conversion is much more important and powerful than the raising of Lazarus. Similarly, in *Dial.* 1.4, Gregory argues that miracles are less important for quality spiritual leadership than purity of heart and commitment to preaching.

6. On the latter, see Gregory, *Mor.* 13.12.15.

7. Gregory, *Ep.* 5.53a. Gregory, of course, famously devises the three-part exegetical model of historical, allegorical, and moral, which becomes the dominant interpretive method in the Middle Ages.

8. See Gregory, *Hom. Ez.* 1.3.5–6; *Hom. Ez.* 1.9.14; and *Hom. Ez.* 1.11.12–22. Augustine was likewise very concerned about the preacher's ability to speak well; see, especially, his *On the Catechism of the Ignorant*. See also Demacopoulos, *Five Models*, 89–92.

9. While this section will emphasize Gregory's understanding of discernment as a trait that spiritual directors employ for the supervision of others, I should note Straw's analysis of Gregory's concept of discernment as a feature of an individual's own reflection and reformation. See, for example, the extent to which she understands discernment to function within a sinner's quest for penance (*Perfection in Imperfection*, 213–15) and the extent to which it enables a proper balance between action and contemplation, therefore making possible a *constantia mentis* (236–38).

10. See Demacopoulos, *Five Models*, 11–12 and 112–13.

11. Gregory, *Mor.* 30.9.35.

12. Gregory, *Mor.* 30.9.35.

13. To be sure, there is an expansive bibliography on the discernment of spirits in early Christianity. See, among other titles, Joseph Lienhard, "On

'Discernment of Spirits' in the Early Church," *Theological Studies* 41 (1980): 505–29; David Brakke, *Demons and the Making of the Monk: Spiritual Combat in Early Christianity* (Cambridge, MA: Harvard University Press, 2006), esp. 80–93; and Antony Rich, *Discernment in the Desert Fathers: "Diakrisis" in the Life and Thought of Early Egyptian Monasticism* (Milton Keynes, UK: Paternoster, 2007).

14. See, for example, Cassian's view that discernment is always a gift of the Holy Spirit that cannot be merited (an intriguing conclusion, given Cassian's proclivity to defend the role of human cooperation). Cassian dedicates the entirety of his second conference to the subject.

15. For an example of the former, see Gregory, *Mor.* 1.34.47; for the latter, see *Hom. Ez.* 1.3.4 or *Hom. Ez.* 1.9.29.

16. Gregory, *Hom. Ez.* 1.9.12–13. He similarly, and not surprisingly, held that the proud would be prevented from ever obtaining discernment. See, for example, *Mor.* 24.23.50.

17. Gregory, *Mor.* 1.9.13; *Mor.* 21.16.25.

18. Gregory, *PR* 2.9; *Hom. Ez.* 1.5.3; *Hom. Ez.* 1.7.2.

19. Gregory, *Hom. Evang.* 12.1.

20. The famous ancient physician Galen maintained that human moods, emotions, and dispositions were linked to imbalances in the physical "humors" within the body. For more on Gregory's discussion of discernment within the context of medical literature, see Straw, *Perfection in Imperfection*, 215–18.

21. Gregory, *Mor.* 6.1.1; *Mor.* 24.8.19; *Hom. Evang.* 17.9; and *Hom. Evang.* 20.8.

22. Gregory, *Mor.* 17.26.37–38; *Mor.* 24.11.28; and *Mor.* 30.8.27.

23. The list of binaries that runs through book 3 of the *Pastoral Rule* was first introduced in Gregory, *Mor.* 30.3.11–13.

24. For more on Gregory's sense of discernment and self-reform as an exercise of the highest reason, see Straw, *Perfection in Imperfection*, 215–20.

25. For example, in *Mor.* 5.52.74, Gregory notes that on certain occasions St. Paul encouraged the drinking of wine, while at other times he warned against the dangers of drunkenness. So, too, the spiritual director needs to conform his message and instruction to the unique situation before him. See also *Mor.* 2.16.28; *Mor.* 20.2.4; and *Hom. Ez.* 2.9.20.

26. Gregory, *Mor.* 20.5.14; *Mor.* 24.16.41–42; and *Hom. Ez.* 1.10.17–19. Gregory speaks here of moderation within a long Stoic tradition, which has its origins with Aristotle's ethical writings.

27. Gregory, *Mor.* 13.5.6; *Mor.* 28.18.41; and *Mor.* 32.22.46.

28. Gregory, *Hom. Ez.* 1.12.25.

29. Gregory, *PR* 3.36–37.

30. Gregory, *Mor.* 19.27.49; *Mor.* 31.13.25; and *Hom. Evang.* 26.6. In this particular framing of *oikonomia* I refer to the ascetic tradition of the lessening of prescribed punishment rather than the broader concept of the divine dispensation for salvation, although the two concepts are obviously connected.

31. Gregory, *Mor.* 26.6.7.

32. The most famous example, of course, concerns the so-called *Responsa* that Gregory sent to Augustine of Canterbury. Gregory's instructions to Augustine demonstrate his willingness to bend the rules (including marriage between cousins and bovine sacrifice) in order to facilitate spiritual progress. An indicative example of one of Gregory's own disciples employing this pastoral technique has been transmitted within Gregory's own corpus of letters (*Ep.* 13.48).

33. Examples include *Ep.* 1.38a (to Peter, his agent in Sicily), 2.30 (to Eusebius, abbot of a monastery in Sicily), 4.1 (to Constantius, bishop of Milan), and, of course the letters of Maximus of Salona and John of Constantinople.

34. A representative example is Gregory, *Mor.* 13.28.32.

35. Gregory, *Mor.* 16.20.25.

36. Gregory, *Mor.* 16.20.25.

37. Gregory, *Mor.* 9.35.55–9.36.58. In this passage, Gregory speaks of both tears of regret (*compunctionis*) and tears of repentance (*paenitentiae*). Here, Gregory suggests that contemplation begins with the compunction of fear. As Straw notes, Gregory understands fear (accompanied by tears) to be the initial stage of moral reform, which then gives way to a different kind of tear, the tears of joy, shed in longing for the kingdom of God. Straw, *Perfection in Imperfection*, 213–21.

38. Gregory, *Mor.* 11.42.57.

39. Gregory, *Mor.* 25.7.14.

40. See, especially, Gregory, *PR* 2.4 and *PR* 3.prol. See also *Hom. Evang.* 5 and *Hom. Evang.* 10.

41. Examples include *Ep.* 3.27, 3.42, 9.25, and 13.48. See Julia Hillner, "Gregory the Great's 'Prisons': Monastic Confinement in Early Byzantine Italy," *Journal of Early Christian Studies* 19 (2011): 433–71.

42. Gregory, *Ep.* 3.4.

43. Gregory, *Ep.* 3.25.

44. An example of errant belief includes *Ep.* 4.30; concerning the treatment of slaves, see *Ep.* 3.57; and concerning the spiritual benefits of charity, see *Ep.* 5.30, 5.38, and 5.39.

45. There are eleven letters addressed to a Venantius of Sicily. John Martyn suggests that there may be have been two men by this name: an ex-monk residing in Syracuse, married to Italica and having two daughters, and a separate aristocrat living in Palermo. Either way, the majority of these letters demonstrate a

long-lasting relationship in which Gregory presents himself as the spiritual counselor of the addressee.

46. Gregory, *Ep.* 1.33.

47. Two letters to the daughters, Barbara and Antonina, survive. The first, *Ep.* 11.23, expresses pastoral consolation at the news of their father's illness; the second, 11.59, rejoices at the news of their engagements.

48. See, especially, Gregory, *PR* 2.1–2.

49. Throughout the *Dialogues* Gregory presents the miracles and behavior of the saints as softening the heart of an otherwise ferocious and problem-causing Totila (the king of the Goths). In some cases, the saint is said to enable the king to believe more fully in the "power of God" (*Dial.* 3.5), sometimes miracles lead the king to respect the power of a particular saint (*Dial.* 3.6, 3.11), and other times they demonstrate how the sanctity of a saint cannot be compromised by the evil of barbarians (*Dial.* 3.13).

50. A similar observation is made in Pellegrini, *Militia Clericatus Monachici Ordines*, 295. It should be noted, however, that the final book of the *Dialogues* does emphasize the sacrifice of the Eucharist, the role of the priest in the ritual, and the power of the celebration of the Eucharist to impact even the deceased.

51. The lack of interest in the sacraments in the *Pastoral Rule* might offer a further indication that Gregory understood the role of spiritual director to extend beyond the clergy and to include nonordained leaders of the ascetic community.

52. Book 1 of the *Moralia* does frequently allegorize Job's actions with respect to his sons as symbolizing a priest's sacramental responsibility for his congregation. See Gregory, *Mor.* 1.8.12; *Mor.* 1.22.30; and *Mor.* 1.24.32.

53. The base text for this, of course, would be the *Pastoral Rule*. See, especially, Gregory, *PR* 1.4; *PR* 2.5; *PR* 2.7; and *PR* 4. See also *Hom. Ez.* 1.7.2.

54. As we will detail in chapter 10, Gregory arranged lumber shipments, negotiated treaties with barbarian tribes, rebuilt Rome's military defenses, and negotiated with the imperial court for financial resources.

55. See, for example, Gregory, *Hom. Ez.* 1.11.6–7 and 1.11.27–28; and *Ep.* 5.53a.

56. See, for example, Gregory, *Hom. Ez.* 2.4.3 or *Hom. Evang.* 11.

57. Just a few examples are Gregory, *Mor.* 2.48.71; *Mor.* 5.14.31; *Mor.* 7.15.18; and *Mor.* 23.20.38. For an analysis of the ways in which *discretio* enables the holy man to strike the proper balance between his own action and contemplation (employing Job as a key example), see Straw, *Perfection in Imperfection*, 236–56.

58. Gregory, *Mor.* 18.43.69–70.

59. Gregory, *Mor.* 19.6.12–13. See also *Mor.* 28.13.33. On this theme, see Straw, *Perfection in Imperfection*, 236–60.

60. Gregory, *Hom. Evang.* 17.

Chapter 8. The Impediments to Effective Leadership

1. See, for example, Gregory, *Mor.* 23.1.6–23.3.12; *Mor.* 31.44.86–87; and *Hom. Evang.* 17.

2. Gregory, *PR* 1.9.

3. Gregory, *PR.* 1.9. In both of these quotations, Gregory stresses the need for the one in power to redouble self-restraint and self-discipline.

4. Gregory formulates this as an opposition between being too strict and too lax. The good *rector* is balanced between extremes so that he is respected and feared rather than flattered or hated. Here, too, Gregory's ideals point toward moderation.

5. See, especially, Gregory, *PR* 2.8. In Gregory's register of vices, vainglory is an aspect of hypocrisy, which he finds to be particularly loathsome among the clergy. On this, see Straw, *Perfection in Imperfection*, 72 and 83.

6. In the opening lines of book 1 of the *Dialogues*, Gregory presents himself as despairing for the loss of monastic *otium* that he had once enjoyed, noting that his soul is now "defiled by contact with worldly men." In the same text he suggests that an unnamed pope's scrutiny of Abbot Equitius stemmed from the bishop's failure to recognize the extent to which he had become consumed by human affairs and, as a consequence, fallen victim to pride. Book 1 of the *Pastoral Rule* (1.3) points to the example of David, who fell into lust, Gregory warns, because he lost sight of the life of contemplation once he became responsible for the well-being of others.

7. Gregory, *Mor.* 1.23.31.

8. "vix ipsa praedicatio sine aliquo transitur admisso." Gregory, *Mor.* 19.14.22.

9. Gregory, *Mor.* 19.14.22

10. Gregory, *Hom. Evang.* 17.

Chapter 9. The Rome of Gregory's Imagination

1. Although my interpretation offers an alternative reading, my thinking about Gregory's *Romanitas* is much informed by Jeffrey Richards, *Popes and the Papacy.*

2. Jeffrey Richards, *Consul of God: The Life and Times of Gregory the Great* (London: Routledge and Kegan Paul, 1980); and *Popes and the Papacy.* Caspar's *Geschichte des Papsttums* offered the first systematic study of the growth of papal ideology from a historical-critical perspective.

3. This was the position of both Caspar and Ullmann. Both they and more recent scholars have shown the extent to which it is possible to explore the ways in which various Roman bishops in the late-ancient and early medieval periods adopted the categories and language of empire for their own initiatives and, in effect, Christianized the imperial message by substituting the Roman bishop for the emperor.

4. See, for example, Nicholas Everett, *Literacy in Lombard Italy 568–774* (Cambridge: Cambridge University Press, 2003); Marcia Colish, *The Stoic Tradition from Antiquity to the Early Middle Ages*, 2 vols. (Leiden: Brill, 1990), 1:253–66; and, especially, Pierre Riché, *Éducation et culture dans l'Occident barbare* (Paris: Seuil, 1962). For studies specific to Gregory, see John Moorhead, "Gregory's Classical Literary Inheritance," in *A Companion to Gregory the Great*, ed. Bronwen Neil and Matthew Dal Santo (Leiden: Brill, 2013), 249–67; Dagens, *Saint Grégoire le grand*, 16–20; and Sofia Boesch Gajano, *Grégoire le Grand: Aux origines du Moyen Âge* (Paris: Éditions du Cerf, 2007), 25–31.

5. By this time it is generally assumed that the *trivium* had supplanted the *quadrivium* in basic education. Averil Cameron, "Education and Literary Culture," in *The Cambridge Ancient History*, ed. Averil Cameron and Peter Garnsey (Cambridge: Cambridge University Press, 1998), 13:673–76.

6. Gregory of Tours, *History of the Franks*, 10.1; Paul the Deacon, *Vita*, 2; Cf. John the Deacon, *Vita*, 1.3.

7. Riché, *Écoles et enseignement dans le Haut Moyen Age*, 17. While Augustine, Jerome, and others cited the Scriptures, Riché believes that Gregory was the first to essentially ignore the classics. Edward Gibbon had been more overtly critical, taking Gregory's lack of classical sources as evidence of a disdain for all things pre-Christian. Edward Gibbon, *Decline and Fall of the Roman Empire*, 4.45, 532.

8. Concerning the number of classical citations in Gregory's corpus, see Moorhead, "Gregory's Classical Literary Inheritance."

9. See Kathleen Brazzel, *The Clausulae in the Works of St. Gregory the Great* (Washington, DC: Catholic University Press, 1939), 65; and Dag Norberg, "Qui a composé les lettres de saint Grégoire le Grand?" *Studi medievali* 21 (1980): 1–17, and "Style personnel et style administratif dans le *Registrum epistularum* de saint Grégoire le grand," in *Grégoire le Grand*, ed. Fontaine, Gillet, and Pellistrandi, 489–97.

10. For an excellent survey of the ways in which the imperial discourse underwent a kind of Christianization in the late-ancient period, see Averil Cameron, *Christianity and the Rhetoric of Empire* (Berkeley: University of California Press, 1994). For Gregory specifically, see Markus, *Gregory the Great and*

His World, 83–96; Dal Santo, "Gregory the Great, the Empire, and the Emperor," in *A Companion to Gregory the Great*, ed. Neil and Dal Santo, 57–81; and David Hipshon, "Gregory the Great's Political Thought," *Journal of Ecclesiastical History* 53 (2002): 439–53.

11. Markus, *Gregory the Great and His World*, 83–96.

12. The *Novellae*, or "new laws," issued mostly by Justinian himself, are especially illustrative of the emperor's conception of diarchy, a system in which the Church and the State constitute two distinct but overlapping spheres of authority. For a brief overview of Justinian's concept of diarchy, see John Meyendorff, "Justinian, the Empire, and the Church," *Dumbarton Oaks Papers* 22 (1968): 43–60. For an overview of what is known about the production, translation, and reception of the *Novellae*, see Detlef Liebs, "Roman Law," in *The Cambridge Ancient History*, edited by Averil Cameron and Peter Garnsey (Cambridge: Cambridge University Press, 1995), 14:251–52.

13. Markus, *Gregory the Great and His World*, 84. See also Claudia Rapp, *Holy Bishops in Late Antiquity* (Berkeley: University of California Press, 2005).

14. Markus, *Gregory the Great and His World*, 84.

15. For more on Gregory's political theology, see Greschat, "Feines Weizenmehl und ungenießbare Spelzen," esp. 69–70; and Hipshon, "Gregory the Great's Political Thought."

16. Markus is particularly alarmed to note that Gregory assumes the role of subservience rather than criticize the emperor Phocas, who had come to the throne through a bloody coup. Markus, *Gregory the Great and His World*, 85.

17. See, especially, Gregory, *Ep.* 11.37 to Ethelbert (king of Kent) and *Ep.* 11.35 to Bertha (Ethelbert's wife).

18. For an overview of imperial consciousness in early Latin Christian literature, see Marc Reydellet, *Le Royauté dans la literature latine de Sidoine Appolinaire à Isidore de Seville* (Rome: Diffusion de Boccard, 1981).

19. On Gelasius's strained relationship with the East, see Demacopoulos, *Invention of Peter*.

20. Recall, for example, Gregory's attempts to persuade Maurice to censure John of Constantinople for his use of the title "Ecumenical Patriarch." Gregory, *Ep.* 5.37. See also Straw, "Gregory's Politics: Theory and Practice," in *Gregorio Magno e il suo tempo*, ed. École française de Rome (Rome: Institutum Patristicum "Augustinianum," 1991) 1:47–63.

21. Walter Ullmann, *The Growth of the Papal Government in the Middle Ages: A Study in the Ideological Relation of Clerical to Lay Power*, 3d ed. (London: Methuen, 1970), 36–37.

22. Robert Markus, "Gregory the Great's Europe," *Royal Historical Society* 31 (1981): 30–35. See also Richards, *Popes and the Papacy*, 26–27.

23. See, especially, the collective trajectory of Neil and Dal Santo, eds., *A Companion to Gregory the Great.*

24. Demacopoulos, "Gregory the Great and a Post-Imperial Discourse."

25. For example, note Gregory, *Ep.* 3.61. See Demacopoulos, "Gregory the Great and a Post-Imperial Discourse."

26. See, for example, Gregory, *Ep.* 5.36.

27. Gregory, *Ep.* 5.36.

28. Gelasius, *Ep.* 12.

29. See Leo, *Sermon* 82; and Gelasius, *Tractate* 6. For an analysis of both events, see Demacopoulos, *Invention of Peter*, ch. 2 and ch. 3 respectively.

30. Although he had many predecessors, Krautheimer's volume remains something of the premier study. Richard Krautheimer, *Rome: The Profile of a City* (repr., Princeton: Princeton University Press, 2000). For a rather different but important study that also incorporates archeological evidence from the Roman world in Gregory's era, see Chris Wickham, *Framing the Early Middle Ages: Europe and the Mediterranean 400–800* (Oxford: Oxford University Press, 2005).

31. See Federico Guidobaldi, "L'organizzazione dei tituli nello spazio urbano," in *Christina Loco: Lo spazio Cristiano nella Roma del primo millennio*, ed. Letizia Pani Ermini (Rome: Fratelli Polombi, 2000), 123–29.

32. Marios Costambeys, "Burial Topography and the Power of the Church in Fifth- and Sixth-Century Rome," *Papers of the British School of Rome* 69 (2001): 169–89.

33. For the possibility of this being a fourth-century development, see John Baldavin, *The Urban Character of Christian Worship: The Origins, Development and Meaning of Stational Liturgy* (Rome: Pontificio Instituto Orientale, 1987). For a useful study of Leo I's effort to be present at various churches and shrines throughout the city, see Michelle Salzman, "Leo's Liturgical Topography: Contestations for Space in Fifth Century Rome," *Journal of Roman Studies* 103 (2013): 208–32.

34. See Demacopoulos, *Invention of Peter.*

35. For Gregory's apocalypticism, see Kisić, *Patria Caelestis*, 54–61; Straw, *Perfection in Imperfection*, 14–26; and Dagens, "La fin des temps et l'église selon saint Grégoire le Grand," *Recherches de Science Religieuse* 58 (1970): 273–88. For an apocalyptic reading of Gregory's *Dialogues*, see Leyser, *Authority and Asceticism*, 134–35.

36. Eusebius famously understood the conversion of the emperor Constantine to have been a pivotal moment in history, one that would both enact God's plan for humanity and bring greater glory to Rome itself.

37. Note, for example, his correspondence with the emperor Maurice as well as his letter to Ethelbert of Kent. Gregory, *Ep.* 3.61 and 11.37. For a concise

overview of Gregory's apocalypticism and how it impacted his thought more generally, see Straw, *Perfection in Imperfection*, 14–15 and 25–26.

38. See Gregory, *Hom. Evang.* 17, which argues that the wars and destruction are the result of the sins of Christians.

39. Gregory, *Hom. Ez.* 2.6.22–24.

40. For more on how the decline of the city of Rome may have shaped Gregory's outlook, see Straw, *Perfection in Imperfection*, 185.

41. Gregory, *Hom. Evang.* 3.

42. Barbara Müller argues, quite convincingly, that Gregory's use of the shipwreck metaphor is quite distinct from previous Christian applications that typically sought to describe the shipwrecked person as either a sinner or heretic. In contrast, Gregory uses the shipwreck as metaphor for all Christians who must persevere in a challenging environment. Barbara Müller, "Nautische Metaphern bei Gregor dem Grossen," *Studia Patristica* 48 (2010): 165–70.

43. See Lucia Saguì, "Roma, i centri privilegiati e la lunga durata della tarda antichità. Dati archeologici dal deposito di VII secolo nell'esedra della Crypta Balbi," *Archeologica Medievale* 29 (2002): 7–42; and Lidia Paroli, "Roma dal V al IX secolo: uno sguardo attraverso le stratigrafie archeologiche," in *Roma: Dall'antichità al medioevo. Archeologia e storia nel Museo Nazionale Romano Crypto Balbi*, ed. Laura Vendittelli, Lidia Paroli, and Maria Stella Arena (Milan: Electa 2004), 11–40.

44. Such an endeavor is of course not without its challenges, and a complete investigation of this matter could be the focus of an entire study.

45. There are also a few letters to Reccared, the Visigothic king of Spain.

46. According to Baun, Gregory concludes the *Moralia* with a very optimistic view of the future coming together of the nations. Jane Baun, "Gregory's Eschatology," in *A Companion to Gregory the Great*, ed. Neil and Dal Santo, 157–76, esp. 73–76.

47. Richards, *Consul of God*, 181.

48. Markus, *Gregory the Great and His World*, 100. Markus here is drawing a rather direct reading of *Ep.* 11.2. He also notes a letter Gregory sent in *Ep.* 5.6, which (according to Markus) implies that if he didn't fear God, Gregory would have orchestrated the assassination of their king.

49. For examples of Gregory's critique of Maurice's policy on monasticism, his indifference to John's use of the ecumenical title, and willingness to support episcopal candidates opposed by the Roman See, see Demacopoulos, "Gregory the Great and a Post-Imperial Discourse."

50. Given the complexities of his relationship with the imperial court, however, it is difficult to untangle in these letters Gregory's attitude concerning the Lombards from his rhetorical objectives with Eastern officials.

51. Unfortunately, Gregory's theological treatises are not much help. Neither the *Pastoral Rule* nor any of his surviving biblical commentaries offer any assistance in resolving the ambiguity of Gregory's correspondence, although the *Commentary on Ezekiel* does seem to break off in the final homily with the lament that Gregory cannot get anyone to attend his discussions of Scripture because they are too dismayed by the impending Lombard siege. Jane Baun offers a nicely nuanced account of the eschatological considerations in Gregory's imperial correspondence. See Jane Baun, "Gregory's Eschatology," in *A Companion to Gregory the Great*, ed. Neil and Dal Santo, 157–76.

52. The *Dialogues* chronicle the lives or posthumous miracles of approximately ninety Italian saints or groupings of saints and martyrs. This figure is inexact because of the complexity of counting the distinct number of stories in book 4, which devotes considerable attention to questions of the soul after death, of heaven, and of hell. My count of twenty-six does not include the four times that the Goths or Lombards are used to mark time — "in the time of the Goths" or "in these days of the Lombards." See, for example, Gregory, *Dial.* 1.2; 2.1; 3.14; and 4.14. Nor does this number include an encounter with the Visigoths of Spain (3.31) or one with the Vandals of North Africa (3.32).

53. For the possibility that the narrative sequence follows the literary pattern found in the *Vita Martini*, which was itself based upon earlier Greco-Roman patterns, see Pearse A. Cusack, "Some Literary Antecedents of the Totila Encounter in the Second Dialogue of Pope Gregory I," *Studia Patristica* 12 (1975): 87–90.

54. Gregory, *Dial.* 2.14.

55. Gregory, *Dial.* 2.15.

56. Gregory, *Dial.* 2.15. The chapter concludes with a conversation between Benedict and the bishop of Canosa about whether or not Totila would destroy Rome. Benedict predicts that it will be hard for Rome, but the Gothic attack will not destroy the city. Gregory, of course, is writing this account nearly fifty years after the siege.

57. Gregory, *Dial.* 2.17.

58. See Cristina Ricci, "Gregory's Barbarian Missions," in *A Companion to Gregory the Great*, ed. Neil and Dal Santo, 29–56. See also Leo Marsicanus, *Chronicon monasterii Casinensis* 1.2, ed. Wihelm Wattenback, MGH SS 7 (Hannover, 1846; repr., Stuttgart, New York, 1963), 580–81.

59. Gregory, *Dial.* 3.1.

60. Some minor exceptions do exist. In *Dialogues* 2.6, Benedict agrees to accept a monk of Gothic origins into his community. More significantly, Reccared's conversion from Arianism to orthodoxy is attributed to the intervention of St. Hermangild in *Dialogues* 3.31.

61. Here, again, the exception is the Visigothic king of Spain, Reccared, who abandons Arianism for orthodoxy.

62. The many stories involving King Totila are especially pertinent here. In *Dial.* 3.5, St. Sabinus's miracle leads Totila to believe more fully in the power of God; in *Dial.* 3.6, St. Cassius's miracle leads the king to have respect for the saintly bishop. A more extreme version of the same theme occurs in *Dial.* 3.11, when Totila tries to have a bishop murdered but then respects him. And then, in *Dial.* 3.13, the body of St. Herculanus, bishop of Perugia, whose murder had been ordered by Totila, is shown to have not decomposed long after it had been buried.

63. See Baun, "Gregory's Eschatology," in *A Companion to Gregory the Great*, ed. Neil and Dal Santo, 157–76.

64. To be sure, not every story in the *Dialogues* conveys Gregory's secular pessimism or his apocalypticism. Indeed, several of the stories reinforce the notion that there is holiness in the countryside, and several of the miracles reflect agrarian concerns, such as crops being saved from flooding rivers or locusts.

65. Cristina Ricci holds a different view. See her "Gregory's Mission to the Barbarians," in *A Companion to Gregory the Great*, ed. Neil and Dal Santo, 157–76.

66. There is a distinction here between the power of ascetic withdrawal (what it does for the individual) and the cause of that power, which is God. The power of the holy man derives from the indwelling of God, which is preconditioned by ascetic training.

67. As noted, the narrative arc in the *Life of Benedict* emphasizes the saint's initial resistance but ultimate willingness to undertake the spiritual supervision of others.

68. As I have argued elsewhere, Gregory's conceptions of leadership, although they reflect Ciceronian and Stoic ideas of statesmanship and mentorship, were more explicitly akin to the models of spiritual formation that occurred in the monasteries of his day. See Demacopoulos, *Five Models*.

Chapter 10. Ever the Praefect

1. Rapp, *Holy Bishops in Late Antiquity*. Although she does not engage Gregory's career extensively, I must acknowledge my debt to Rapp's approach to her subject.

2. Within his correspondence, scholars have identified seventy-four explicit and fifty-four implicit references to the Justinianic Law Code. Gregory's familiarity with the *Codex* can be traced to multiple things, including his education, his time as prefect, his continuous correspondence with Eastern officials,

and his temperament. See G. Damizia, "Il *Registrum Epistolarum* di San Gregorio Magno ed il *Corpus Iuris Civilis*," *Benedictina* 2 (1948): 195–226.

3. As noted, Richards's thesis is that Gregory's *Christianitas* and his *Romanitas* were always in a certain tension with one another.

4. See Richards, *Consul of God*, 89–90.

5. Recall that Gregory's father, Gordianus, was a property manager for one of the papal patrimonies. This service would have been in addition to the administration of his own lands, which were located primarily in Sicily.

6. The farms in Sardinia and Corsica came under the administrative control of the Exarch of Africa.

7. The initial grants were from the imperial family. Those were supplemented by a variety of different benefices. The patrimonies were organized into fifteen separate landholdings, four of which were outside of Italy and Sicily. See Richards, *Consul of God*, 127. See also Vincenzo Recchia, *Gregorio Magno e la società agricola* (Rome: Studium, 1978); and Dominic Morneau, "Les patrimoines de l'Église romaine jusqu' à la mort de Grégoire le Grand," *Antiquité tardive* 14 (2006): 79–93.

8. In large part this was because the Roman See became one of the primary beneficiaries of the land previously owned by the Arian Church, which was seized by Justinian's armies at the conclusion of the Gothic Wars in 554. In addition, Gregory himself had added to the Roman patrimony by disposing of his family's estates (mostly in Sicily) at the time he entered the monastic life in 574.

9. By Gregory's tenure, Sicily was the location of roughly four hundred agricultural estates owned by the Roman Church. A fully functioning administrative system in the Sicilian patrimony likely began during the tenure of Pope Pelagius I (556–561).

10. For a cogent assessment of the various administrative roles and the types of clerics Gregory employed, see Pellegrini, *Militia Clericus Monachici Ordines*.

11. We gain a strong sense of Gregory's efforts to enforce ascetic standards upon the clerics of lower orders through his activity in Sicily, for which we have extensive documentation of his efforts. See Demacopoulos, *Five Models*, 145–53.

12. For more on Gregory's activity in Sicily and the role of his *rectores*, see chapter 11, "Gregory's Ascetic Program and its Opponents."

13. For a survey of Gregory's interactions with the local nobility and what that interaction tells us about the shifting contours of the political and religious structures on Sicily at the end of late antiquity, see Roberta Rizzo, *Papa Gregorio Magno e la Nobiltà in Sicilia* (Palermo: Officina di Studi Medievali, 2008).

14. Because Gregory's surviving correspondence is so extensive, and because that correspondence provides exponentially more detail of the inner workings of

the patrimonial system than we have for any other late-ancient or early medieval pope, there is a certain temptation to view Gregory's oversight of the patrimonial system as a premeditated and well-executed business strategy that would ultimately make the Roman Church the wealthiest entity in Europe during the Middle Ages. More than simply anachronistic, however, such a reading of Gregory's administrative efforts fails to account for the real challenges and haphazard circumstances under which he operated. In one sense, we might say that Gregory brought order, efficiency, and accountability to the patrimonial estates because had he not done so, the people of Rome might have starved to death. That reading also fails to account for the fact that Gregory seeks the proper balance of stewardship—he needs the farms to flourish, but not at the expense of mistreating their peasants.

15. Gregory, *Ep.* 12.6. Here Gregory writes to his agent John, whom he expects to press the exarch for support in this matter.

16. Concerning the ransoming of prisoners, see, for example, *Ep.* 6.32.

17. Gregory, *Ep.* 5.30. John the Deacon, *Vita*, 2.27. Richards takes John's figure as accurate, which is problematic because Gregory simply informs the emperor that "some nuns from various parts" have arrived in Rome. See Richards, *Consul of God*, 98.

18. See, for example, Gregory, *Ep.* 5.30, 5.38, and 7.23.

19. Gregory, *Ep.* 3.40, 3.41, 3.42, 4.17, and 9.52. Although Gregory did believe that it was perfectly reasonable to melt church-plate to raise money for the ransoming of prisoners, he was deeply concerned about refugee priests who had taken the plate with them when they fled the Lombards, only to sell this plate and use the resources to fund their livelihoods. See, for example, *Ep.* 1.63, 9.93, and 9.94.

20. See, for example, St. Fortunatus's role in gaining the liberation of two young boys from Goths (*Dial.* 1.10) or St. Paulinus's heroic liberation of all the Italian captives who had become slaves of the Vandals in North Africa (*Dial.* 3.1).

21. Richards notes that one consequence of the continued threat of war was that the patrimonial estate managers, the *defensores*, also took on additional clerical responsibilities, including ransoming of prisoners and placement of refugees. In response to this, Gregory organized the order of *defensores* into a separate *scholia*, or college, giving them formal corporate status like that of the deacons and notaries. See Richards, *Consul of God*, 93–94.

22. See Gregory, *Ep.* 2.4, 2.10, 2.27, and 2.28. In a letter to two of these generals, *Ep.* 2.27, Gregory encourages his correspondents that the Lombards have set themselves against St. Peter, who will himself aid in the defense of Rome.

23. Gregory, *Ep.* 2.47.

24. Gregory twice purchased peace. In 592 he paid the duke of Spoleto an undisclosed amount to abandon his attack on Rome. In 593 he allegedly paid Agilulf, the Lombard king, five hundred pounds of gold to negotiate a peace.

25. See Peter Llewellyn, "The Roman Church in the Seventh Century: The Legacy of Gregory I," *Journal of Ecclesiastical History* 25 (1974): 363–80, esp. 365–66.

26. A decade or so later, Pope Pelagius II implored Gregory, then serving as *apocrisiarius*, to make every possible effort to ensure that the imperial court came to understand the gravity of the threat posed by the Lombards. Pelagius II, *Ep.* 2 (MGH *Ep.* 2, appendix 2). See Markus, *Gregory the Great*, 98–99.

27. See Richards, *Consul of God*, 182–85. Although some scholars since Richard's writing have questioned previous assessments of the scope of the plague in Italy during the sixth century, it is nonetheless clear that illness and the fear of illness compounded the difficulty in Rome.

28. Whether Gregory wrote directly to Romanus is unknown, as no letter survives. What is known is that he wrote to John, the bishop of Ravenna, seeking his assistance with the exarch. Gregory, *Ep.* 2.38. For Müller's account of this string of events, see *Führung im Denken*, 205–7.

29. Gregory, *Ep.* 5.36 is Gregory's defense of his actions to Maurice. Richards cites this letter as evidence of Gregory's payment, but there is nothing specific mentioned in the letter. There is a brief mention that he made peace with no cost to the imperial treasury.

30. Gregory, *Ep.* 5.36.

31. Gregory, *Hom. Ez.* 2.10.24.

32. Although there is ample evidence in the Gregorian materials (esp. *Ep.* 5.36) that he concluded a specific treaty with Agilulf, those documents make no mention of the precise arrangements. A Lombard chronicle known as the *Continuatio prosperi havniensis* mentions that Gregory purchased the peace with Agilulf with five hundred pounds of gold. Richards (*Consul of God*, 184–86) takes this document at face value. Markus (*Gregory the Great*, 103), who also cites the text, privileges an earlier passage, which suggests that Agilulf spared Rome out of respect for Gregory. The *Continuatio* is an anonymous manuscript, dated to the period around 625, that proposes to be a continuation of the chronicle of Prosper of Aquitaine. It is a pro-Lombard document that castigates the Romans for the failure to protect Italy and praises the Lombards for protecting the region from Frankish invasion. The text was edited by T. Mommsen, MGH *AA* 9 (Berlin, 1892). The passage in question is to be found at 9.339.

33. This included working through the Archbishop of Milan, Constantius (see *Ep.* 4.2) as well as Romanus's own advisors (see *Ep.* 5.34).

34. Gregory, *Ep.* 5.36. Gregory's overly defensive response to the charge of foolishness and treason was prompted by a now-lost missive from the imperial court censoring the pope's intrusion into negotiations with the Lombards.

35. Gregory, *Ep.* 5.34.

36. Gregory, *Ep.* 5.34.

37. Gregory, *Ep.* 6.34.

38. For the continuing back-and-forth between Ravenna and Lombards, see Richards, *Consul of God*, 188–91.

39. For Kaufman's treatment of Gregory and the Lombards, see *Church, Book, and Bishop*, 118–22.

40. Gregory, *Ep.* 1.30.

41. See Kaufman, *Church, Book, and Bishop*, 121–22.

42. The lone exception is Gregory, *Ep.* 1.17, which encourages the northern bishops to exploit the death of King Autharit to their advantage. According to Gregory, Autharit had decreed that it would be a capital offense for anyone of the Lombard dukes to have a son baptized by a Catholic priest. But, Gregory tells us, the king dropped dead shortly after making this decree, and so he (i.e., Gregory) wanted the Italian bishops to narrate these events as a judgment from God.

43. Richards, *Consul of God*, 191–94. A year before Gregory's election, Theodelinda (a Bavarian Catholic) married Autharis, the king of the Lombards. Autharis died in September of 590, the same month as Gregory's election. In May of 591 Theodelinda remarried—this time to one of Autharis's relatives, the chieftain Agilulf of Turin, who was soon elected king of the Lombards.

44. Markus, for his part, says next to nothing about Gregory's missionary activity among the Lombards apart from his efforts to convince Queen Theodelinda to drop her opposition to the condemnation of the Three Chapters; see Markus, *Gregory the Great*, 137–40.

45. Richards's argument, in fact, is largely one from silence. Recall that it is generally assumed that only a small fraction of Gregory's letters survive, and decisions about what to preserve were largely made by Carolingian editors who may well have had a bias against the Lombards. It may be the case, in fact, that Richards's conclusion that Gregory "hated" the Lombards has colored his interpretation of the pope's willingness to convert them.

46. As scholars have shown with increasing sophistication, the motives behind the collection of papal records were often anything but innocent. See, for example, Kate Cooper and Julia Hillner, eds., *Religion, Dynasty, and Patronage*, esp. 1–18.

47. This involved a gentle and deferential approach that combined theological argument with healthy dose of Petrine authority. See Demacopoulos, *Inven-*

tion of Peter, ch. 5. See also Demacopoulos, "Gregory the Great and the Appeal to Petrine Authority," *Studia Patristica* 48 (2010): 333–46.

48. See Markus, *Gregory the Great*, 125–42; and Müller, *Führung im Denken*, 286–88.

49. Although the Three Chapters schism persisted, Agilulf baptized his son into the Catholic faith.

50. See Paul the Deacon, *History of the Lombards [Historia Langobardorum]*, ed. Ludwig Bethmann and Georg Waitz (MGH 48), 5.28. See also Gregory, *Ep.* 14.12, where Gregory responds happily to the news. Agilulf, despite Paul's statements to the contrary, likely remained an Arian.

51. *Liber Pontificalis*, ed. Louis Duchene, 312. The most important exception is the anonymous *Life of Gregory*, written by a monk of Whitby who offers a series of apocryphal accounts of Gregory's interventions among the Lombards.

52. While it is possible that Leo may have "met" Attila, there is no reason to believe that he played any active role in Attila's decision to spare Rome. Leo, in fact, says nothing about a meeting between them. For an example of the apocryphal myths of Leo's role in the preservation of Rome from Attila's forces, see his entry in the *Liber Pontificalis*.

53. Gregory, *Ep.* 1.3.

54. Gregory, *Ep.* 1.5.

55. Gregory, *Ep.* 1.6.

56. Gregory, *Ep.* 1.7.

57. Kaufman, *Church, Book, and Bishop*, 120–21.

58. We should never lose sight of the fact that all of Gregory's theological treatises were either written or edited during his pontificate. Even the *Moralia*, which was ostensibly delivered as a series of sermons during his time in Constantinople, was "published" a few years into his tenure as bishop.

59. Kaufman, *Church, Book, and Bishop*, 122.

Chapter 11. Gregory's Ascetic Program and Its Opponents

1. See Conrad Leyser, *Authority and Asceticism*, esp. 136–50; "Temptation of Cult: Roman Martyr Piety in the Age of Gregory the Great," *Early Medieval Europe* 9 (2000): 289–309; and "Expertise and Authority in Pope Gregory the Great," 38–61.

2. In addition to Leyser, see Llewellyn, "Roman Church in the Seventh Century"; and Richards, *Popes and the Papacy*, 280–306, and *Consul of God*, 80–84.

3. On the variety of worship spaces in late-antique Rome and the role of the aristocracy in their creation, see Kimberly Bowes, *Private Worship, Public*

Values, and Religious Change in Late Antiquity (Cambridge: Cambridge University Press, 1998).

4. There is considerable scholarly literature on this process. Of recent note, see Kristina Sessa, *The Formation of Papal Authority in Late Antique Italy: Roman Bishops and the Domestic Sphere* (Cambridge: Cambridge University Press, 2012); and Hannah Jones, "Agnes and Constantia: Domesticity and Cult Patronage in the *Passion of Agnes*," in *Religion, Dynasty, and Patronage*, ed. Kate Cooper and Julia Hillner (Cambridge: Cambridge University Press, 2007), 115–39.

5. The origins and organization of the *tituli* churches in Rome is complex, and we should resist the temptation to think of them as parish churches scattered throughout the city. Although they ultimately came under papal control, they did not originate as papal sites—they were independently funded, and their clergy were often appointed and supported by lay patrons. For the most current assessment of the *tituli* churches, see Julia Hillner, "Families, Patronage, and the Titular Churches of Rome, c. 300–c. 600," in *Religion, Dynasty, and Patronage*, ed. Kate Cooper and Julia Hillner, 225–61.

6. Leo Mohlberg, "Historisch-kritische Bemerkungen zum Ursprung der sogennaten 'Memoria Apostolorum' an der Appischen Straße," in *Colligere fragmenta: Festschrift Alban Dold zum 70. Geburstag am 7.7.52*, ed. Bonifatius Fischer and Virgil Fiala (Beuron: Beuroner Kunstverlag, 1952), 52–74; and Kate Cooper, "The Martyr, the *Matrona*, and the Bishop," *Early Medieval Europe* 8 (1999): 297–317, at 311–13.

7. In the end, Damasus secured the papal throne, but not without considerable damage to his reputation. For this reason, most scholars view Damasus's subsequent building program at the martyr shrines as a dual attempt to harness the city's enthusiasm for the martyrs and to purge his enemies from those partisan strongholds. See Marianne Sághy, "*Scinditur in partes populous*: Damasus and the Martyrs of Rome," *Early Medieval History* 9 (2000): 273–87; Dennis Trout, "Damasus and the Invention of Early Christian Rome," *Journal of Medieval and Early Modern Studies* 33 (2003): 517–36; and Demacopoulos, *Invention of Peter*, 34–35

8. See Demacopoulos, *Invention of Peter*, 103–7.

9. Peter Llewellyn, "The Roman Church during the Laurentian Schism (496–506): Priests and Senators," *Church History* 45 (1976): 417–27, and "The Roman Clergy during the Laurentian Schism (498–506): A Preliminary Analysis," *Ancient Society* 8 (1977): 245–75. Llewellyn continues this theme in the seventh century as well: Llewellyn, "The Roman Church in the Seventh Century."

10. See Llewellyn, "The Roman Clergy during the Laurentian Schism (496–506)," 248.

11. For example, see Charles Pietri, "Le Sénat, le people chrétien et les partis du Cirque à Rome sous le Pape Symmaqhe," *Mélanges d'Archéologie et d'Histoire* 78 (1966): 123–39.

12. On the origins and social makeup of the diaconal and priestly orders, consult Charles Pietri, *Roma christiana: Recherches sur l'église de Rome, son organization, sa politique, son idéologie de Miltiade à Sixte III* (Rome: École Française de Rome, 1976), vol. 1.

13. That evidence strongly belies the notion that the contest was one that pitted priests against deacons. See Richards, *Popes and the Papacy*, 83–85.

14. Gregory of Tours, *History of the Franks*, 10.1.

15. A similarly styled sermon was included in the MGH publication of Gregory's words and listed as *Ep.* 13.2. A translation of that sermon is provided by John R. C. Martyn in *The Letters of Gregory the Great*, Appendix 9, 3:887.

16. Gregory of Tours, *History of the Franks*, 10.1: "Conversionis nobis aditum dolor aperiat, et cordis nostri duritiam ipsa, quam patimur, poena dissolvat."

17. Gregory of Tours, *History of the Franks*, 10.1: "orationis nostrae studium merito bonae operationis erigere."

18. Gregory of Tours, *History of the Franks*, 10.1.

19. Leyser, *Authority and Asceticism*, 145–46.

20. Leyser, *Authority and Asceticism*, 146.

21. Whereas the biblical commentaries were largely designed for Gregory's ascetic inner community and are generally thought to have gone through several editorial efforts, the *Homiliae in Evangelia* were often preached to mixed audiences and convey a more extemporaneous style.

22. Antoine Chavasse, "Aménagements liturgiques à Rome, au VIIe et VIIIe siècles," *Revue Ben.* 99 (1989): 75–102. This essay assigns precise dates to many of the forty Gospel homilies using a calendar of early medieval martyr festivals in Rome and a contemporary list of titular churches. The ten sites are St. Felicity, St. Andrew, St. Sylvester, St. Agnes, St. Felix, St. Pancras, Sts. Nereus and Achilles, Sts. Processus and Martin, St. Mennas, and St. Sebastian. See also Leyser, "Temptations of Cult."

23. Leyser, "Temptations of Cult."

24. Gregory, *Hom. Evang.* 37. The final verse of the biblical text reads, "So, therefore, any one of you who does not renounce all that you possess cannot be a disciple of mine."

25. Gregory, *Dial.* 4.56.

26. See Leyser, "Temptations of Cult," 305–7.

27. Constantius was not a "graduate" of St. Andrews, but he was a monk that Gregory knew from Constantinople. There are also the famous cases of

Augustine, who became the bishop of Canterbury, and Mellitus, who eventually became bishop of London.

28. John the Deacon, *Vita*, 2.11–12. John's statement about the removal of laymen is partially corroborated by evidence of Gregory's removal of laymen from the papal *cubiculum*. See *Ep.* 5.57A.

29. See Richards, *Consul of God*, 70–84; cf. John the Deacon, *Vita*, 2.11–12.

30. Richards, *Consul of God*, 70–84.

31. Richards, *Consul of God*, 80.

32. Reflecting a more indirect initiative to co-opt the clerical establishment's control of Roman martyr cults and the potential heterodoxy of the *Gesta Martrium*, several scholars have argued that we should see Gregory's *Dialogues* as a means by which the pontiff simultaneously recalibrated the narrative of saintliness according to his ascetic standards and undermined the aristocratic control of popular religious devotion. See, especially, Sofia Boesch Gajano "La proposta agriografia dei 'Dialogi' di Gregorio Magno," *Studi Medivali* 3 (1980): 623–64, and "'Narratio' e 'expositio' nei Dialoghi di Gregorio Magno," *Bullettino dell'Istituto per il Medio Evo e Archivio Muratoriano* 88 (1979): 1–33.

33. Gregory claims that he has heard complaints from laypersons in the neighborhood that they frequently go to the church expecting to participate in the liturgy, only to return home when they found no one presiding over the Mass.

34. He encourages the abbot, Maurus, to employ a foreign priest for the continuation of Eucharistic services, if there is no member of Maurus's community who is a priest.

35. John the Deacon, *Vita*, 2.15. Leyser refers to it as "nothing less than a coup d'état"; *Authority and Asceticism*, 146. Also from the twentieth century, see Richards, *Popes and the Papacy*, 305; and Llewellyn, "Roman Church in the Seventh Century," 365.

36. The deacons were led by the archdeacon; the priests by the archpriest; the notaries by the *primicerius*; and the *defensores* also by a *primicerius*. Each of these groups had its own hierarchical structure based upon gerontocracy. See Richards, *Popes and the Papacy*, 290.

37. Llewellyn, "Roman Church in the Seventh Century," 365; and Peter Llewellyn, *Rome in the Dark Ages* (London: Praeger, 1971), esp. ch. 4 and 5. Richards offers an extensive overview of the papal administration. See *Popes and the Papacy*, 289–306.

38. According to this formulation, some scholars view episcopal efforts to bring the popular devotion to the cult of martyrs under papal control as a usurpation of a localized religious identity that had been initially supported by lay patrons. See Leyser, especially *Authority and Asceticism* and "Temptations of

Cult"; Sessa, *Formation of Papal Authority*; and Llewellyn, "Roman Church in the Seventh Century."

39. Llewellyn, "Roman Church in the Seventh Century," 365; and Leyser, "Temptations of Cult," 304.

40. Leyser, *Authority and Asceticism*, 147. Leyser recognizes that "precise parallels and connections remain, as yet, out of view," but later proposes that Gregory's selection of St. Andrew as the patron of his monastery in the 570s would have been interpreted as a partisan act because Symmachus had been an important patron for the cult of St. Andrew.

41. Gregory himself offers a mixed assessment of the affair in one of the stories in his *Dialogues*: a saint is culpable for having supported Laurentius during the schism, but he was so holy that his tomb became a locus for miraculous healing. Gregory, *Dial.* 4.42.

42. This would appear to be the animating concept of Leyser's approach to Gregory in *Authority and Asceticism*.

43. "propter superbiam et mala sua." *Ep.* appendix 3.

44. *Ep.* appendix 3.

45. Richards, *Popes and the Papacy*, 299.

46. For an analysis of the actions regarding the papal *cubiculum*, see Sessa, *Formation of Papal Authority*, 108–9.

47. In large part, the assumption of pro- or antimonastic bias is predicated upon whether or not the *Liber Pontificalis* claims that the pontiff in question was a lover of the clergy (if yes, then it suggests an anti-Gregorian bias) and whether or not their epithets declare an affiliation between the pontiff and Gregory. See Richards, *Consul of God*, 80–84; and Llewellyn, "Roman Church in the Seventh Century."

Chapter 12. Prefect of the Roman Church

1. In late antiquity, a bishop's diocese consisted of a geographic space (mapped according to imperial bureaucratic divisions) in which he possessed administrative and sacramental authority. With time, the bishops of large urban areas gained more grandiose titles (e.g., archbishop, metropolitan, or patriarch) and were able to extend their administrative authority beyond the specific geographic space of their original see. The most obvious outcome of this expansion was the ability to oversee the election of bishops in smaller neighboring regions. During the latter part of the fourth century and especially during the fifth century, the See of Rome was able to extend its influence far beyond the neighboring

diocese of Rome, such that it had administrative authority over a vast network of dioceses throughout Central and Southern Italy, and the Balkans. By "super-jurisdiction" I refer to those non-neighboring dioceses in which Rome exerted administrative authority, namely through the ability to oversee episcopal elections.

2. For an examination of ways in which the individual parties and concerns overlapped in this context, see the collection of essays in Celia Chezelle and Catherine Cubitt, eds., *Crisis in the Oikoumene: The Three Chapters and the Failed Quest for Unity in the Sixth-Century Mediterranean* (Turnhout: Brepols Publishers, 2007).

3. Gregory, *Ep.* 1.35.

4. Gregory, *Ep.* 2.25.

5. Gregory, *Ep.* 2.25.

6. Gregory, *Ep.* 2.34.

7. Gregory, *Ep.* 2.38.

8. Gregory, *Ep.* 3.54.

9. For more on the election, see Demacopoulos, *Five Models*, 147–48.

10. Gregory criticized Marinianus for failing to give adequately to the poor (*Ep.* 6.33). For evidence of Gregory's approval, see *Ep.* 7.39, 9.139, 9.140, and 9.156.

11. See Ralph Mathisen, *Ecclesiastical Factionalism and Religious Controversy in Fifth-Century Gaul* (Washington, DC: Catholic University Press, 1989), 11.

12. See Markus, *Gregory the Great and His World*, 133–37.

13. Markus, *Gregory the Great and His World*, 133–37.

14. Gregory, *Ep.* 1.80. To be clear, not everyone in Milan accepted a pro-Roman and anti-Three Chapters metropolitan. Characteristically, a schism in the Milanese church ensued that lasted through the end of the sixth century.

15. Gregory, *Ep.* 3.29, 3.30, and 3.31. See Demacopoulos, *Five Models*, 148–49.

16. Though Constantius was not from St. Andrews like Marinianus, Gregory had known Constantius from their time together in Constantinople.

17. Cf. Gregory, *Ep.* 4.37.

18. Gregory, *Ep.* 3.29, 4.37, and 5.18.

19. Some examples include *Ep.* 4.1, 4.2, 4.3, 4.22, 4.33, 4.37, 5.18, 5.37, and 7.14.

20. Although Sicilian clergy largely accepted Roman ecclesiastical jurisdiction, they did not always embrace Rome's moral policies, especially regarding celibacy of the lower clergy. On the circumstances and dimensions of Roman authority in Sicily in the time of Leo, see Demacopoulos, *Invention of Peter*, chapter 2.

21. A fully functioning administrative system in the Sicilian patrimony likely began during the tenure of Pope Pelagius I (556–561). Gregory personally contributed to the Sicilian landholdings when he disposed of his share of the family property upon taking his monastic vows in 574. According to Gregory of Tours, a contemporary account, Pope Gregory also endowed six monasteries on this property in Sicily. Gregory of Tours, *History of the Franks*, 10.1. See also John the Deacon, *Vita*, 1.5–6. For more on the Sicilian patrimony of the Roman Church, see Richards, *Popes and the Papacy*, 307–22. See also Dominic Morneau, "Les patrimoines de l'Église romaine," 79–93; and Vincenzo Recchia, *Gregorio Magno e la società agricola*.

22. The particular forms of Gregory's strict governance of the island (especially his concerns for questions of justice, the conditions of peasants, social policies, and so on) exemplify the extent to which his practical administrative talents enabled the promotion of a particular form of moral theology that reflected his ascetic concerns.

23. While it is not entirely clear when the Sicilian patrimony was divided into two administrative units, it likely preceded Gregory. Gregory's contribution in this regard was to formalize a division in ecclesiastical organization of the island that mirrored the economic one. The Syracusan bishop was made the senior of the two. See Gregory, *Ep.* 2.50.

24. Concerning the Roman Church's involvement in estate management, see Sessa, *Formation of Papal Authority*, esp. 90–126.

25. Even the title *rector*, at this time, was a title of honor, not office.

26. See, for example, Pelagius I, *Ep.* 91, in *Pelagii I papae epistulae quae supersunt (556–561)*, crit. ed., ed. Pius Gassó and Columba Batlle (Barcelona: Abadia de Montserat, 1956), which ordered his agent to deprive the bishop of Tauromenium of the pallium. See Robert Markus, *Gregory the Great*, 114n23.

27. See, for example, *Ep.* 1.70 and 13.35. See also Demacopoulos, *Invention of Peter*, ch. 5.

28. By this I mean that Gregory simultaneously selected for leadership in the church men who possessed ascetic credentials and encouraged those men to develop a kind of spiritual supervision of those under their care that reflected the type of spiritual mentoring that was occurring in organized ascetic communities at the time. Demacopoulos, *Five Models*, esp. ch. 5.

29. For example, several Sicilian bishops do not seem to have shared Gregory's views concerning clerical celibacy. See Gregory, *Ep.* 1.42, 4.34. See also Demacopoulos, *Five Models*, 144–53.

30. Concerning Gregory's involvement in Maximian's election, see Gregory, *Ep.* 2.5. Examples of Gregory's criticisms include *Ep.* 3.12, 4.11, and 4.12.

31. Gregory, *Ep.* 1.18.

32. For a critique of Richards's and Martyn's assessment that Gregory deliberately stacked the Sicilian bench with Roman clerics, see Demacopoulos, *Invention of Peter*, 142–46. Müller similarly interprets Gregory's action in Sicily to constitute a systematic assertion or Roman authority, but she refrains from going as far as Richards and Martyn. Müller, *Führung im Denken*, 176–82.

33. See, for example, Gregory, *Ep.* 2.29. See also Demacopoulos, *Invention of Peter*, 141–42.

34. According to the surviving evidence, Gregory never justified his intervention in Sicily by reciting the scriptural basis for Petrine authority, never claimed that an uncontrollable bishop was guilty of insulting Peter's *principium*, and never availed himself of the canonical grounds for his Petrine authority. See Demacopoulos, *Invention of Peter*, 147.

35. The letters preserved in the *Collectio Thessalonicensis* reveal the complicated history of Roman pretensions in the region and help to differentiate the papacy's actions and expectations there from elsewhere. *Epistularum Romanaroum pontificium ad vicarios per Illyricum aliosque episcopos collection Thessalonicensis*, crit. ed., ed. C. Silva-Tarouca (Rome: Pontificia Università gregoriana, 1937).

36. Gregory informs Jobinus, the prefect of Illyria, of his decision in *Ep.* 2.20.

37. Letters to Antoninus include *Ep.* 2.19, 3.9, and 3.22. For the many tasks performed by Gregory's *rectores*, see Markus, *Gregory the Great and His World*, 112–21.

38. The first being the case of the archdeacon Honoratus (see *Ep.* 2.19); the second was that of Bishop Florentius of Epidaurus (see *Ep.* 3.8 and 3.9).

39. See *Ep.* 2.44, where Gregory rails against Natalis's lack of abstemiousness and general failure to adhere to the ascetic expectations of spiritual leaders.

40. Gregory, *Ep.* 5.6. See Demacopoulos, "Gregory the Great and the Sixth-Century Dispute over the Ecumenical Title," 606–7.

41. One of Gregory's criticisms of Maximus was that he had purchased the support of the imperial exarch, Romanus.

42. Gregory, *Ep.* 4.20, 5.6, and 5.39.

43. Gregory, *Ep.* 5.6, 6.3, and 6.25.

44. Gregory, *Ep.* 5.39.

45. For an examination of the entire affair, see Richards, *Consul of God*, 201–7.

46. See, for example, Gregory, *Ep.* 1.46, 1.47, 1.63, 1.65, 3.1, and 3.5.

47. See Gregory, *Ep.* 1.48, 1.77, 2.38, and 2.42.

48. See, for example, Gregory, *Ep.* 1.60–62, 1.81, 3.4, 3.36, 3.39, 7.21, and 9.222. His frequent rebukes of Januarius of Cagliari and Lucillus of Malta offer

a prime example of moral policing of malcontent bishops. See *Ep.* 4.8, 4.9, 4.10, and 9.25. See also Demacopoulos, *Five Models*, 150–53.

49. The origins of the pallium are uncertain. The *Liber Pontificalis* suggests that its first distribution was by Pope Marcus (d. 336). The vita that likely serves as the source material for the *LP* dates to the beginning of the sixth century.

50. Gregory, *Ep.* 2.18.

51. Gregory, *Ep.* 3.54.

52. Gregory, *Ep.* 5.61.

53. See John Martyn, introduction to *Letters of Gregory the Great*, 78–80.

54. The request itself could be interpreted in multiple ways: it could simply have been an act of patronage by Brunhilde on behalf of her bishop; it could also be seen as an indirect attempt at self-aggrandizement—few suffragan bishops possessed a pallium, and having her own advisor receive one could be symbolically powerful.

55. Gregory, *Ep.* 8.4.

56. Gregory, *Ep.* 8.4.

57. See Gregory, *Ep.* 5.58, 5.59, and 5.60.

58. See Gregory, *Ep.* 5.58, 5.59, and 5.60.

59. Concerning his view that the relics of Peter possessed miraculous power, see Gregory, *Ep.* 1.25, 1.29, 6.58, 8.33, and 13.43.

60. According to Thomas Noble, Symmachus was the first bishop of Rome to distribute a relic of St. Peter (he sent one to the Burgundian king, Sigismund). It was Gregory, however, who first developed the distribution of relics as a repeatable and deliberate act of diplomacy. Thomas Noble, "Review: Michele Maccarrone on the Medieval Papacy," *Catholic Historical Review* 80 (1994): 518–33, at 527.

61. Gregory, *Ep.* 1.25 (the exiled patriarch of Antioch), 1.29 (a member of Constantinopolitan court), 1.30 (also a member of the royal court), 3.33 (a patrician in Gaul), 3.47 (an African bishop), 6.6 (Childebert), 6.58 (Brunhilde), 7.23 (the emperor's sister), 7.25 (a Constantinopolitan physician), 8.33 (a Sicilian official), 9.229b (Reccared), 11.43 (a patrician in Gaul), 12.2 (three African noblewomen), 12.14 (the bishop of Istria), and 13.43 (the patriarch of Alexandria). On a few occasions, the gift was accompanied by relics of other saints, such as St. Paul (*Ep.* 6.58) and St. John the Baptist (*Ep.* 9.229b), or a fragment of the cross of Christ (*Ep.* 9.229b). Concerning Gregory's distribution of the relics of St. Peter to members of royal elite, see Grazia Rapisarda, "I doni nell'epistolario di Gregorio Magno," in *Gregorio Magno e il suo tempo* (Rome: Institutum Patristicum "Augustinianum," 1991), 2:285–300.

62. Gregory, *Ep.* 4.30. Gregory seems to have been uncomfortable with the idea of partitioning the actual bones of a saint, which was already a common

practice in the East, although he was willing to allow the translation of relics from one place to another. See *Ep.* 14.7.

63. Gregory, *Ep.* 1.25.

64. Gregory, *Ep.* 6.6.

65. Gregory, *Ep.* 9.229b.

66. Gregory, *Ep.* 6.58.

67. Gregory, *Ep.* 6.58.

68. Placement of these relics within a key symbolized the link between the historic authority of Peter and his contemporary arbiter, the bishop of Rome. Christ's granting of the keys of heaven to Peter (Mt. 16:18–19), more than anything else, provided the biblical justification for Peter's leadership among the apostles and, as a consequence, Rome's privilege in the Church of Gregory's day. Gregory no doubt hoped that the recipients of these gifts would be reminded of this connection every time that they viewed the key or called upon it for help. As bishop of Rome, Gregory was the contemporary steward to the gates of heaven—yet another point subtly reinforced by his distribution of the keys.

Chapter 13. Spreading Christianity beyond the Roman World

1. See, for example, Gregory, *Ep.* 6.5 and 6.6.

2. See, for example, Robert Markus, "Gregory the Great and a Papal Missionary Strategy," *Studies in Church History* 6 (1970): 29–38, and *Gregory the Great and His World*, 80–82; Richards's position is less explicit: *Consul of God*, 212–16.

3. See Demacopoulos, "Gregory the Great and the Pagan Shrines of Kent." Note, also, the way that Gregory refers to his own spiritual advancement to the life of asceticism as a "conversion" in the prefatory letter to the *Moralia*, which he sent to Leander of Seville.

4. Indeed, it was quite common for ascetic authors such as Benedict to refer to a Christian's decision to embrace the monastic life as a "conversion." Moreover, as Straw has demonstrated, there is a certain parallelism between Gregory's efforts to bring non-Christians to Christianity and his notion of the need to bring (Christian) sinners to repentance. See Straw, *Perfection in Imperfection*, 194–235. For more on the linguistic use of *convertere* and *conversio* in Gregory's works, see Demacopoulos, "Gregory the Great and the Pagan Shrines of Kent."

5. See, for example, Gregory, *Ep.* 8.4 and 9.214.

6. Gregory, *Ep.* 6.5. 6.6, 6.51, 6.59, and 6.60.

7. Gregory, *Ep.* 6.52, 6.54, 6.55, and 6.56.

8. Gregory struggled to collect back revenues from Virgilius, who had been serving as the de facto steward of the patrimony. See *Ep.* 6.55.

9. See Gregory, *Ep.* 11.46. In this particular letter, which repeatedly complains about the evil behavior of priests, Gregory never actually identifies the immoral behavior. Other letters sent to Gaul at the same time complain about simony and married clergy.

10. Gregory's approach to the Jews is typically understood to be more generous than that of other early Christian authors. For example, he repeatedly condemned forced conversions or acts of violence against the Jews. But he was also perfectly willing to induce conversion through a relaxation of the rents of Jews who lived on Church property. For a recent examination, see Darius Makuja, "Gregory the Great, Roman Law, and the Jews: Seeking 'True' Conversions," *Sacris Erudiri* 48 (2009): 35–74.

11. See Gregory, *Ep.* 7.21 and 9.214. The pontiff demanded that the local rulers and ecclesiastical officials put an end to the practice, but he also adjusted the financial accounts so that Candidus might purchase the freedom of any Christian slaves he encountered.

12. Gregory, *Ep.* 6.5 and 6.6.

13. Some of the more notable studies include Markus, "Gregory the Great and a Papal Missionary Strategy" ; Robert Markus, "Gregory the Great's Pagans," in *Belief and Culture in the Middle Ages: Studies Presented to Henry Mayr-Harting*, ed. Richard Gameson and Henrietta Leyser (New York: Oxford University Press, 2001), 23–34; Rob Meens, "A Background to Augustine's Mission to Anglo-Saxon England," *Anglo-Saxon England* 23 (1994), 5–17; Clare Stancliffe, "Kings and Conversion: Some Comparisons between the Roman Mission to England and Patrick's to Ireland," *Frühmittelalterliche Studien* 14 (1980): 59–94; Ian Wood, "The Mission of Augustine of Canterbury to the English," *Speculum* 69 (1994): 1–17; and Wood, "Some Historical Re-identifications and the Christianization of Kent," in *Christianizing Peoples and Converting Individuals*, ed. Guyda Armstrong and Ian Wood, International Medieval Research 7 (Turnhout: Brepols, 2000), 27–35.

14. For Bertha's marriage, her Christianity, and the implications for both upon the mission, see Ian Wood, "Augustine and Gaul," in *St. Augustine and the Conversion of the English People*, ed. Richard Gameson (Stroud: Sutton, 1999), 68–82.

15. Gregory, *Ep.* 6.10. For more on the dating of the mission, see Robert Markus, "The Chronology of the Gregorian Mission to England: Bede's

Narrative and Gregory's Correspondence," *Journal of Ecclesiastical History* 14 (1963): 16–30; and Wood, "Mission of Augustine of Canterbury to the English."

16. See Wood, "Mission of Augustine of Canterbury to the English."

17. Gregory, *Ep.* 6.51.

18. Gregory, *Ep.* 6.51.

19. Gregory, *Ep.* 6.60: "sed sacerdotes qui in vicino sunt pastoralem erga eos sollicitudinem non habere."

20. Gregory, *Ep.* 6.52 (to the bishops of Turnis and Marseilles), 6.54 (to Virgilius of Arles), 6.55 (to Desidrius, bishop of Vienne, and Syagius of Autun), and 6.55 (to Protasius of Aix).

21. Gregory, *Ep.*6.53. Gregory hints that the physical difficulty of the journey and the trouble of finding adequate translators were two of the primary challenges.

22. Gregory, *Ep.* 8.29.

23. See Margaret Truran, "The Roman Mission," in *The Monks of England: Benedictines in England from Augustine to the Present Day*, ed. Daniel Rees (London: SPCK 1997), 19–36.

24. Gregory, *Ep.* 11.37 (to Aethelbert), 11.35 (to Bertha), and 11.36 (to Augustine).

25. Gregory, *Ep.* 11.56.

26. See Demacopoulos, "Gregory the Great and the Pagan Shrines of Kent." Perhaps the most concise alternative interpretation is that of Markus, "Gregory the Great and a Papal Missionary Strategy."

27. The *Responsa* is not contained in any of the early Roman collections of Gregory's letters. As noted previously, the oldest surviving evidence of its existence stems from Bede, *Ecclesiastical History of the English People* 1.27.

28. The most recent analysis of the *Libellus responsionum* is that of Müller, *Führung im Denken*, 341–60. See also Margaret Deansly and Paul Grosjean, "The Canterbury Edition of the Answers of Pope Gregory I to St. Augustine," *Journal of Ecclesiastical History* 10 (1959): 1–49; and Paul Meyvaert, "Le libellus responsionum à Augustin de Cantorbéry: Une oeuvre authentique de saint Grégoire le Grand," in *Grégoire le Grand*, ed. Jacques Fontaine, Robert Gillet, and Stan Pellistrandi (Paris: Éditions du CNRS, 1986), 543–50.

29. See Demacopoulos, *Five Models*, 156.

30. Gregory, *Ep.* 8.4.

31. Gregory, *Ep.* 8.4.

32. Gregory, *Ep.* 11.37.

33. See Demacopoulos, "Gregory the Great and the Pagan Shrines of Kent."

34. Gregory, *Ep.* 11.35.

Chapter 14. The Steward of Peter's Tomb

1. This is the principal argument of Demacopoulos, *Invention of Peter*.

2. For a brief overview of the scholarly understanding of the original Constantinian basilica, see Joseph Alchermes, "Petrine Politics: Pope Symmachus and the Rotunda of St. Andrew's at the Old St. Peter's," *Catholic Historical Review* 81 (1995): 1–40, esp. 3–6. See also Turpin Bannister, "The Constantinian Basilica of St. Peter at Rome," *Journal of the Society of Architectural Historians* 27 (1968): 3–32; and Krautheimer, *Rome*.

3. Concerning the archeological evidence for third-century activity, see Gitte Lonstrup, "Constructing Myths: The Foundation of *Roma Christiana* on 29 June," trans. Lene Ostermark-Johansen, *Analecta Romana* 33 (2008): 27–64; and Joseph Donalla Alchermes, "'Cura pro mortuis' and 'Cultus Martyrum': Commemoration in Rome from the Second through the Sixth Century" (Ph. D. diss., New York University, 1989), 64–125.

4. This particular epigram has been transcribed as *Epigrammata* 20. Damasus, *Epigrammata*, ed. Antonio Ferrua (Vatican City: Bibliotheca Apostolica Vaticana, 1942). Damasus does not tell us where Peter's relics are or when they were moved—in fact, he does not actually say that they were moved; he simply acknowledges that pilgrims will come to this site looking for the relics. Damasus informs the visitors that they should instead take note of the star-like quality of Peter and Paul and be heartened that pilgrims, too, can be inscribed as stars by the patron for the shrine (i.e., Damasus). In effect, Damasus seems to continue the cult of Peter on the Via Appia, even though relics no longer existed there. Perhaps this was because the *Memoria Apostolorum* offers him an opportunity to link himself to Peter's cult in a way that he could not achieve at the Vatican, where patronage was still primarily in the hands of the imperial family and wealthy elite.

5. See Demacopoulos, *Invention of Peter*, 110.

6. Krautheimer, *Rome*, 87; B. Brenk, "Der Kultort, seine Zugänglichkeit und seine Besucher," in *Akten des XII Internationalen Kongresses für christliche Archäologie, Bonn September 1991*, ed. E. Dassmann and J. Engemann (München: JAC Ergänzungsband, 1995), 29–122, esp. 79–81. The most prominent attempt to link Gregory's building program to his theology is Barbara Müller, "*Fecit ut super corpus beati Petri missas celebrarentur:* Gregory the Great and St. Peter's Tomb," *Studia Patristica* 40 (2006): 69–74.

7. See Krautheimer, *Rome*; and Müller, "*Fecit ut super corpus.*"

8. Krautheimer maintains (*Rome*, 86) that Gregory's construction introduced distance between the pilgrim and the saint, which fit with the pontiff's aversion to the movement of relics. Müller, however, successfully argues that

building the crypt in this way allowed a much larger number of pilgrims to gain access to the site, even if it was at a greater distance.

9. Gregory, *Ep.* 8.28.

10. Guy Philippart, "Grégoire le Grand et les *gesta martyrum*," in *Gregorio Magno e L'Agiografia fra IV e VII Secolo*, ed. Antonella Degl'Innocenti, Antonio De Prisco, and Emore Paoli, 257–283.

11. See, for example, Gregory, *Ep.* 1.70, written to Peter, who was likely Gregory's most trusted administrator. See also *Ep.* 13.35.

12. See, for example, Gregory, *Ep.* 2.29.

13. Gregory, *Ep.* 4.30.

14. Demacopoulos, *Invention of Peter*, ch. 5.

15. Demacopoulos, "Gregory the Great and the Appeal to Petrine Authority."

16. See Demacopoulos, *Invention of Peter*, ch. 2 and ch. 3.

17. See Demacopoulos, "Gregory the Great and the Appeal to Petrine Authority."

Conclusion

1. As Sessa demonstrates, the Roman bishops of late antiquity were dual figures of authority (in both private households and public administration).

BIBLIOGRAPHY

Primary Sources

Augustine. "New Letters." Critical ed. Edited by Johannes Divjak. CSEL 88.

———. *On Marriage and Concupiscence [De nuptiis et concupiscentia]*. Critical ed. Edited by Carl Franz Urba. CSEL 42.

———. *On the Grace of Christ and Original Sin [De gratia Christi et de peccato originale]*. Edited by J.-P. Migne. PL 44.

Bede. *Ecclesiastical History of the English People*. Critical ed. Edited by Bertram Colgrave. Oxford: Clarendon Press, 1969.

Cassian, John. *Conferences [Conlationes]*. Critical ed. Edited by Michael Petschenig. CSEL 13.

———. *Institutes [Institutiones]*. Critical ed. Edited by Michael Petschenig. CSEL 17.

Continuatio prosperi havniensis. Edited by Theodor Mommsen. MGH AA 9. Berlin, 1892.

Damasus. *Epigrammata*. Critical ed. Edited by Antonio Ferrua. Vatican City: Bibliotheca Apostolica Vaticana, 1942.

Epistularum Romanaroum pontificium ad vicarios per Illyricum aliosque episcopos collection Thessalonicensis. Critical ed. Edited by C. Silva-Tarouca. Rome: Pontificia Università gregoriana, 1937.

Gregory. *Book of Pastoral Rule [Liber regulae pastoralis]*. Critical ed. Edited by Floribert Rommel. SC 381–82.

———. *Dialogues [Dialogorum libri IV]*. Critical ed. Edited by Adalbert de Vogüé. SC 251, 260, 265.

———. *Homilies on Ezekiel [Homiliae in Hiezechihelem]*. Critical ed. Edited by Marcus Adriaen. CCSL 142.

———. *Homilies on the Gospels [Homiliae in Evangelia]*. Critical ed. Edited by Raymond Étaix. CCSL 141.

———. *Letters [Epistulae]*. Critical ed. Edited by Dag Norberg. CCSL 140–140A.

———. *Morals on the Book of Job [Moralia in Iob libri]*. Critical ed. Edited by Marci Adriaen. CCSL 143, 143A, 143B.

———. *Responsa [Libellus responsionum]*. In Bede, *Ecclesiastical History of the English People*. Critical ed. Edited by Bertram Colgrave. Oxford: Clarendon Press, 1969.

Gregory of Tours. *History of the Franks [Historia Francorum]*. Critical ed. Edited by Rudolf Buchner. Berlin: Rutten & Loening, 1955.

John the Deacon. *Vita Sancti Gregorii Magni*. PL 75.

Leo Marsicanus. *Chronicon monasterii Casinensis*. Edited by Wilhelm Wattenbach. MGH SS 7.

Liber Pontificalis. 2d ed. Edited by Louis Duchesne. 2 vols. Paris: E. de Boccard, 1955.

Paul the Deacon. *History of the Lombards [Historia Langobardorum]*. Edited by Ludwig Bethmann and Georg Waitz. MGH 48.

———. *Vita Sancti Gregorii Magni*. 2 vols. Critical ed. Edited by Sabina Tuzzo. Pisa: Scuola normale superiore, 2002.

Palladius. *The Lausiac History [Historia Lausiaca]*. Critical ed. Edited by Cuthbert Butler. Cambridge: Cambridge University Press, 1904.

Pelagius. *Pelagii I papae epistulae quae supersunt (556–561)*. Crit. ed. Edited by Pius Gassó and Columba Batlle. Barselona: Abadia de Montserat, 1956.

Procopius. *The Wars [De bellis]*. Critical ed. Edited by Jakob Haury. Leipzig: Teubner, 1905–1913; revised by Gerhard Wirth, 1976.

Sulpicius Severus. *Life of St. Martin of Tours [Vita S. Martini]*. Critical ed. Edited by Jacques Fontaine. SC 133.

Gregory's Works in English Translation

Book of Pastoral Rule. Translated by George E. Demacopoulos. Crestwood, NY: St. Vladimir's Seminary Press, 2007.

Dialogues. Translated by Odo John Zimmerman. FC 39. Washington, DC: Catholic University Press, 1959.

Forty Gospel Homilies. Translated by David Hurst. Kalamazoo, MI: Cistercian Publications, 1990.

The Homilies of St. Gregory the Great on the Book of the Prophet Ezekiel. Translated by Juliana Cownie. Etna, CA: Center for Traditionalist Orthodox Studies, 1990.

The Letters of Gregory the Great. Translated by John R. C. Martyn. 3 vols. Toronto: Pontifical Institute of Medieval Studies, 2004.

Morals on the Book of Job by St. Gregory the Great. Translated by the Faculty of Oxford. Oxford: John Henry Parker, 1844.

Secondary Sources

Alchermes, Joseph Donalla. "'Cura pro mortuis' and 'Cultus Martyrum': Commemoration in Rome from the Second through the Sixth Century." Ph. D. dissertation. New York University, 1989.

———. "Petrine Politics: Pope Symmachus and the Rotunda of St. Andrew's at the Old St. Peter's." *Catholic Historical Review* 81 (1995): 1–40.

Baldavin, John. *The Urban Character of Christian Worship: The Origins, Development and Meaning of Stational Liturgy.* Rome: Pontificio Instituto Orientale, 1987.

Bannister, Turpin. "The Constantinian Basilica of St. Peter at Rome." *Journal of the Society of Architectural Historians* 27 (1968): 3–32.

Batiffol, Pierre. *Saint Gregory the Great.* Translated by John Stoddard. London: Burns, Oates & Washbourne, 1929.

Beyschlag, Karlmann. *Grundriß der Dogmengeschichte.* Vol. 2, *Gott und Mensch,* part 2, *Die abendländische Epoche.* Darmstadt: Wissenschaftliche Buchgesellschaft, 2000.

Boesch Gajano, Sofia. "Dislivelli culturali e mediazioni ecclesiastiche nei *Dialogi* di Gregorio Magno." *Quaderni storici* 14 (1979): 398–415.

———. *Grégoire le Grand: Aux origines du Moyen Âge.* Paris: Éditions du Cerf, 2007.

———. *Gregorio Magno: Alle origini del Medioevo.* Rome: Viella, 2004.

———. "'Narratio' e 'expositio' nei Dialoghi di Gregorio Magno." *Bullettino dell'Istituto per il Medio Evo e Archivio Muratoriano* 88 (1979): 1–33.

———. "La proposta agiografica dei 'Dialogi' di Gregorio Magno." *Studi Medievali* 3 (1980): 623–64.

Bolton, W. F. "The Super-Historical Sense in the Dialogues of Gregory I." *Aevum* 33 (1959): 206–13.

Bowes, Kimberly. *Private Worship, Public Values, and Religious Change in Late Antiquity.* Cambridge: Cambridge University Press, 1998.

Brakke, David. *Athanasius and the Politics of Asceticism.* Reprint, Baltimore: Johns Hopkins Press, 1998.

———. *Demons and the Making of the Monk: Spiritual Combat in Early Christianity.* Cambridge, MA: Harvard University Press, 2006.

Brazzel, Kathleen. *The Clausulae in the Works of St. Gregory the Great*. Washington, DC: Catholic University Press, 1939.

Brenk, B. "Der Kultort, seine Zugänglichkeit und seine Besucher." In *Akten des XII Internationalen Kongresses für christliche Archäologie, Bonn September 1991*, edited by Ernst Dassmann and Josef Engemann, 29–122. München: JAC Ergänzungsband, 1995.

Brown, T. S. *Gentlemen and Officers: Imperial Administration and Aristocratic Power in Byzantine Italy, A.D. 554–800*. Rome: British School at Rome, 1984.

Cameron, Averil. *Christianity and the Rhetoric of Empire*. Berkeley: University of California Press, 1994.

———. "Education and Literary Culture." In *The Cambridge Ancient History*. vol. 13, *The Late Empire, A.D. 337–425*, edited by Averil Cameron and Peter Garnsey, 673–76. Cambridge: Cambridge University Press, 1998.

Caspar, Eric. *Geschichte des Papsttums*. 2 vols. Tubingen: J. C. B. Mohr, 1930–33.

Chadwick, Owen. *John Cassian: A Study in Primitive Monasticism*. Cambridge: Cambridge University Press, 1950.

Chavasse, Antoine. "Aménagements liturgiques à Rome, au VIIe et VIIIe siècles." *Revue Ben.* 99 (1989): 75–102.

Chezelle, Celia, and Catherine Cubitt, eds. *Crisis in the Oikoumene: The Three Chapters and the Failed Quest for Unity in the Sixth-Century Mediterranean*. Turnhout: Brepols Publishers, 2007.

Chryssavgis, John. *Soul Mending: The Art of Spiritual Direction*. Brookline, MA: Holy Cross Orthodox Press, 2000.

Clark, Elizabeth. *Reading Renunciation: Asceticism and Scripture in Early Christianity*. Princeton: Princeton University Press, 1999.

Clark, Francis. *The Pseudo-Gregorian Dialogues*. Leiden: Brill, 1987.

Colish, Marcia. *The Stoic Tradition from Antiquity to the Early Middle Ages*. 2 vols. Leiden: Brill, 1990.

Cooper, Kate. "The Martyr, the *Matrona*, and the Bishop." *Early Medieval Europe* 8 (1999): 297–317.

Cooper, Kate, and Julia Hillner, eds. *Religion, Dynasty, and Patronage in Early Christian Rome, 300–900*. Cambridge: Cambridge University Press, 2007.

Costambeys, Marios. "Burial Topography and the Power of the Church in Fifth- and Sixth-Century Rome." *Papers of the British School of Rome* 69 (2001): 169–89.

Cusack, Pearse A. "Some Literary Antecedents of the Totila Encounter in the Second Dialogue of Pope Gregory I." *Studia Patristica* 12 (1975): 87–90.

Dagens, Claude. "La 'Conversion' de saint Grégoire le Grand." *Revue des Études Augustiniennes* 15 (1969): 149–62.

———. "La fin des temps et l'église selon saint Grégoire le Grand." *Recherches de Science religieuse* 58 (1970): 273–88.

———. *Saint Grégoire le Grand. Cultre et experience chrétiennes.* Paris: Études Augustiennes, 1977.

Daley, Brian. "Position and Patronage in the Early Church: The Original Meaning of the 'Primacy of Honour.'" *Journal of Theological Studies* 44 (1993): 429–53.

Dal Santo, Matthew. "Gregory the Great and Eustrathios of Constantinople: The *Dialogues on the Miracles of the Italian Fathers* as an Apology for the Cult of the Saints." *Journal of Early Christian Studies* 17 (2009): 421–57

———. "The Shadow of a Doubt?: A Note on the *Dialogues* and *Registrum Epistolarum* of Gregory the Great." *Journal of Ecclesiastical History* 61 (2010): 3–17.

Damizia, G. "Il *Registrum Epistolarum* di San Gregorio Magno ed il *Corpus Iuris Civilis.*" *Benedictina* 2 (1948): 195–226.

Deansly, Margaret, and Paul Grosjean. "The Canterbury Edition of the Answers of Pope Gregory I to St. Augustine." *Journal of Ecclesiastical History* 10 (1959): 1–49.

Degl'Innocenti, Antonella, Antonio De Prisco, and Emore Paoli, eds. *Gregorio Magno e L'Agiografia fra IV e VII Secolo.* Firenze: Edizioni del Galluzzo, 2007.

Demacopoulos, George. *Five Models of Spiritual Direction.* Notre Dame, IN: University of Notre Dame Press, 2007.

———. "Gregory the Great." In *The Spiritual Senses in the Western Christian Tradition*, edited by Paul Gavrilyuk and Sarah Coakley, 71–85. Cambridge: Cambridge University Press, 2012.

———. "Gregory the Great and a Post-Imperial Discourse." In *Power and Authority in the Eastern Christian Experience*, edited by Fevronia K. Soumakis, 120–37. New York: Theotokos Press, 2011.

———. "Gregory the Great and the Appeal to Petrine Authority." *Studia Patristica* 48 (2010): 333–46.

———. "Gregory the Great and the Pagan Shrines of Kent." *Journal of Late Antiquity* 1 (2008): 353–69.

———. "Gregory the Great and the Sixth-Century Dispute over the Ecumenical Title." *Journal of Theological Studies* 70 (2009): 600–21.

———. *The Invention of Peter.* Philadelphia: University of Pennsylvania Press, 2013.

———. "The Soteriology of St. Gregory the Great: A Case against the Augustinian Interpretation." *American Benedictine Review* 54 (2003): 312–28.

de Vogüé, Adalbert. "Le pape qui persécuta saint Equitius. Essai d'identification." *Annolecta Bollandiana* 100 (1982): 319–25.

Dudden, F. Homes. *Gregory the Great: His Place in History and Thought.* 2 vols. New York: Russell and Russell, 1905.

Everett, Nicholas. *Literacy in Lombard Italy 568–774.* Cambridge: Cambridge University Press, 2003.

Folliet, Georges. "Les Trois categories de chrétiens, survie d'un theme augustinien." *L'Année théologique augustinienne* 14 (1954): 81–96.

Fontaine, Jacques, Robert Gillet, and Stan Pellistrandi, eds. *Grégoire le Grand.* Paris: Éditions du Centre National de la Recherche Scientifique, 1986.

Foucault, Michel. *The Courage of Truth: Lectures at the Collège de France 1983–1984.* Translated by Graham Burchell. New York: Picador, 2011.

———. *The Government of Self and Others: Lectures at the Collège de France 1982–1983.* Translated by Graham Burchell. New York: Picador, 2010.

———. *The Hermeneutics of the Subject: Lectures at the Collège de France 1981–1982.* Translated by Graham Burchell. New York: Picador, 2005.

Gessel, Wilhelm. "Reform am Haupt: Die Pastoralregel Gregors des Grossen und die Besetzung von Bischofsstühlen." In *Papsttum und Kirchenreform: Historische Beiträge. Festschrift für Georg Schwaiger zum 65. Geburtstag*, edited by Manfred Weitlauff and Karl Hausberger, 17–36. St. Ottilien: EOS Verlag, 1990.

Gibbon, Edward. *The Decline and Fall of the Roman Empire.* 12 vols. London, 1806.

Godding, Robert. "Les *Dialogues* . . . de Grégoire le Grand. A propos d'un livre récent." *Analecta Bollandiana* 106 (1988): 201–29.

Greschat, Katharina. "Feines Weizenmehl und ungenießbare Spelzen: Gregors des Großen Wertschätzung augustinischer Theologie." *Zeitschrift für antiques Christentum* 11 (2007): 57–72.

———. *Die* Moralia in Job *Gregors des Großen: Ein christologisch-ekklesiologischer Kommentar.* Tübingen: Mohr Siebeck, 2005.

———. "Die Verwendung des Physiologus bei Gregor dem Grossen: Paulus als gezähmtes Einhorn in *Moralia in Job XXI.*" *Studia Patristica* 43 (2006): 381–86.

Guidobaldi, Federico. "L'organizzazione dei tituli nello spazio urbano." In *Christina Loco: Lo spazio cristiano nella Roma del primo millennio*, edited by Letizia Pani Ermini, 123–29. Rome: Fratelli Polombi, 2000.

Hadot, Pierre. *Philosophy as a Way of Life: Spiritual Exercises from Socrates to Foucault.* Translated by Michael Chase. Oxford: Blackwell, 1995.

Harnack, Adolf von. *History of Dogma.* Translated by Neil Buchanan. 7 vols. New York: Dover, 1961.

Hausherr, Irénée. *Spiritual Direction in the Early Christian East.* Translated by Anthony Gythiel. Kalamazoo, MI: Cistercian Publications, 1990.

Hillner, Julia. "Gregory the Great's 'Prisons': Monastic Confinement in Early Byzantine Italy." *Journal of Early Christian Studies* 19 (2011): 433–71.

Hipshon, David. "Gregory the Great's Political Thought." *Journal of Ecclesiastical History* 53 (2002): 439–53.

Holman, Susan. *The Hungry are Dying: Beggars and Bishops in Roman Cappadocia*. Oxford: Oxford University Press, 2001.

Hwang, Alexander, Brian Matz, and Augustine Casiday, eds. *Grace for Grace: After Augustine and Pelagius*. Washington DC: Catholic University Press, 2012.

Jones, A. H. M. *The Later Roman Empire: 284–602*. 2 vols. 1964. Reprint, Baltimore: Johns Hopkins University Press, 1986.

Kaufman, Peter. *Church, Book, and Bishop: Conflict and Authority in Early Latin Christianity*. Boulder, CO: Westview Press, 1996.

Kisić, Rade. *Patria Caelestis: Die eschatologische Dimension der Theologie Gregors des Großen*. Tübingen: Mohr Siebeck, 2011.

Krautheimer, Richard. *Rome: The Profile of a City*. Reprint, Princeton: Princeton University Press, 2000.

Leyser, Conrad. *Authority and Asceticism from Augustine to Gregory the Great*. Oxford: Oxford University Press, 2000.

———. "Expertise and Authority in Pope Gregory the Great: The Social Function of *Peritia*." In *Gregory the Great: A Symposium*, edited by John Cavadini, 38–61. Notre Dame, IN: University of Notre Dame Press, 1995.

———. "Temptations of Cult: Roman Martyr Piety in the Age of Gregory the Great." *Early Medieval Europe* 9 (2000): 289–309.

Liebs, Detlef. "Roman Law." In *The Cambridge Ancient History*, vol. 14, *Late Antiquity: Empire and Successors, A.D. 425–600*, edited by Averil Cameron, Bryan Ward-Perkins, and Michael Whitby, 251–52. Cambridge: Cambridge University Press, 1995.

Lienhard, Joseph. "On 'Discernment of Spirits' in the Early Church." *Theological Studies* 41 (1980): 505–29.

Llewellyn, Peter. "The Roman Church during the Laurentian Schism (496–506): Priests and Senators." *Church History* 45 (1976): 417–27.

———. "The Roman Church in the Seventh Century: The Legacy of Gregory I." *Journal of Ecclesiastical History* 25 (1974): 363–80.

———. "The Roman Clergy during the Laurentian Schism (498–506): A Preliminary Analysis." *Ancient Society* 8 (1977): 245–75.

———. *Rome in the Dark Ages*. London: Praeger, 1971.

Lonstrup, Gitte. "Constructing Myths: The Foundation of *Roma Christiana* on 29 June." Translated by Lene Ostermark-Johansen. *Analecta Romana* 33 (2008): 27–64.

Loofs, Friedrich. *Leitfaden zum Studium der Dogmengeschichte.* Halle-Saale: Niemeyer, 1906.

Makuja, Darius. "Gregory the Great, Roman Law, and the Jews: Seeking 'True' Conversions." *Sacris Erudiri* 48 (2009): 35–74.

Markus, Robert. "The Chronology of the Gregorian Mission to England: Bede's Narrative and Gregory's Correspondence." *Journal of Ecclesiastical History* 14 (1963): 16–30.

———. "Gregory the Great and a Papal Missionary Strategy." *Studies in Church History* 6 (1970): 29–38.

———. *Gregory the Great and His World.* Cambridge: Cambridge University Press, 1997.

———. "Gregory the Great's Europe." *Royal Historical Society* 31 (1981): 30–35.

———. "Gregory the Great's Pagans." In *Belief and Culture in the Middle Ages: Studies Presented to Henry Mayr-Harting,* edited by Richard Gameson and Henrietta Leyser, 23–34. New York: Oxford University Press, 2001.

Mathisen, Ralph. *Ecclesiastical Factionalism and Religious Controversy in Fifth-Century Gaul.* Washington, DC: Catholic University Press, 1989.

McCulloh, John. "The Cult of Relics in the Letters and 'Dialogues' of Pope Gregory the Great." *Traditio* 32 (1976): 145–84.

McGinn, Bernard. "Contemplation in Gregory the Great." In *Gregory the Great: A Symposium,* edited by John Cavadini, 146–167. Notre Dame, IN: University of Notre Dame Press, 1995.

McReady, William. *Signs of Sanctity: Miracles in the Thought of Gregory the Great.* Toronto: Pontifical Institute of Medieval Studies, 1989.

Meens, Rob. "A Background to Augustine's Mission to Anglo-Saxon England." *Anglo-Saxon England* 23 (1994): 5–17.

Meyendorff, John. "Justinian, the Empire, and the Church." *Dumbarton Oaks Papers* 22 (1968): 43–60.

Meyvaert, Paul. "Bede's Text of the *Libellus Responsionum* of Gregory the Great to Augustine of Canterbury." In *England before the Conquest,* edited by Peter Clemoes and Kathleen Hughes, 15–33. Cambridge: Cambridge University Press, 1971.

———. "The Enigma of Gregory the Great's *Dialogues*: A Response to Francis Clark." *Journal of Ecclesiastical History* 39 (1988): 335–81.

Mohlberg, Leo. "Historisch-kritische Bemerkungen zum Ursprung der sogennaten 'Memoria Apostolorum' an der Appischen Straße." In *Colligere Fragmenta: Festschrift Alban Dold zum 70. Geburstag am 7.7.52,* edited by Bonifatus Fischer and Virgil Fiala, 52–74. Beuron: Beuroner Kunstverlag, 1952.

Morneau, Dominic. "Les patrimoines de l'Église romaine jusqu' à la mort de Grégoire le Grand." *Antiquité tardive* 14 (2006): 79–93.

Müller, Barbara. "*Fecit ut super corpus beati Petri missas celebrarentur:* Gregory the Great and St. Peter's Tomb." *Studia Patristica* 40 (2006): 69–74.

———. *Führung im Denken und Handeln Gregors des Grossen.* Tübingen: Mohr Siebeck, 2009.

———. "Nautische Metaphern bei Gregor dem Grossen." *Studia Patristica* 48 (2010): 165–70.

Munz, Peter. "John Cassian." *Journal of Ecclesiastical History* 11 (1960): 1–22.

Neil, Bronwen, and Matthew Dal Santo, eds. *A Companion to Gregory the Great.* Leiden: Brill, 2013.

Newhauser, Richard, and Susan Ridyard, eds. *Sin in Medieval and Early Modern Culture: The Tradition of the Seven Deadly Sins.* York: York Medieval Press, 2013.

Niespolo, Aelred. "Authority and Service in Gregory the Great." *Downside Review* 122 (2004): 113–28.

Noble, Thomas. "Review: Michele Maccarrone on the Medieval Papacy." *Catholic Historical Review* 80 (1994): 518–33.

Norberg, Dag. "Qui a composé les lettres de saint Grégoire le Grand?" *Studi medievali* 21 (1980): 1–17.

Paroli, Lidia. "Roma dal V al IX secolo: uno sguardo attraverso le stratigrafie archeologiche." In *Roma: Dall'antichità al medioevo. Archeologia e storia nel Museo Nazionale Romano-Crypta Balbi*, edited by Laura Vendittelli, Lidia Paroli, and Maria Stella Arena, 11–40. Milan: Electa, 2004.

Pellegrini, Pietrina. *Militia Clericatus Monachici Ordines: Istituzioni Ecclesiastiche e Società in Gregorio Magno.* 2d ed. Catania: Edizioni del Prisma, 2008.

Petersen, Joan. *The Dialogues of Gregory the Great in their Late Antique Cultural Background.* Toronto: Pontifical Institute for Medieval Studies, 1984.

Pietri, Charles. "Aristocratie et société cléricale dans l'Italie chrétienne au temps d'Odoacre et de Théodoric." *Mélanges de l'École française de Rome. Antiquité* 93 (1981): 417–67.

———. *Roma christiana: Recherches sur l'église de Rome, son organisation, sa politique, son idéologie de Miltiade à Sixte III.* 2 vols. Rome: École Française de Rome, 1976.

———. "Le Sénat, le people chrétien et les partis du Cirque à Rome sous le Pape Symmaqhe." *Mélanges d'Archéologie et d'Histoire* 78 (1966): 123–39.

Pitz, Ernst. *Papstreskripte im frühen Mittelalter: Diplomatische und rechtsgeschichtliche Studien zum Brief-Corpus Gregors des Grossen.* Sigmaringen: Thorbecke, 1990.

Rapisarda, Grazia. "I doni nell'epistolario di Gregorio Magno." In *Gregorio Magno e il suo tempo*, edited by École francaise de Rome, 2:285–300. Rome: Institutum Patristicum "Augustinianum," 1991.

Rapp, Claudia. *Holy Bishops in Late Antiquity*. Berkeley: University of California Press, 2005.

Recchia, Vincenzo. *Gregorio Magno e la società agricola*. Rome: Studium, 1978.

Reydellet, Marc. *Le Royauté dans la literature latine de Sidoine Appolinaire à Isidore de Seville*. Rome: Diffusion de Boccard, 1981.

Rich, Antony. *Discernment in the Desert Fathers: "Diakrisis" in the Life and Thought of Early Egyptian Monasticism*. Milton Keynes, UK: Paternoster, 2007.

Richards, Jeffrey. *Consul of God: The Life and Times of Gregory the Great*. London: Routledge and Kegan Paul, 1980.

———. *Popes and the Papacy in the Early Middle Ages*. London: Routledge and Kegan Paul, 1979.

Riché, Pierre. *Écoles et enseignement dans le Haut Moyen Age*. Paris: Aubier Montaigne, 1979.

———. *Éducation et culture dans l'Occident barbare*. Paris: Seuil, 1962.

Rizzo, Roberta. *Papa Gregorio Magno e la Nobiltà in Sicilia*. Palermo: Officina di Studi Medievali, 2008.

Rousseau, Philip. *Ascetics, Authority, and the Church in the Age of Jerome and Cassian*. Oxford: Oxford University Press, 1978.

Sághy, Marianne. "*Scinditur in partes populus*: Damasus and the Martyrs of Rome." *Early Medieval History* 9 (2000): 273–87.

Saguì, Lucia. "Roma, i centri privilegiati e la lunga durata della tarda antichità. Dati archeologici dal deposito di VII secolo nell'esedra della Crypta Balbi." *Archeologia Medievale* 29 (2002): 7–42

Salzman, Michelle. "Leo's Liturgical Topography: Contestations for Space in Fifth Century Rome." *Journal of Roman Studies* 103 (2013): 208–32.

Seeberg, Reinhold. *Lehrbuch der Dogmengeschichte III: Die Dogmengeschichte des Mittelalters*. Leipzig: A. Deicherts Nachf, 1913.

Sessa, Kristina. "Domestic Emergencies: Pelagius (556–561) and the Challenge of Managing the *domus dei* in Post-Gothic War Italy." Paper delivered at Oxford Patristics Conference, August 2011.

———. *The Formation of Papal Authority in Late Antique Italy: Roman Bishops and the Domestic Sphere*. Cambridge: Cambridge University Press, 2012.

Sotinel, Claire. "Emperors and Popes in the Sixth Century: The Western View." In *The Cambridge Companion to the Age of Justinian*, edited by Michael Maas, 267–90. Cambridge: Cambridge University Press, 2005.

Stancliffe, Clare. "Kings and Conversion: Some Comparisons between the Roman Mission to England and Patrick's to Ireland." *Frühmittelalterliche Studien* 14 (1980): 59–94.

Stewart, Columba. *Cassian the Monk*. Oxford: Oxford University Press, 1998.

Straw, Carole. *Gregory the Great: Perfection in Imperfection.* Berkeley: University of California Press, 1988.

———. "Gregory's Politics: Theory and Practice." In *Gregorio Magno e il suo tempo*, edited by École française de Rome, 1:47–63. Rome: Institutum Patristicum "Augustinianum," 1991.

Trout, Dennis. "Damasus and the Invention of Early Christian Rome." *Journal of Medieval and Early Modern Studies* 33 (2003): 517–36.

Truran, Margaret. "The Roman Mission." In *The Monks of England: Benedictines in England from Augustine to the Present Day*, edited by Daniel Rees, 19–36. London: SPCK, 1997.

Ullmann, Walter. *The Growth of the Papal Government in the Middle Ages: A Study in the Ideological Relation of Clerical to Lay Power.* 3d ed. London: Methuen, 1970.

Wickham, Chris. *Framing the Early Middle Ages: Europe and the Mediterranean 400–800.* Oxford: Oxford University Press, 2005.

Wilken, Robert. "Interpreting Job Allegorically: The *Moralia* of Gregory the Great." *Pro Ecclesia* 10 (2001): 213–26.

Wood, Ian. "Augustine and Gaul." In *St. Augustine and the Conversion of England*, edited by Richard Gameson, 68–82. Stroud: Sutton, 1999.

———. "The Mission of Augustine of Canterbury to the English." *Speculum* 69 (1994): 1–17.

———. "Some Historical Re-identifications and the Christianization of Kent." In *Christianizing Peoples and Converting Individuals*, edited by Guyda Armstrong and Ian Wood, International Medieval Research 7, 27–35. Turnhout: Brepols Press, 2000.

INDEX

active contemplative life, 21–22,
28–30, 58–69, 77–78, 172n76,
188n18. *See also* Scripture, Luke
10:38–42
Adam, 22, 25, 30, 32–34, 174n9
Aethelbert of Kent, 140, 144, 147
allegory, 63–64, 164n35, 167n17,
195n52
Ambrose of Milan, 188n7
apocrisiarius, 3, 205n26
*Apophthegmata Patrum/Sayings of the
Fathers. See* desert fathers
Arichis of Benevento, 107
Ariulf of Spoleto, 106–8
asceticism, 17–30, 31–32, 33,
35, 117–18, 121–23; for
others, 28–30; ascetic
hermeneutic, 20–23, 24; ascetic
qualifications, 3. *See also*
humility and/or pride
Athanasius of Alexandria, 45
Athanasius of Isauria, 179n38,
180n5, 191n37
Augustine of Canterbury, 46,
143–46, 182n15, 194n32

Augustine of Hippo, 162n16, 165n2;
theology, 4, 7, 9, 13–14, 31–34,
173n2, 174n5, 175n11, 176n25.
See also grace; participationist
soteriology

Basil of Caesarea, 28
Bede, 145, 174n10. *See also* Gregory
the Great, *Libellus
responsionum/responsa*
Benedict of Nursia, Saint, 27,
29–30, 68–69, 96–97, 172n85,
202n67. *See also* Gregory the
Great, *Dialogues*
Bertha of Kent, 140, 143–47
Boniface of Reggio, 76
Brakke, David, 180n5, 191n37
Britain. *See* England
Brunhilde, 136–47

Candidus, 141–44
Carolingian editors and biographers,
5, 120, 206n45
Caspar, Erich, 5–6, 177n6
Cassiodorus, 87

232

George E. Demacopoulos

is the Fr. John Meyendorff and Patterson Family Chair
of Orthodox Christian Studies at Fordham University.
He is the author and editor of a number of books,
including *Five Models of Spiritual Direction in the Early Church*
(University of Notre Dame Press, 2007).